Where the Sacred
and Secular Harmonize

Where the Sacred and Secular Harmonize

Birmingham Mass Meeting Rhetoric
and
the Prophetic Legacy of the Civil Rights Movement

DAVID G. HOLMES

Foreword by Keith D. Miller

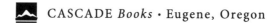 CASCADE *Books* • Eugene, Oregon

WHERE THE SACRED AND SECULAR HARMONIZE
Birmingham Mass Meeting Rhetoric and the Prophetic Legacy of the Civil Rights
Movement

Cascade Books
An imprint of Wipf and Stock Publishers
199 W. 8th Ave., Suite 3
Eugene, OR 97401

www.wipfandstock.com

PAPERBACK ISBN: 978-1-5326-1527-6
HARDCOVER ISBN: 978-1-5326-1529-0
EBOOK ISBN: 978-1-5326-1528-3

Cataloging-in-Publication data:

Names: Holmes, David G., author.

Title: Where the sacred and secular harmonize : Birmingham mass meeting rhetoric and
    the prophetic legacy of the Civil Rights Movement / David G. Holmes.

Description: Eugene, OR: Cascade Books, 2017 | Includes bibliographic data and index.

Identifiers: 978-1-5326-1527-6 (paperback) | 978-1-5326-1529-0 (hardcover) |
    978-1-5326-1528-3 (ebook)

Subjects: LCSH: King, Martin Luther, Jr., 1929–1968—Oratory | King, Martin Luther,
    Jr., 1929–1968—Political and social views | United States—Race relations | Oratory—
    United States.

Classification: E185.97 K5 H65 2017 (print) | E185.97 (ebook).

Manufactured in the U.S.A.   11/13/17

Chapter 2 is a revision of "(Re) Dressing the KKK: Fred Shuttlesworth's Precept Hermeneutic
and the Rhetoric of African American Prophetic Patriotism." *Journal of Black Studies* 42/5 (2011)
811–827. Portions from this article are used in chapter 2 by stipulated permission.

Chapter 4 is based on two articles: "'Hear Me Tonight': Ralph Abernathy and the Sermonic
Pedagogy of the Birmingham Mass Meeting." *Rhetoric Review* 32/2 (2013) 156–73. "Speaking of
Moses and the Messiah: Ralph Abernathy's Rhetoric for and by the People." *Journal of Communi-
cation and Religion* 35/1 (2012) 1–11. Portions of both articles are used by permission.

For my sons, Jonathan David and Gregory Matthew—
head and heart prophets in the making.

"Beware of false prophets (Talk sir) who come to you in sheep's clothing (Yes) but inwardly they are raving wolves (Yeah). Whenever a man will not take a proper stand for freedom (Yeah)—talking is all right, but no sentence is completed unless it has a verb in it (Alright). A verb is a word that shows action (Yeah). This is a time for action and not for much talking (Right)."[1]

—Calvin Woods, Alabama Christian Movement for Human Rights

---

1. April 22nd, 1963, mass meeting, transcribed by the author.

Contents

Foreword

Valley Forge. The Alamo. Pearl Harbor. When I was growing up in Alice, Texas, our teachers informed us that these were not places, but moments, moments of great suffering that supplied heroes with necessary fortitude and courage. I eagerly devoured books in our town library that confirmed the significance of those moments.

Yorktown. San Jacinto. Normandy. Iwo Jima. Our teachers and books told us that these were not places, but events, events of suffering but also of victories, victories that vindicated, fortified, and extended democracy.

Gettysburg. We heard and read that it served as the pivot in the clash between the brave soldiers on both sides of the Civil War. The South couldn't win after the Union army rebuffed the charge of General George Pickett at Cemetery Ridge.

Appomattox. My childhood guides named it the moment that one shrewd and noble general surrendered to another shrewd and noble general, ending the conflict and pivoting the nation toward unity.

No one ever mentioned Birmingham. Not a word.

But, if you are looking for a pivot in American history, I suggest Birmingham.

That's because the Emancipation Proclamation, the Civil War, and the Thirteenth Amendment did not achieve what I was told. In a Pulitzer Prize-winning book, Douglas Blackmon declares that Gettysburg, Appomattox, the Emancipation Proclamation, and the Thirteenth Amendment failed to erase slavery. Instead, as Blackmon carefully documents, slavery continued "by another name."

In 2013 the national news media lavished attention on the celebration, at the National Mall, on the fiftieth anniversary of the March on Washington, where Martin Luther King Jr., delivered "I Have a Dream." But the reporters who related that commemoration largely ignored the fiftieth anniversary of

Birmingham, which occurred three and a half months earlier. They failed to notice that Diane McWhorter did not peg the March on Washington as the apex of the civil rights movement. Instead, she subtitled her Pulitzer Prize-winning book: *Birmingham, Alabama: The Climactic Battle of the Civil Rights Revolution*. Nor did they hear Glenn Eskew's verdict that Birmingham "broke the stalemate"[2] on civil rights in the U.S. Nor did they read or talk to King's confidante and best fundraiser, Harry Belafonte, who observes that, had King been defeated in Birmingham, he would have "lost the last of his power and credibility."[3]

As these and other writers note, the triumph of Birmingham spawned many other, Birmingham-like protests. Together, they spurred a reluctant President John Kennedy to propose what became the landmark Civil Rights Act of 1964, propelled people to attend the March on Washington, and ensured that the March became momentous. For that reason, orations at the mass meetings in Birmingham *as a whole* prove at least as important as "I Have a Dream."

In this book David Holmes provides a fresh look at Birmingham and a fresh look at King. Holmes's first step is to analyze vital speeches that—with so many journalists, historians, and textbook authors magnetized by "I Have a Dream"—had never been analyzed before. Holmes thoroughly grasps that one can only understand Birmingham by understanding how *numerous* gifted speakers ignited listeners at the mass meetings there. For that reason, he refuses the common procedure of treating King as the great protagonist with other participants serving as a Greek chorus. By portraying the dynamic interplay among six major orators in Birmingham, Holmes enriches our comprehension not only of Birmingham, but also of King. As Holmes indicates, the contrast between King's elevated style and Ralph Abernathy's down-home humor blended successfully at the mass meetings. Similarly, the secular rationality that James Farmer and Roy Wilkins supplied at the mass meetings complemented the passionate sermons of Fred Shuttlesworth and James Bevel. To extract King from these other orators is to misunderstand King.

In his study of these crucial speeches, Holmes concentrates on key tropes. He examines Shuttlesworth's legerdemain with the initials "KKK"—which the preacher translates as "King, Kennedy, Khrushchev"—to diminish African Americans' fear of the extremely dangerous Ku Klux Klan.

2. Eskew, *But for Birmingham*, 299.

3. Belfonte, *My Song*, 265.

Holmes also explores Bevel's use of a story in the Gospel of John to shame certain African Americans who, having accustomed themselves to the illness of segregation, "don't want to get well." As Holmes notes, Abernathy locates Birmingham in a large, historical panorama by portraying whites as newcomers in a land already well-settled by Native Americans. An additional chapter spotlights Wilkins's explanation that New Yorkers' federal taxes uplift the relatively impoverished state of Alabama—a statistic that effectively refutes segregationists' emphasis on the notion of states' rights. This chapter also describes Farmer mocking whites who obsessively and mindlessly chase African Americans out of town after dark.

Prophecy is an extremely important genre of Judeo-Christian rhetoric that resists any easy definition. In his analysis of these addresses, the well-read Holmes weighs valuable perspectives on prophecy and—without forcing the Birmingham messages into any single, well-defined box—contemplates them while developing his own understanding of prophecy and persuasion in Birmingham.

After thoughtfully relating the ascendency of King to that of Barack Obama, Holmes reports his own personal journey from being a boy preacher to becoming a professor at Pepperdine University. He explains his sometimes conservative, usually white students' encounters with the books that he assigns them, books that challenge their preconceptions. He also reports his experience leading a group of students on a travel course to Birmingham. There they visited Sixteenth Street Baptist Church, where four girls were murdered in a Klan bombing not long after the March on Washington. Serving as the students' tour guide for the rebuilt church was Carolyn McKinstry, who knew the girls well and who barely survived the bombing herself.

By weighing the poignancy of McKinstry's words inside the church and the fire of the orators urging listeners to withstand police dogs and water cannons, Holmes's students began to reconsider race in America.

If Gettysburg was a pivot, it wasn't a very good one. Another convulsion in the cataclysm of the Civil War, Gettysburg served as a model for future warfare. By contrast, despite the tragedy of the church bombing, Birmingham offers a gift of courage and a model for nonviolence. This book helps us to understand that gift and that model. Now, more than ever, we need Birmingham to serve as our pivot.

Keith D. Miller
Arizona State University

BIBLIOGRAPHY

Belafonte, Harry, with Michael Shnayerson. *My Song: A Memoir.* New York: Knopf, 2011.

Blackmon, Douglas. *Slavery by Another Name: The Re-Enslavement of Black Americans from the Civil War to World War II.* New York: Anchor, 2008.

Eskew, Glenn. *But for Birmingham: The Local and National Movements in the Civil Rights Struggle.* Chapel Hill: University of North Carolina Press, 1997.

McWhorter, Diane. *Carry Me Home: Birmingham, Alabama: The Climactic Battle of the Civil Rights Revolution.* New York: Simon & Schuster, 2001.

Preface

The civil rights movement represents one of the most ambitious attempts in American history to reconcile democratic ideals with social realities. Birmingham, Alabama, epitomized the key moral, political, and social issues of the civil rights movement. Moreover, Birmingham was a critical city for understanding the inception and end of this movement. In 1963 particularly, a watershed year for the nation and for civil rights, Birmingham became pivotal to the larger movement's continued success and the nation's democratic future. Less than one month after the March on Washington and Martin Luther King's timeless "I Have Dream" speech, a bomb killed four little black girls in the basement of the Sixteenth Street Baptist Church in Birmingham.

Given this tragic event and Birmingham's well-established reputation as "the most thoroughly segregated southern city," it became the last stand for the civil rights movement. The climate of increasing violence and bolder demands for civil rights began to accentuate the growing rifts among King, student-led organizations, and black nationalists. There were some opponents of King within the movement who ironically wanted the Birmingham campaign to fail, for this would likely remove King from the national spotlight.

But the Birmingham campaign did succeed, to a great extent because of King but not due exclusively to his exceptional oratory and leadership. Much of the success of the Birmingham campaign and of the civil rights movement more broadly can be attributed to the mass meetings. Hailing back to the Montgomery Bus Boycott of 1955–56, these religious rallies housed in churches were inimitable forums for variegated rhetorical practices. The mass meetings were crucial to the organization, motivation, and mobilization of participants within most cities involved in the civil rights movement, including Birmingham. While historians like Taylor Branch,

David Garrow, and Glenn Eskew, as well as scholars of rhetoric and homiletics, like Richard Lischer, Kirt H. Wilson, Davis Houck, and Keith D. Miller, have written rich narratives about the civil rights movement that include brief reflections on the mass meetings, a rhetorical study concentrating on these Birmingham rally speeches has not been undertaken largely due to the scarcity of primary sources, namely recordings of the mass meetings. Sociologist, Jonathan Rieder, has written two fine books that include citations from the Birmingham mass meetings, which largely focus on Martin Luther King as a master of a number of communication styles.

My introduction to the Birmingham mass meetings was coincidental or providential—depending on one's worldview. In 2001, I won a summer fellowship from the Lilly Foundation. Sponsored by Samford University in Birmingham, Alabama, seven colleagues from a variety of mostly Christian colleges and I studied the theme "Spirituality and Social Justice: Lessons from the Civil Rights Movement." This informative and inspirational seminar spanned one month and three Southern states: Alabama, Tennessee, and Mississippi. We read much, ate more, and dialogued about the civil rights movement with several scholars and a few luminaries of the movement. And then there were the field trips. The most memorable for me would turn out to be the spark for my interest in the mass meetings—a trip to the Birmingham Civil Rights Institute. It was there, during a lecture, that I heard a recording of a part of Martin Luther King Jr.'s mass meeting speech of May 3rd 1963. King delivered this riveting speech the evening after dogs and water cannons were unleashed on school-age children who, like their parents, were marching for their right to be treated equally and humanely.

To say I was transfixed would be an understatement. Some longing was born in me that transcended my scholarly interest in rhetoric and religion. From 2004 to 2013, I was on an intellectual, cultural, and spiritual journey to learn more about the Birmingham mass meetings of 1963. During this vocational odyssey, I interviewed over a dozen people who participated in the mass meetings, including one C. Herbert Oliver who recorded the meetings and donated copies of those recordings to the Birmingham Civil Rights Institute. I also spent several research trips over the years scouring over the archives in the Birmingham Public Library, trying to not only reassemble the events of those revivalist rallies but to resuscitate the spirit that inhabited them as well.

My research includes several recorded speeches that I have selected from the nine Birmingham mass meetings that I have transcribed. Hence, this book is in part a reclamation project. To some degree, the communicative dynamics of the mass meeting speeches can be analyzed using classical, contemporary, sacred, and secular rhetorical approaches. The medium of mass meeting rhetoric conforms to the traditions of the African-American church, including passionate sermons, as well as other vocal, written, and gestural modes of communication and spirited, interactive audience feedback (call-and-response). The content of these oral performances falls within the traditions of American democratic rhetoric, while the intent was to secure civil rights and civil liberties for disenfranchised people of color.

This book contends that prophecy ranks among the best frames to account for the ideological range, political traction, and, primarily, rhetorical effectiveness of the Birmingham mass meeting speeches. By *prophecy*, I mean a spiritual, moral, conceptual, and pragmatic orientation to speak truth to power, point out injustices, and defend the marginalized. Prophecy is rooted in religion but, as many thinkers across disciplines have argued, is not restricted to places or people of faith. Like the larger civil rights movement, the Birmingham campaign of 1963 was about more than racial equality; it was about whether or not the soul of American democracy could be and remain saved. I hope and trust that my prophetic analysis of Birmingham mass meeting oratory will be about more than how these speeches captivated the minds and hearts of the nation back then. The more pressing issue is whether or not we can recapture and expand upon that forthright, righteous rhetoric for our times.

Acknowledgments

Acknowledging everyone that encouraged me with this book is harder than writing an Academy Award acceptance speech. I'm not going to even attempt thank everyone. I do wish to thank Professors H. Hugh Floyd and Penny Long Marler (emeriti of Samford University) for a stimulating seminar during the summer of 2001. While I had read about the Birmingham mass meetings before then, I had never heard excerpts from them. Once I did, I was hooked. Laura Caldwell Anderson, archivist of the Birmingham Civil Rights Institute, and Jim Baggett, archivist of the Birmingham Public Library, enabled me to feed this addiction over the next several years, as I listened to rare recordings, read primary documents, and obtained names for over one dozen interviews.

However, like many African Americans, this addiction to religious language began in my home congregation—the Normandie Church of Christ in Los Angeles, where the late Carroll Pitts Jr. was my minister. I thank him and other preachers that struggled to feed my wayward soul but, in the process, definitely whet my rhetorical appetite during my formative years, including the late Dr. R. N. Hogan, the late Dr. Calvin Bowers, Dr. Carl C. Baccus, and Dr. Billy Curl.

Over the past several years, a chorus of scholars have directly and indirectly influenced my thinking, reading, and writing—perhaps none more formidably than have Professors Keith Gilyard, Jacqueline Jones-Royster, Shirley Wilson Logan, Sharon Crowley, and Keith D. Miller. Their robust vision of scholarship challenges and inspires me. Knowing the quality and quantity of their work, I can be neither a competitor nor a spectator. I also extend my sincere thanks to those that have read various drafts of this work: Professors Patricia Bizzell, Martin Medhurst, Jack Selzer, Vorris Nunley, Ersula Ore, Richard Hughes, Raymond Carr, Gary Selby, and Roselyn Satchel. A special thanks to my former student, Nate Barton.

Acknowledgments

I began drafting a few chapters of this book during the spring of 2013, while I was the Langston Hughes Visiting Professor at the University of Kansas. A stellar company of colleagues made this Californian's wintry stay both pleasant and productive. J. Edgar Tidwell, Randal Maurice Jelks, and Tanya Hart were particularly hospitable and helpful. There are literally no appropriate words to capture my enduring gratitude for my family: Veronica, Jonathan, and Gregory. I deeply appreciate you letting me be myself—with all of the quirks that this reality entails.

Abbreviations

ACMHR   Alabama Christian Movement for Human Rights

CORE   Congress of Racial Equality

NAACP   National Association for the Advancement of Colored People

SCLC   Southern Christian Leadership Conference

SNCC   Student Nonviolent Coordinating Committee

1

Framing the Fragments

Remembering the Civil Rights Movement and Recovering Mass Meeting Prophetic Rhetoric

"Well, it [mass meeting] was similar to the church service, because we saw ourselves as doing God's work. King saw himself as being an instrument in God's hands. And our civil rights anthem marching song was 'We Shall Overcome.' We are not afraid. Black and white together.' Sometimes we said, 'The Lord is on our side, and the Lord will see us through.' So the meetings were shot through with our Christian faith. I don't think we could have had any without that. We had old-fashioned prayer meetings, old-fashioned warriors, singing in the choir."[1]

—Abraham Woods, Alabama Christian Movement for Human Rights

"In terms of the mass meetings, particularly, I guess one thing you see definitely is how worship can be used as a tool for liberation, because that's what the mass meetings were about. It was a place where people came to affirm their faith, affirm their hope . . . The mass meetings concretized the black experience particularly through worship."[2]

—Wilson F. Fallin Jr., Baptist preacher and historian

1. Interview with this author, June 2005.
2. Interview with this author, May 24th, 2006.

1

Now, beyond the one-half-century mark, the civil rights movement continues to captivate our national and global imagination. Much of this sustained attention has to do with how we remember or romanticize certain people, places, and events. Martin Luther King Jr. and Rosa Parks have long since become icons; we tend to remember Montgomery, Selma, the March on Washington, King's assassination in Memphis, as well as the passage of the Civil Rights and Voting Rights Acts of 1964 and 1965. To some extent what we don't remember nevertheless remains sacrosanct, insolated, preserved, and sanctified by the selective memories of a grand movement that changed the course of the world and that most everyone (now in retrospect) believes was a good idea. Countless numbers of people, regardless of political stripe, recall marching with Martin Luther King Jr., intending to, or knowing someone who did. For most, including many academics who should know better, the civil rights movement is a moment that American society has moved on from, like the Civil War or slavery.

Those who teach and research about the civil rights movement, while searching for contemporary links, implications, and resonances, represent a broad swath of disciplines: African American studies, history, religion, theology, literary studies, philosophy, politics, law, communication, and composition. The cataloged and emergent scholarly treatments of the civil rights movement are legion. Given that much of civil rights rhetoric focuses on oratory, the work done on this subject is more than abundant. Scholars include, but are not excluded to, Keith D. Miller, Kirt Wilson, Eric King Watts, John Hatch, Mark Lawrence McPhail, John Louis Lucaites, and David Zarefsky. While remarkable studies continue to emerge on King, scholars such as Maegan Parker Brooks, Davis W. Houck, and David Dixon have produced substantive work on lesser known civil rights orators.

I pitch my tent in relatively unknown territory as well, rhetorically speaking. This book focuses on Birmingham mass meeting rhetoric of 1963. The history of the Birmingham campaign has been sufficiently covered in broader historical studies of the civil rights movement by the likes of Taylor Branch, Clayborne Carson, and David Garrow, as well as in specific treatments of this city in works by Jonathan Bass, Glenn T. Eskew, Andrew Manis, J. Mills Thornton, and Diane McWhorter, to name a few. When one turns to those scholars who mention or focus on the persuasive oratory and writing produced during the Birmingham campaign, the list shrinks considerably. Gary Selby, Richard Lischer, Davis W. Houck, and Jonathan Riedar have given rich and, in some cases, robust attention to Birmingham rhetors, most prominently, and, understandably, concentrating on Martin Luther King Jr.

Because King remains a practically incomparable figure in fathoming not only the Birmingham campaign but also the larger civil rights movement and its reverberating global impact, one should expect close readings of his rhetorical feats wherever they might be found. However, what abiding rhetorical and cultural relevance might be derived from a study of other Birmingham orators? Most historians agree that thirty-eight days in Birmingham saved the civil rights movement. How did other Birmingham orators help to facilitate this grand rhetorical experiment? What can be learned from them about the sources of African American preaching and its relationship to African American expressive culture, American political rhetoric, community-level civic engagement, and, by extension, public pedagogy, and popular culture? In short, do the Birmingham mass meeting rhetors—pastors and other visiting orators who were not clergy—have something salient to reveal about this pivotal moment in the civil rights movement and, by extension, to our politically charged culture?

Obviously, I believe they do, or I wouldn't have written this book. The speeches that have been recovered from the Birmingham campaign are few. While my transcriptions cover several of these mass meetings in their entirety, I have chosen to examine the speeches of six speakers, including King. The others speakers are Fred Shuttlesworth, James Bevel, Ralph Abernathy, James Farmer, and Roy Wilkins. My examination of their speeches could hardly afford readers of this book with a full picture of the form, function, and force of these sociopolitical rallies steeped in the African American revivalist, worship tradition. So much has been written on the use of religious music in the black struggle for freedom for example. For better or worse, this book assumes a basic knowledge of the political history of black religious music—that the spirituals, anthems, gospel, and other genres of religious music inspired blacks to fight for equality for over three hundred years by redefining the terms of human struggle. These speeches I examine hail from the same rich cultural tradition, and though examining them alone does not afford readers with an understanding of the whole drama enacted during the Birmingham mass meetings, this book, nevertheless, opens up new scenes that might invoke richer insights.

Even with this relatively modest sampling, a full-on engagement of Birmingham mass meeting oratory, not to mention other rhetorical strategies, would require several books and spates of articles. As a result, I have opted to frame my analysis primarily through the concept of prophecy. When I use the word *prophecy*, I am not referring to supernatural fore-telling. By *prophecy*, I mean a spiritual, moral, conceptual, and pragmatic orientation to speak truth to power, point out injustices, and defend the marginalized. Among the several reasons for choosing this term, I here note three principal ones. First, prophecy foregrounds the rhetorical strategies to be discussed within their most immediate and pertinent contexts. The oratory practiced during the civil rights mass meetings in general grew out of the African American preaching tradition and, for the most part, was done by black preachers. While there were mass meeting orators who were not preachers, that rhetorical tradition was the overriding standard by which they were judged to some degree. Second, as a number of scholars of religion, homiletics, communication, and composition-rhetoric have not-ed, prophecy or the prophetic is one of the most fruitful ways to describe civil rights discourse. Third, thinkers across disciplines have shown how prophetic discourses, while rooted in religion, possess sociopolitical and communicative potential beyond the walls of institutional or organized religion. Writers ranging from Cornel West and David L. Chappell to Sharon Crowley and George Shulman have argued that prophecy divorced from dogma can constitute a set of fertile resources for democratic deliberations as well as social critique of status quo injustices, including those perpetuated by religious institutions.

In this chapter, I will undertake two tasks. First, I consider the religious and ceremonial sources of Birmingham mass meeting rhetoric. Second, I introduce how prophecy, as one viable frame for analyzing mass meeting oratory, suggests productive rhetorical and ideological tensions that will be explored throughout the rest of the book. These tensions include the expressive and epistemic, literacy and orality, hierarchal and grassroots leadership, the political and subversive, and the sectarian and the secular.

MASS MEETING SOURCES

As used today, the phrase *mass meetings* likely conjures up images of public events such as concerts and political conventions. Obviously, this is not the sense in which I use the term here. While Martin Luther King Jr. eventually consulted Billy Graham and tried to model the mass meetings after the famous evangelist's mass crusades,[3] the idea of black religionists assembling

3. Chappell, *Stone of Hope*, 96–97.

4

in houses of worship for sociopolitical purposes predates both men. In terms of the modern civil rights movement, most scholars will trace the words "mass meeting" back to the assembly at the Holt Street Baptist Church in December 1955. Prompted by the arrest of Rosa Parks for refusing to give up her seat to a white man and the subsequent plans made for a bus boycott, a twenty-six-year-old Martin Luther King Jr. preached at a mass meeting that, according to Kirt Wilson, was "part political rally, part religious revival, and part business meeting."[4] For all intents and purposes, given the African American sociocultural proclivity to draw little if any distinction between spiritual and political liberation, Wilson's description rings as historically sound. Sociologist Aldon Morris's now classic description of the mass meetings likewise remains pertinent:

> The new movement organizations inherited a vibrant church culture, with its tradition of bringing whole congregations into community activities, a guarantee of mass participation. When the masses assembled at the meetings, everyone sang the black spirituals they knew so well. They all bowed their heads when the traditional prayers of the church were offered. When the leaders addressed the meetings their style of presentation was rooted in the tradition of the church sermon, which elicited the mass response of "amen." Indeed, mass participation at the meetings was usually guaranteed because scripture reading, prayer, and hymns were built directly into the program.[5]

Richard Lischer, renowned professor of homiletics and author of the critical acclaimed *The Preacher King: Martin Luther King Jr. and the Word that Moved America*, echoes Morris's assessment, specifically focusing on Birmingham:

> From the beginning, observers and participants noticed that the mass meetings resembled evangelistic church services. Like the typical week-long revival, these assemblies tested the endurance of the faithful; the mass meetings in Birmingham, for example, began in January and ended in May 1963, and at one stretch ran an astonishing fifty consecutive nights. All preaching and exhorting was borne along by the lively and sometimes haunting music of the movement . . . Also like revivals, the meetings closed with an appeal to members of the audience to make a decision to

4. Wilson, "Interpreting the Discursive Field," 304.
5. Morris, *Origins*, 47.

participate in the Movement and to signal their commitment by coming forward.[6]

Lischer will go on to point out how a "praise" service (a time of prayer) before the meeting characterized a patterned ritual for many black Baptist churches. Walter F. Pitts Jr. offers a more expansive description of what he calls, the "Afro-Baptist Ritual," consisting of a two parts: (1) "Devotion" (which includes a series of prefacing prayers and songs) and (2) "Service" (including the headlining activities like choir singing, the main prayer, and the sermon).[7] Pitts, like many other scholars of African American Christianity, traces this worship structure to the cultural synthesis of the outdoor camp meetings of the Second Great Awakening and West African spirituality. While the camp meetings entailed a modicum of structure to the services, the diverse participation of blacks and rural, working-class whites, as well as the more fervent preaching, created an atmosphere where West African rituals like call-and-response could flourish. The West African belief in spiritual forces taking possession of participants during ceremonial services also informed the mood of these camp meetings. Though the levels of emotional intensity, education, and class would vary, especially by the time of the civil rights movement, most black church services would retain evidence of the fusion between camp religion and West African spirituality

A salient component of West African spirituality is *nommo*. Rhetorical scholars recognize *nommo* as the power, energy, or "life force" of the word.[8] Far from being neutral, static, or detached, *nommo* represents a textured view of language—particularly oral language—doing more than conveying meaning. Words animate the ideas and objects they described. For Africans taken from their motherland and dispersed across the Diaspora, *nommo* encapsulated, indeed embodied, the wisdom of the ancestors, the will to survive, and the words to bring liberation into existence. Understandably, then, *nommo* would manifest itself in the black preacher's ardent, emotive, almost histrionic vocal delivery, and in dramatic bodily gestures (often convulsive to the untutored eye). By the time of the civil rights movement, strands of *nommo* would remain evident in the congregations where black folk preachers resided. However, traces of *nommo* could be found in most forms of African American oral performance, then and now, including in

---

6. Lischer, *Preacher King*, 248.

7. Pitts, *Old Ship*, 18–19.

8. Karenga, "Nommo," 8.

sermons, spoken word presentations, raps, poetry readings, and, in a few cases, political speeches.

Hence, *nommo* constitutes one link between black religion and black politics; the mass meetings suggest one site for this linkage. However, while all the scholars I have mentioned so far, as well as many others, recognize an amalgamated relationship between black religion and black politics, they also feel the need to unravel some distinctions as well. Lischer, for example, notes that,

> Despite the nimbus of "church" that accompanied these meetings, King and his associates intentionally modified the traditional Sunday-morning gospel in order to accommodate the equally traditional African-American quest for political freedom.[9]

A range of scholars on black religion agree that a structure underlies the most ostensibly spontaneous moments in a black church service. That King and his associates recognized the potential malleability of the structured rituals within the black church arrests my attention for slightly different reasons than it might Lischer. Both of us are interested in religious rhetoric on the one hand and civil rights on the other. However, I find myself consumed with unearthing, exploring, and exploiting the language of racial liberation wherever and however I can.

The African American church has been and, to a larger extent, remains a bulwark site of African American history, literacy, rhetoric, culture, and politics. C. Eric Lincoln, Wilson Fallin Jr., and a host of others have noted that black church was the space where African Americans could develop the whole person—body, mind, and spirit. Fallin's books on Alabama's black Baptist churches provides a particularly helpful context for this study.[10] For one thing, the vast majority of Protestant leaders and participants in the civil rights movement were Baptist. Since the major campaigns of the civil rights movement were situated in Alabama, any attention on that state provides context for my analysis. According to Fallin, from the Reconstruction through the civil rights movement to the present, black Baptists in Alabama epitomized how African Americans multitasked their fight against disenfranchisement by promoting social and artistic activities; building private schools; passing resolutions at the community, regional, and state level; sponsoring literary societies; fundraising; and registering voters;

9. Lischer, *Preacher King*, 249.

10. See Fallin, *African American Church in Birmingham*; and Fallin, *Uplifting the People*.

among many other undertakings. Local churches collectively morphed into and, in many cases, supported numerous causes. And what could be said of black Baptists could be said (to greater or lesser degrees) of many black denominations during slavery and segregation across regions and regardless of denomination. Given the discriminatory practices foisted upon African Americans in the school, the marketplace, and the artistic arena, African American churches oft became multipurpose institutions, where members' financial, aesthetic, and other intellectual literacies were forged.

In short, the black church became a canonized or normative space for variegated iterations of African American expressive modes. In terms of Aristotelian rhetoric, African American sermons, Sunday school lessons, convention presentations, newsletters, and bulletins (to name a few examples) often employed overlapping strands of ceremonial, deliberative, and forensic language. Obviously, sermons, songs, and the call-and-response frame itself constituted a brand of epideictic or ceremonial rhetoric. However, within the cultural context of ongoing, systematic, and institutional oppression, African Americans rarely engaged in the ceremonial modes of communication simply to celebrate or pass the time; instead they did so for some higher purpose: existential, social, political, cathartic—often all of the above, and almost always wrapped in the language of Christian spirituality. And even as some conservative black church leaders drew a distinction between the concerns of God and Caesar, they reserved the option to combine the two when necessity dictated.

This is not to claim some sense of off limits idealization for the African American church historically, ethically, or ideologically. As a host of self-identified scholars of faith have attested to, including Michael Eric Dyson and Cornel West, the black church, like American Protestantism more broadly, should be called into question for its complicity with and sometimes downright participation in discourses that attempt to mute the voices and bookshelf the experiences of women, gays, and the poor. The African American church has not always done the best job policing its own social transgressions or rooting out its own instances of ethical failings.

That said (only in terms of expositional transition rather than ending the conversation), the church mattered for the civil rights movement. For all the lynching, bombings, beatings, political disenfranchisement, economic devastation, and human humiliation inflicted upon people of color by religionists, the church still mattered to most blacks. Obviously, there are legions of philosophical, theological, literary, communicative, and existential reasons why this was the case. And whereas I have stated that my investment in these questions is rhetorical, even the reasons rooted in specialties of that field are too daunting to address in one book.

Instead, I think a partial answer to the questions, why and how did the church advance the cause of civil rights for black citizens? as well as more particularly, why study Birmingham mass meetings of 1963? are that both can offer perches for sociopolitical critique, spaces to conceptualize and cultivate communal values, rhetorics, and literacies and to suggest routes to reading liberating discourses within popular culture and incorporating them into how one teaches. But I am referring to more than teaching confined by classroom walls. Rather, the lessons to be learned from studying Birmingham civil rights oratory are important enough to reconsider as what scholars call *public pedagogy*. Simply put, public pedagogy entails the social, cultural, and political lessons taught nationally and globally through formal and informal, traditional and nontraditional means. Public pedagogy lessons are as likely—sometimes more likely—to be learned watching a film as reading a textbook, listening to the latest hip hop song as hearing a lecture. The Birmingham campaign mattered not simply because of the history books that recorded that event; the campaign still matters because of the ways—spoken and tacit—that it still inhabits the nation's political and popular consciousness.

PROPHECY AS MASS MEETING THEORY AND PRACTICE

For these reasons, I use prophecy to frame most of my analysis of the Birmingham mass meeting rhetorics of 1963. According to Keith Gilyard, the Afro-American jeremiad, along with the black church and the slave narratives, not only constitute the sources of African American rhetorics and literacies, but these discursive fountainheads further expose the streams of a wide range of African American discourses.[11] Most, arguably all, forms of African American expression can be politically liberating—indeed must be in many critical instances. The Afro-American jeremiad, as David Howard Pitney's now classic work explains, evolved from the New England Puritan jeremiad. Named for the prophet Jeremiah, both iterations of this form of religiously inflected rhetoric entailed a discursive cycle of calling a community to repent of its sins with promise of restoration and receiving God's blessings. Puritan preachers lamented their fellow colonists' failure to live

11. Gilyard, "African American Contributions," 62.

up to biblical standards. After all, the Puritans enacted the Exodus narrative when they left Europe and would eventually experience new Canaan, or the promised land, if they lived up to God's expectations in their new home. The New England jeremiad, Sacvan Bercovitch observes, evolved in to more culturally pervasive forms during the First Great Awakening (or American revivals) and the American Revolution, forms that would suture biblical spirituality to American success economically and militarily.[12] Mainstream efforts to fuse the sacred and the secular, from these early forms of the American jeremiad to the contemporary appeals of the Religious Right remain just that—mainstream.

African Americans also appealed to the jeremiad from exposing the sins of slavery and later segregation to envisioning, albeit ever so dimly, America's prospects of becoming the inclusive nation that God called it to be. However, the African American exodus was never confined to international geography. Their promised land was not to be found in another country as it had been for the Puritans. A wholesale spiritual conversion of white enslavers and later segregationists would contribute to full enfranchisement for black people and would transform America into the promised land. During the American Revolution and the Civil War, according to Howard-Pitney, Americans broadly speaking came to see the exodus as a transition that was not necessarily geographical but spiritual or "political."[13] Consequently, both the white and black strands of the jeremiad saw America as deviating from its chosen destiny as the Old Testament Eden and the New Testament city on a hill. But while white practitioners of the jeremiad maintained the privilege of doing so as insiders to the culture they critiqued, Africans in Americans critiqued America as aspirant insiders but actual outsiders.

While many civil rights rhetors, therefore, worked from the assumption of America as a chosen nation, I intend on using prophetic rhetoric to critique this assumption as well, and in doing so will uncover some of the limitations of the very rhetorics (from the Birmingham mass meetings) that I seek to promote. Granted, myriad scholars have demonstrated how global concerns and the international community captivated the imagination of Martin Luther King, Malcolm X, Stokely Carmichael, and Angela Davis, to name a few. But my recovery and rhetorical examination of Birmingham mass meeting speeches suggest another shading of the prophetic critique

12. Bercovitch, *American Jeremiad*, ch. 5.

13. Howard-Pitney, *Afro-American Jeremiad*, 11.

of American exceptionalism. In fact, I envision my use of prophecy at its core as a hermeneutic and heuristic. Prophetic critique provides vistas for interpreting and interrogating American traditionalism, including traditional readings of the prophetic. But prophetic critique—as I will attempt to reconfigure it from the Birmingham mass meetings—also can evoke commonplaces for creating democratically sustainable and inclusive politics, rhetorics, and pedagogies or ways of teaching.

As a result, I contend that making this choice to use prophecy as the major framework for this project is indeed productive. Untangling prophecy from its sanctimonious etymology, prescribed rhetorical formulations, and—most significantly—dogmatic politics is an undertaking not to be taken lightly. Preaching and prophesying have been used interchangeably as a way of describing stuck-up diatribes designed to put down anyone and anything that does not fit within a myopic definition of what the religious rhetor deems right or wrong. Although these negative associations between and about prophecy and preaching can be accurate, the links are hardly comprehensive or conclusive. Of late, the notion of prophecy or the prophetic has recaptured the collective imaginations of scholars across a range of disciplines. Just as it is difficult to separate out the notion of the church from negative sociopolitical notions, so it is hard to disentangle prophetic discourse from the negative sociopolitical notions that the term *prophecy* conjures up. However, a number of scholars, only a few of whom have religious affiliations or investments, deem freeing the concept of prophecy from its baggage to be worth the risk.

Of the many scholars that call upon and even celebrate the prophetic as an effective means of civic engagement and democratic deliberation, I will place my primary focus on three: Cornel West, David L. Chappell and George Shulman. I have chosen these three for at least two reasons. First, their works display common yet quite distinct ways of linking the notion of prophecy to the civil rights movement and African American rhetorics; taken together, they will ensure a reasonably well-rounded, though hardly comprehensive, reading of Birmingham mass meeting oratory. Second, their respective readings, when extended to my project, suggest how a prophetic analysis of Birmingham mass meeting rhetoric constitutes a reciprocal set of readings: the prophetic enhances our understanding of the mass meeting rhetorics, and mass meeting rhetorics enrich our understanding of the prophetic.

Cornel West may be the best known among the scholars I have chosen who examines the prophetic. As an African American popular culture intellectual whose Ivy League training concentrated on religion and philosophy, West seems like a natural fit for this discussion. The corpus of his writings spans a wide range, from pragmatic philosophy to American imperialism, subjects that also push West towards a rigorous cultural analysis of American literature and other forms of national expressive culture, like films and music. One of West's most widely read early works, *Race Matters*, catapulted him into the popular square as an heir to the civil rights movement. The book provided a lucid yet textured examination of race for popular consumption, as West summarily critiqued essentialist views that confined the American race problem exclusively to individual bigotry or intuitional discrimination, opting instead for a both/and rather than an either/or analysis of America's complex racial legacy.

Race Matters engages what West considered to be a crisis in black leadership. Rather than upholding the culturally entrenched boundaries that pit Martin Luther King Jr. against Malcolm X, West argues that both men were "race transcending prophetic leaders."[14] While both were fully invested in social justice for black people, neither engaged by compromising their own integrity or their people's humanity. For West, the two leaders' dark suits signified how seriously they took their mission as well as their determination to distance themselves from the glitter and gold that West perceived some contemporary black leaders pursuing. That Martin and Malcolm spoke with absolute power without being absolutely corrupted by power placed them within the prophetic tradition. Yet West discusses what he calls "prophetic witness" in more comprehensive terms in *Democracy Matters.*

Democracy Matters reveals prophetic witness as a major theoretical trope in West's thought. One way to apprehend and appreciate the ideological range of prophetic witness is to note how West contrasts the phrase to center philosophical, religious, and cultural ideas within Western and African American culture. First, West draws a distinction between prophetic and "Constantinian Christianity."[15] Named for the Roman emperor Constantine, "Constantinian Christianity" reveres and, as a result, reinforces the values of the cultural status quo or the political hegemony. "Prophetic Christianity," conversely, suggests a set of critical and rhetorical stances that

14. West, *Race Matters*, 61.
15. West, *Democracy Matters*, 148.

are rooted in Christianity but not regulated by any form of that religion that is complicit in the oppression of others. This constitutes the principal reason why West expands the semantic purview of this critical concept from prophetic Christianity to "prophetic witness." Any one, West argues, with or without a religious affiliation, can practice prophetic witness.

However, West does more than extend the linguistic reach of the idea of prophetic witness. By aligning the phrase with "Socratic questioning" and "tragic-comic hope,"[16] West engages in a level of disciplinary crossover that enriches our understanding of how an interdependent, interracial, and intercultural democracy might function. The highest aspirations of Western education and politics are rooted in Socrates's preference for dialectic or ongoing, rigorous dialogue. While few could or would ever hope to scale the highest peak of his endless quest for truth, Socrates's valorizing of that quest has provided all interested in authentic democracy with a standard for which to aspire. West shares Western culture's admiration for Socratic questioning with qualification: Socratic questions may satisfy our cognitive aspirations but not our affective longings, may expand our intellect but not account for our experience. West sees this as particularly true for people on the margins of society, like Africans in America, people who saw knowing as showing, as a matter of survival, as an existential journey more than an epistemic exercise, however philosophically consequential that exercise might seem. For African Americans, knowledge had to do more than mean something; it had to mean something to them.

This is where, according to West, "tragic-comic hope" entered or, better yet, shaped the worldview of the enslaved Africans whose ancestors became the segregated blacks, who fought the battle for civil rights. Tragic-comic hope is that spiritual, psychological, social, and existential space carved out somewhere between the sacred and the secular, the personal and the political or, as the theologian James Cone might opine, between the spirituals and the blues. West focuses on the blues as a cultural expression of tragic- comic hope, as the African Americans' penchant and potential for seeing reality at its worst but anticipating the best. Given the uniquely horrifying experiences that enslaved and segregated African Americans faced, they had to fashion unique coping strategies. This is not to say that some people of color were not crushed (physically, psychologically or spiritually) under the heels of colonialism and racism. But surprisingly, downright miraculously, African Americans on the whole learned to hope against

16. Ibid., 21

hope—not hope as wishful thinking or pie-in-the sky idealism. But hope as confident expectation of a slice of pie on earth and perhaps, depending on how fundamental one's worldview, a slice in the sky later.

In short, West's project towards a "deep democratic tradition"[17] encompasses Socratic questioning and tragic-comic hope being ideally tethered to yet tempered by prophetic witness. Prophetic witness pulls exclusively academic approaches to Socratic questioning from the brink of abstract irrelevance and rescues those who can't see beyond the tragic from an incapacitating nihilism. As a result, elements of prophetic witness can be excavated from the most unlikely discourses, disciplines, and dogmas. Prophetic witness, according to West, can be articulated in hip hop lyrics and within the walls of the United Nations. Prophetic witness can be preached by Christians, Jews, Muslims, or secularists who dare to speak out against oppressive or duplicitous status quo politics, even at the risk of losing status within their respective ideological communities. And prophetic witness can provide a source of rhetorical resources that cognitively and affectively prepare people—from the classroom to the community center—to be civically active and politically engaged.

David Chappell focuses not on the prophetic legacy of the civil rights movement as West does. Rather, he considers how what he calls "prophetic Christian realism"[18] largely, though not exclusively, accounts for the movement's success. Chappell begins his book *A Stone of Hope: Prophetic Religion in the Age of Jim Crow* by pointing out white liberals' failed efforts to address racism. Intellectuals as well regarded as John Dewey and Arthur Schlesinger set their reflective, philosophically informed critiques of racism within a larger narrative of progress. In keeping with the liberal doctrines of education and, subsequently, cultural enlightenment, a host of philosophers and theologians believed that the key to eradicating racism was for whites to disseminate the right information about blacks.[19] The ongoing process of civilization, liberal thinkers believed, would arch towards many benefits, including more civil behavior toward all humankind. The white liberals of the 1930s placed an almost unshakeable faith in this narrative of progress, therefore, believing that it was a cultural cure-all for every evil, from war to poverty to racism.

17. Ibid., ch. 3.
18. Chappell, *Stone of Hope*, ch. 4.
19. Ibid., chs. 1 and 2.

Like the pre-twentieth-century classical liberals[20] that Sharon Crowley discusses in her provocative *Toward a Civil Discourse,* twentieth-century liberals' *religion* was reason; their dogma was rationality. And during the long, meandering ebb and flow of rationality—through the Enlightenment in the eighteenth century to industrialization in the nineteenth century to the Scopes trial and ultimate triumph of science in the twentieth century—disciples of reason never completely lost faith in its power. But American racism, born of slavery, matured in segregated southern towns, and sequestered in northern inner cities, was anything but reasonable. American racism was no more rational than German Nazism or Russian Communism, each ideology attempting to justify the unjustifiable, to make sense of the senseless, and to humanize inhumanity. In short, the advocates of racism, Communism, and Nazism crafted well thought out, rhetorically executed reasons to do the unthinkable: finding a group to scapegoat, segregate, and oppress.

And if liberals like Dewey felt put upon by this onslaught of the irrational, horrific treatment that one group of people foisted upon another, how did the victims feel? More important, what did the victims do? Where conventional reason and rationality did not work, African Americans during the civil rights movement turned to their tried-and-true religious traditions. While Chappell understands and aptly explores this choice, he struggles with why this move was not only effective politically for African Americans but socially transformative for the entire nation as well. How could southern black Christianity, which according to Chappell was rooted in superstition and fundamentalism, succeed where white liberal reason had failed? Further, Chappell wonders why this same religion did advance (yet did not ultimately ensure success for) the cause of the segregationists. One of the major reasons Chappell adopts the moniker "prophetic Christian realism" is to address these two questions.

In a pragmatic sense, prophetic politics represent a more realistic set of ethical, rhetorical, and political strategies than did white liberalism. No matter how irrational black religious faith appeared to outside observers, for most black southerners, Christianity constituted a worldview that had sustained them and for good reasons. When I say *good* here, I am referring to more than southern African Americans' belief in the veracity of Scripture. Rather, they had come to view the Bible as "good"[21] in the sense

---

20. Crowley, *Toward a Civil Discourse,* 3.

21. Fisher, *Human Communication,* 106–10.

that Walter Fisher describes when discussing "narrative rationality."[22] Rooted in communal or institutional values, these types of good reasons are justifications, rationales, and evidences that are not confined to logical or even rhetorical modes of argument. Said differently, these are the claims, explanations, and convictions that ring true for a community that shares collective experiences—experiences that may fall within the range of what West calls the "tragic-comic."

The black church in the South was more than a compartmentalized experience for African Americans. Instead, black spirituality (shaped by Christianity in the United States) informed, influenced, and ultimately inspired African American religionists to face, fight, and overcome the struggles they encountered. Particularly in Alabama, where the canonized civil rights movement began and ended, the church, as Wilson Fallin Jr. effectively argues, became everything that segregationist society would and, in some cases, could not be. Fallin's *Uplifting the People: Three Centuries of Black Baptists in Alabama* points to how many churches actively sought to meet the educational, social, political, and economic needs of their congregants, with varying degrees of success or autonomy from the white power structure.[23]

The main reason, therefore, that southern blacks found the church and its attendant prophetic rhetoric to be a more reasonable choice than white liberal rationality was that the former had served them before and, as a result could persuade, motivate, and move them like no other ideological discourse, no matter how elaborately reasoned. So while Chappell is quite right to raise and even marvel at the question of how black fundamentalism could galvanize arguably the most successful mass political movement in American history, to some degree the question misses the point: even the most rational people must be persuaded, and persuasion is rooted in the affective as much as, if not more than, it is rooted in the cognitive. As deplorable, domineering, and demeaning as Sharon Crowley finds the apocalyptic rhetoric of the Religious Right, she concedes that religious rhetoric appeals to pathos in ways that classical liberalism did not. That is, classical liberal rationality could hardly capture the imagination of a large segment of the body politic the way right-wing fundamentalism has. Classical liberalism lacked in some cases, or failed to use effectively in others, the rhetoric of affect.

22. Ibid., 48.
23. Fallin, *Uplifting the People*, chs. 6, 7, and 10.

Similarly, Chappell claims that the liberal discourses of Dewey did not fully resonate with southern black Christians in their fight for freedom. But I believe that there was more to this disconnect than just a lack of familiarity with the tenets of liberalism or being steeped in what Chappell dismissively, to my mind, characterizes as southern religious fundamentalism. Despite its strides in other sociopolitical contexts, early twentieth-century liberalism was not the one size that could fit the struggles of all Americans. In his book *Racism without Racists,* Eduardo Bonilla-Silva critiques that idea that the civil rights movement led to a largely postracist, colorblind society. He foregrounds his argument in the evolution of the word *liberal. Liberalism* in the classical sense, he contends, while promoting individualistic goals like discipline, diligence, and merit, was neither a culturally nor a racially neutral term. Many of the Europeans who coined and circulated the term did so while embracing racist and colonialist assumptions. The next stage for the concept, "social reform liberalism," emerged as some mainstream Europeans and Americans during the 1950s and 1960s began applying the tenets of liberalism to the struggles of the marginalized. The drawback for Bonilla-Silva is that proponents for social reform liberalism never sufficiently interrogated the cultural and racial underpinnings of liberalism. As a result, social reform liberalism could not navigate the rising tides of the highly politicized ethnic, class, and gender differences that surfaced after the civil rights movement.[24]

To be clear, Chappell does not believe that prophetic Christian realism worked for African Americans during the civil rights movement simply as a default position when liberalism did not. Many, if not the majority, of southern segregationists preferred Christianity to liberalism. Why wasn't their cause successful? For Chappell, the answer to this question can be captured in two words: *division* and *commitment.* According to Chappell, southern white politicians and clergy were divided on how or, in some cases, whether the Bible should be used to promote segregation.[25] Chappell documents a number of incidents when southern white clergy defended segregation based on custom rather than Scripture. More significantly, when segregationist politicians pressed these clerics to publicly use the Scriptures to combat desegregation, many of them emphatically refused. Obviously some white clergy used Scripture to advanced segregation; some of these individuals were members of the Klan. However, Chappell's

24. Bonilla-Silva, *Racism,* ch. 2.
25. Chappell, *Stone of Hope,* chs. 6 and 7.

principal claim is that on the whole, southern white clerics did not exegete Scripture to support segregation to the extent that their counterparts had done earlier with slavery.

For this reason, Chappell views southern clerics and politicians to be at a standoff during the height of the civil rights movement. The more educated the clerics, the less likely they were to be buttonholed into a position of using Scripture to defend segregation. Apparently some southern politicians became so incensed with the clergy's intransigence that their commitment to attending or supporting these churches was dampened. These politicians saw the clergy's lukewarm commitments to upholding segregation as more than disingenuous; they saw it as destructive to the southern way of life. For their part, these clerics would hardly characterize their commitments to segregation as lukewarm. While most of them opposed desegregation based on law and custom, a few would draw vague connections between principles taught in Scripture and the status quo of segregation.

Whereas southern white clerics and politicians were mostly divided on the use of Scripture, Chappell argues that southern black Christians were mostly united. Chappell realizes that the advocates for civil rights were not monolithic in their religious outlook. He reviews the differences in opinion that abounded within the movement regarding methods and strategies. However, Chappell convincingly argues that southern blacks were able to capitalize on prophetic rhetoric in a way that southern whites did not. But how did they? Clearly southern segregationists were not entirely uniform in their opinions about how to advance their cause. But it would seem that—as the regional powers that were—they should have been better able to manage their disagreements than would the proponents of civil rights.

Combining crusaders' zeal and revivalists' sensibilities, advocates of the civil rights movement advanced their cause. In fact, Chappell, like a host of other scholars, claims that the entire movement could be described as a revival, and not just the mass meetings.[26] While Chappell does not play this concept out, his observation illustrates how significant a study of mass meeting rhetoric would be, as I will demonstrate in subsequent chapters. However, Chappell does point out how this revivalist consciousness carried the movement across geographical, ethnic, and ideological lines. The mainstream civil rights movement remained rooted in the African American church, but it sprouted in a number of unexpected places and to a plethora

26. Ibid., ch. 5.

of unlikely people. Given her fundamentalism, so notes Chappell, many might have expected the rural, black Mississippian Fannie Lou Hamer to have been sympathetic to voting rights campaign in her state, but few would have expected her meteoric rise as a spokesperson within that campaign, given racism, sexism, and her lack of formal education. Similarly, even fewer might have expected the one thousand plus students who came down from the North to help with the Mississippi campaign—nearly all white and scarcely a few that claimed religious faith. Aside from being black, Bob Moses (the leader of what became known as Freedom Summer) and Fannie Lou Hamer, could not be any more different. Moses held a masters degree in mathematical logic and was working towards a doctorate before he felt the call to travel down to Mississippi. Where Hamer was unlettered, passionate, and outspoken, Moses was cerebral and soft spoken. Yet both comported a spiritual aura and exuded a charisma that many movement participants, according to Chappell, deemed divine in origin.

Thus, there were two interrelated, biblically inspired narratives, so observes Chappell, that largely accounted for the sociopolitical success of the civil rights movement: "conversion" and "miracles."[27] Many of the leaders were convinced that they were doing more than changing the social, political, or even moral climate of the nation. From Martin Luther King Jr. to Fannie Lou Hamer, civil rights advocates ideally hoped to convert their opponents to the more spiritual point of view of accepting their fellow citizens of a different racial hue. Where that conversion could not be brought about in the hearts of segregationists, it would be approximated in their actions through civil rights legislation, which constituted a necessary philosophical paradox for King. Those already thoroughly committed to the cause, most notably leaders like Fred Shuttlesworth and Fannie Lou Hamer, were delivered from circumstances so dangerous that they and others described the escapes as miraculous.

Prophetic Christian realism, then, is the paradigmatic language Chappell uses to capture the consciousness and commitment that mobilized black religionists—but also secularists of different races—to speak against the segregationist status quo. This commitment and consciousness was as entrenched in realism as it was in the rhetoric of biblical prophecy. As fundamentalist as Chappell describes some of the movement followers to be, they were not so heavenly minded that they were no earthly good. They adopted the language of the Jewish prophets to confront the horrors

27. Ibid., 91–95.

of post–World War II racism head on and in a way that the most lettered liberal philosopher could not manage.

Where West partly envisions prophetic witness as a legacy of the civil rights movement and Chappell coins *prophetic Christian realism* to account for the movement's historical success, George Shulman situates and explains prophecy within the context of political theory. Like West and Chappell, Shulman argues that prophecy is not necessarily restricted to religious codes or regulated by religious people. Among the examples he uses to buttress this point are James Baldwin and Martin Luther King Jr. A celebrated author of novels, essays, and plays, Baldwin was a formidable voice during the civil rights movement. As a renowned writer, he could speak from a perch and with an ethos not accessible to most preachers. While he was not a preacher, Baldwin had mastered the rhetoric and poetics of the black church. In fact, as Shulman reminds us, Baldwin had been a teenage preacher who left the church and "fashion[ed] a nontheist prophetic voice as an artist bearing witness to human finitude."[28] He was openly and proudly gay at a time when, not only mainstream society and the black church frowned upon this lifestyle, but also the emerging militants within the black freedom struggle—one of whom derisively called Baldwin "Martin Luther Queen."[29] But Baldwin's prophetic stance could not be compromised by the restrictive dogmas of racism or homophobia any more than could his style as a creative artist. As a prophet of humanism, Baldwin largely entrenched his critiques of American society in a raw, demanding, socially conscious, and ethically responsible definition and practice of love. Conceptually elusive but a reality for all Americans to come to grips with, Baldwin declares in *The Fire Next Time*, if God cannot teach us to be more loving, perhaps it is time we got rid of him.

Martin Luther King Jr. once declared, as Shulman reminds us, that "not every minister can be a prophet."[30] Obviously, given King's background, he did not see this comment as a wholesale put-down of pastors. As a preacher hailing from a generation of preachers, King had nothing but the highest regard for ministers. However often, as King's own experience during the freedom struggle indicated, even the most socially conscious preachers were often beholden to the status quo. Many black ministers in King's day were controlled by regional economic pressures, social customs,

28. Shulman, *American Prophecy*, 132.
29. Ibid., 160.
30. Ibid., 105.

personal choices, or a combination of the three. King noted that to step out as a prophet required not only courage, but also a willingness to see sacrifice as a lifestyle, rather than as isolated acts of charity. On a secondary yet substantive level, as King disentangles the necessary connection between prophet and preaching, he implies a pertinent idea for my examination of mass meeting rhetoric: preaching can be prophetic in the broader terms that I am laying out here, but not all preaching is prophecy.

For Shulman, prophecy is endemic to and pervasive within American culture. In fact, he refers to prophecy as a "social practice,"[31] a global phenomenon that has captured the imagination of a number of cultures and is part of or parcel to various religious rituals. Shulman finds the notion so dominant within the American imagination that he conceptualizes prophecy as a "genre"[32] of American politics. Perfectly aware of the denotative and connotative perceptions of prophecy as religiously inflected and socially restrictive, Shulman uses political theory and political theology to carve out an alternative reading. While readily acknowledging that prophecy can be employed to dominate, discriminate, and inhibit (he offers the Puritans and Jerry Falwell as examples), he acknowledges that prophetic discourse can conversely be used to critique oppressive politics and social practices. The principal target of this alternative brand of prophecy is white supremacy. And prophets, from various occupations and communicating in a variety of genres, adapt the language of prophecy to critique white domination. Shulman mentions not only Baldwin and King but also Henry David Thoreau and Toni Morrison. Prophecy, then, becomes a master trope that cuts across and potentially inhabits other genres of expression, particularly those that possess the promise of liberation.

Said differently, prophecy at its pragmatic best is largely about politics but ultimately about persuasion. Even within Old Testament narratives, prophets had to endure extraordinary odds to critique the powers that were. For the most part, these prophets were about as displaced from the individuals and institutions they criticized as enslaved blacks were from reaping the benefits of the antebellum economy or segregated blacks were from fully participating in southern politics. Still, I realize that asserting that prophetic discourse can be used rhetorically within secular public arenas carries its own problematic baggage and cannot be easily untangled from how that form of rhetoric is linked to top-down dictating rather than

31. Ibid., 1.
32. Ibid., 6.

one-to-one deliberation. True, Shulman argues that the war against white supremacy, including the battles that King waged, salvaged prophecy from being exclusively oppressive. However, one could view even this brand of prophecy as inhibiting the free flow of grassroots democracy, as some members of the Student Nonviolent Coordinating Committee (SNCC) accused King of doing.

Shulman is obviously aware of this problem. This is why he recognizes prophecy as a genre of American politics and also how it has functioned as "cadences of speech," "registers of voice," "tropes," "narrative forms," and "idioms."[33] Understanding vernacular as prophecy exposes the rhetorical potential of linguistic terms applied to the prophetic. As a result, while Shulman claims that prophecy can be deployed to combat white supremacy (hence sucking some of the antidemocratic venom from the word *prophecy*), the body politic should be on guard lest the poison of oppression begin circulating in other forms, just as the overt sexism and covert homophobia functioned within civil rights movement. Shulman opts to describe politically viable prophecy as vernacular because, like language, such a description affords users more sociopolitical flexibility. No one party or denomination would, in theory at least, own this kind of prophetic speech. For example, although Shulman considers both King and Baldwin to be prophets, he claims that they viewed America's past differently. Similar to the New England jeremiads, King viewed America's past as a promise yet to be fulfilled for black Americans. Baldwin, on the other hand, eyed America's past as a horror to be faced and acknowledged.

Like all forms of language use, adopting prophecy as vernacular is not without its own limitations, as Shulman well knows. But prophecy as vernacular has afforded African Americans greater rhetorical range to revise political discourses more than liberal rationalism alone. Shulman seems to share Chappell's sentiment about liberalism but takes prophecy more seriously. As a rhetorician, I am particularly struck by the link between prophecy and narrative.

Renowned black language scholar Geneva Smitherman represents one among many scholars who argues that narrative, specifically "narrative sequencing,"[34] constitutes a more persuasive form of rhetorical discourse than linear argumentation within Euro-American rhetorical traditions. Narrative sequencing comprises a major rhetorical strategy that evolved

33. Ibid., 6.
34. Smitherman, *Talkin and Testifyin*, 149.

from West African oral traditions. For the enslaved Africans kidnapped and brought to the Americas, narrative sequencing took on various life affirming and liberating forms including folk tales, sermons, spirituals and (into the twentieth century) the blues, gospel, and hip hop. Throughout African American history, narrative sequencing inhabited the consciousness of black essayists, novelists, poets, preachers, politicians, and musicians. As one of the clearest examples of *nommo*, storytelling was and is a ubiquitous and indispensable force in the struggle for African Americans to express their humanity and exercise agency.

For Shulman, aesthetics (signified by terms like *genre, vernacular*, and *idiom*) describes how prophecy functions politically; such descriptions also afford oppressed groups more linguistic range to advance their cause. This is why Shulamn views vernacular prophecy as more allied with rhetoric than with philosophy. I would add that any approach to black politics that stalls at debates but never demonstrates, that thinks about without being about progress constitutes a static form of language, regardless of subject matter—one that remains confined to the classroom and restricted within church walls. As Baldwin could not abide an art-for-art's-sake approach to his writings about black life—indeed themes of affirmation and liberation ooze out of his fiction and nonfiction—Martin Luther King Jr.'s theology was political, even before that term gained traction in the works of thinkers such as James Cone.

This is not to say, however, that narrative or other forms of aesthetic communication precludes incorporating Western rationality into various genres of African American rhetoric, including the prophetic. Yet, as I have suggested, syllogisms, induction, or other forms of analytic reasoning can be found to be less reasonable to black people when these strategies are employed to stifle or slow down black progress—primarily because Western rationality has not resonated as persuasively with blacks and other oppressed people as has expressive discourse. In fact, the possibility of latching onto modes of communication more in keeping with a people's experience and needs has been discussed by a legion of thinkers, including the Greek philosopher Aristotle and the communication theorist Walter Fisher.

One way Shulman explains vernacular prophecy, therefore, is by describing what prophets do. Borrowing from biblical terminology, Shulman views political prophets as occupying an "office," by which he means a key, rather than popularly elected, role. A prophet is a "messenger," "witness," "watchman," and "singer."[35] As messengers, prophets "announce" or declare the unpleasant truths often left unsaid. These announcements carry authority, Shulman contends, not necessarily because of theism but because of the quality of the claims. And if politics generally represent a taboo topic, then those who speak aloud about white supremacy or other institutionalized practices of subordinating some completely violate mainstream mores. But prophets do more than speak against societal wrongs: they "bear witness" against those who do wrong and on behalf of the wronged, or as Shulman says, borrowing from Morrison, the "disremembered and unaccounted for."[36] I think of those who do not have access to the political process, who lack the literacy or access to participate, or who will be ignored by those controlling the process. As a watchperson, the prophet warns not of an inevitable future based on the nation's undesirable course of action but a conditional one. Past injustices that have been institutionalized or ignored or both must be addressed. And this is one reason why prophets lament a nation's state. Turning again to the force of aesthetic rhetoric, Shulman points out how a lament, rather than a celebrative song conveying tones of narrow nostalgia or naïve hope, compels us to face harsh national realties with the determination to do something about them, even when these challenges appear irresolvable.

Ultimately, West, Chappell, and Shulman acknowledge the rhetorical potential of prophecy as a viable political option for African Americans seeking and promoting freedom and equality. West sees prophetic witness as grounded in and shaped by African American religious and artistic culture. As a central legacy of the civil rights movement, prophetic witness cuts across ethnicity and crisscrosses the sacred and the secular as an ethical imperative for anyone interested in social justice. Chappell explicates what he calls "prophetic Christian realism" as an underemphasized historical phenomenon that accounts for the success of the movement, a success that neither liberal, pragmatic philosophy could advance nor southern racist politics obstruct. Shulman borrows from political theory to interpret how African Americans have invoked a number of genres (mostly artistic) to craft prophecy as a genre and vernacular with idiomatic accessibility and rhetorical force. Though they interpret the civil rights movement through different disciplinary lenses, taken together, West, Chappell, and Shulman offer a critical conceptual framework for appreciating, interpreting,

35. Shulman, *American Prophecy*, 5.
36. Ibid., 8.

and explaining the historical and contemporary efficacy of civil rights discourses considered broadly or particularly. Tracing resonances of West, Chappell, and Shulman to read Birmingham civil rights oratory, therefore, will be most promising.

While this book focuses on what I consider the prophetic oratory practiced during the Birmingham mass meetings of 1963, prophetic rhetoric, similar to rhetoric as it has been debated and redefined over several millennia, cannot be confined to preaching or other religiously centered rhetorical acts. As West and Chappell, for instance, stretch the concept of prophecy beyond religious ideology and oral performance, this book attempts to do the same. Following their and other thinkers' lead, I will introduce the implications of Birmingham mass meeting oratory for unearthing the prophetic in various genres, disciplinary perspectives, and public practices.

Put another way, my close reading of selected orators from the Birmingham mass meetings of 1963 is framed by prophecy in part to bear witness to an extended, richer, robust definition of both the prophetic and the role of the prophet. In chapter 2, I examine the master of ceremonies rhetoric that Fred Shuttlesworth exercised during the Birmingham mass meetings. While the bulk of his remarks appeared to constitute impromptu, fundamentalist exhortations couched in reports about the Birmingham campaign, I argue that a closer reading of his reflections further confirms how black prophetic discourses are confined to neither classical definitions of rhetoric nor traditional homiletics (the art of preparing and delivering sermons). Chapter 3 analyzes James Bevel's April 12th speech. Speaking during Martin Luther King's first night of imprisonment, Bevel tries to persuade his listeners to adopt the grassroots rhetoric of mobilization. Thereby, African Americans regardless of gender, economic, or educational standing, could speak and act against injustices with or without ministerial leadership. Chapter 4 turns to the May 3rd speech of Martin Luther King's closest confidant, Ralph Abernathy. Though Abernathy is often dismissed as a folksy warm-up act for King even by noted historians and rhetoricians, this chapter demonstrates Abernathy to be a shrewd orator, one who at once identified with his black audience using an earthy rhetorical style while offering sophisticated critiques of white racism and mainstream, so called *neutral* historical and journalistic narratives.

Chapter 5 takes up the pertinent and practical issue of secular prophecy by considering two speeches: one by James Farmer of CORE and the other by Roy Wilkins of the NAACP. Neither man was a pastor, but both addressed the mass meetings in ways that would place their messages within West's, Chappell's, and especially Shulman's respective definitions of the prophetic. In chapter 6, I turn to the popular and contested subject of Martin Luther King's legacy and Barack Obama's presidency. I argue that President Obama found himself in a full-court press of controversies partly because of the broad cultural inability to distinguish between the oft subtle convergences and divergences of prophecy and politics within the African American rhetorical tradition. And the last chapter, "Birmingham on My Mind," includes my personal and professional reflections on why the civil rights movement inhabits my consciousness as well as how the movement does and, perhaps should, inform popular culture, politics, and pedagogy.

2

Prophecy, Poetry, and Hermeneutics

Fred Shuttlesworth's Presidential Mass Meeting Rhetoric

"Fred was a ball of fire. He wouldn't dress anything up. You know, he's an eloquent
man, but he's a ribald man. He'd get up and preach for the big cause, and the
police would listen . . . And he was well-read on current events. He knew what
was going on across the country, and he knew what was going on in the city."[1]

—Calvin Woods, Alabama Christian Movement for Human Rights

Perhaps more than David Chappell, Cornel West and George Shulman
insist that the exercise of prophecy is not genre bound. West, for example, would likely view liberal pragmatism and black revivalist prophecy as
having meaningful connection with each other at points. Moreover, West
would not portray prophecy in such a way as to enshrine the expressive over
the epistemic as Shulman suggests. Similar to the way Eddie Glaude does,
West argues that the goal of liberation has often infused African American
modes of artistic expression with an epistemic edge. Glaude contends that
because of ongoing struggle African Americans have manufactured their

---

1. Interview with this author.

27

own brand of pragmatism from politics as well as highbrow and popular culture art.[2]

On the other hand, Shulman considers the prophetic critique employed by African Americans as being more about rhetoric than philosophy, more about aesthetics than rationality. Much of what drives Shulman's contention may have to do with the accessibility of aesthetic modes of communication. As much as I am indebted to Shulman's analysis, the dividing lines between rhetoric and philosophy or, as I will suggest in this chapter, between African American prophecy as poetry and prophecy as hermeneutics are neither indelibly nor easily drawn. Shulman rightly views poets, preachers, essayists, and novelists as exploiting the racially liberating potential of prophecy. However, I see further challenges that can be made as to how broadly one might define black preaching as a type of prophetic rhetoric. If preaching can constitute one form of prophetic discourse, which additional genres of church speech might one include? Testimonies, prayers, spontaneous, and structured recitations of biblical passages, and announcements compose part of the repertoire many ordained and lay ministers use to spiritually, existentially, socially, or politically edify their congregations. Equally important, therefore, is how a study of any politically inflected genre of black preaching or church speech might likely entail a hermeneutical function.

As Vincent L. Wimbush remarks, one would be hard pressed to chronologically or topically produce a study that could calculate, let alone codify, every individual and institutional biblical hermeneutic practice among (and I would add about) African Americans from the eighteenth century to the present. Indeed, the West African penchant for epistemological eclecticism substantively and stylistically, according Wimbush, practically ensured that enslaved blacks could "adapt themselves to different understandings of reality," including the religion (Christianity) coming out of a sacred book used to oppress them.[3] The same could be said of civil rights activists who took the Bible literally and their fight against segregation seriously.

This chapter inserts Fred Shuttlesworth, founder and president of the Alabama Christian Movement for Human Rights, into this discussion about black religious interpretation, aesthetics, and communication. In 1963, Shuttlesworth invited Martin Luther King Jr. and the Southern Leadership Conference to participate in the campaign against racial injustice in

2. Glaude, *Shade of Blue*, ch. 1.

3. Wimbush, "Bible and African Americans," 85.

Birmingham. I argue that many of the presidential remarks Shuttlesworth shared during the mass meetings illustrate how black preaching often blurs the Western dichotomy between informal and formal discourse as well as blends the contours of poetics and hermeneutics. In many instances, black preaching style is indivisible from substantive content. Nor is black preaching confined to a particular space or length. When the Spirit moves, veteran preachers can find a sermon anywhere, anytime, and in anything. The poetics of African American preaching function rhetorically to produce, communicate, interpret, and interrogate knowledge. Given both the syncretism expressed in West African religions and the racism practiced by many white clergy during slavery and segregation, black Christians quite understandably blurred the semantic lines that their mainstream oppressors established. Semantic dissent became a matter of sociopolitical advancement as well economic and cultural survival.

One noteworthy illustration of Shuttlesworth's blurring the genre lines between preaching and presidential remarks on the one hand and black poetic style and hermeneutics on the other is his acrostic reinvention of the initialism KKK. During the Birmingham mass meetings of 1963, Shuttlesworth extended KKK from Ku Klux Klan to alternatively signify Martin Luther King Jr., John F. Kennedy, and Nikita Khrushchev. He employed this reinvention to critique southern racism, Communism, and other institutions or individuals directly or indirectly opposed to the civil rights movement. The strategy also suggested the range of speech genres within the black church that can be considered prophetic. In Shuttlesworth's particular case, the genres of prophecy included his formal addresses and informal remarks as president of the Alabama Christian Movement for Human Rights (ACMHR for the remainder of this chapter). The itialism KKK, therefore, may represent poetic shorthand for interpreting the ways Shuttlesworth examined democracy on regional, national, and global scales in speeches regardless of their genre classification. These vital themes become commonplaces that—similar to the prophetic tone that infuses much of black preaching—can be confined to classical definitions of neither rhetoric nor homiletics (the art of sermon preparation and delivery).

Shuttlesworth's place in more popular readings of civil rights history has been limited for the most part to the *Eyes on the Prize* documentary series, where he, like other civil rights notables, serves as a historical warm-up act for Martin Luther King's more prominent role. *Eyes on the Prize* also covers approximately one minute of footage of Shuttlesworth being brutally beaten as he attempted to integrate four black children (two of his own) into the all-white Phillips High School in 1957.[4] Additionally, the Birmingham Civil Rights Institute catalogs a part of Shuttlesworth's biography beginning with a lifelike statue displayed prominently near the building's entrance. The institute houses other materials, including some of his speeches and personal papers that afford one a more nuanced reading of Shuttlesworth. However, the Birmingham Civil Rights Institute caters primarily to tourists. Cultural critic Robyn Wiegman examines the institute to comment on how white narrative privilege may be subtly entrenched within popular efforts to promote racial inclusion: what she styles "the paradox of particularity."[5]

As might be expected, rich historical analyses (Taylor Branch, Aldon Morris, J. Mills Thornton, and Glenn Eskew to mention a few) mention Shuttlesworth. However, aside from Andrew Manis in his unsurpassed biography, very few scholars have analyzed Shuttlesworth's rhetorical abilities. A notable leader of the civil rights movement in his own right, Shuttlesworth was a bold, passionate, and folksy preacher who was convinced that God not only had called him to lead his people in Birmingham but had also given him a hard head to endure blows from the most rabid racists. He led bus and business boycotts, had his house bombed twice, and received numerous death threats. After Shuttlesworth escaped the first bombing of his house with relatively minor injuries, one police officer cautioned that if he were Shuttlesworth, he would leave town. Shuttlesworth's response illustrates the intrepid tone that inflected his rhetoric:

> Officer you are not me. And you go back and tell your Klan brothers that if God can keep me through this, that the war is on; the battle has just begun, and I'll be around for the duration.[6]

BACKGROUND SKETCH OF A POETIC PROPHET

A few months after identifying with the Baptists in 1943, according to Manis, Shuttlesworth, a former African Methodist, began preaching occasionally. Cedar Grove Academy, organized by the Moonlight Baptist Association, provided a convenient place for Shuttlesworth to attain his initial ministerial training, given its location and class times. Located in

---

4. Else and Vecchione, prods., *Eyes on the Prize*, vol. 1.

5. Wiegman, "Whiteness Studies," 115.

6. From Lee, dir., *Four Little Girls* (Holmes transcript).

Prichard just twelve miles north of Mobile where Shuttlesworth worked for an air force base, Cedar Grove Academy held classes a couple to a few days per week. Among the classes Fred took were systematic theology and New Testament. As Manis recalls, while discussing the book of Acts one day, Shuttlesworth's teacher, the renowned U. J. Robinson, secretary of the National Baptist Convention, said something that aroused Shuttlesworth's fiery convictions regarding Scripture. Robinson claimed that two characters in the book of Acts chapter 5, Ananias and Sapphara, were cursed because the couple gave away all they had to other Christians in their congregation. In Robinson's mind, sharing all they had actually amounted to Communism. Shuttlesworth questioned, then challenged Robinson, who became increasingly angry at his unlettered student's presumption and persistence. Shuttlesworth clung to a literalist reading of the text, that these two characters were punished for lying about the amount they were going to share. Manis views this as a stalwart foundation for Shuttlesworth's unwavering faith in formalist interpretation of Scripture:

> Although never showing the typical fundamentalist fervor to root out heresy, Shuttlesworth remained a strong Biblicist, later commenting, "I disagreed with some of what I learned in theology. I must remember that some of it was what man thought and . . . always, when anybody got on theories, it has been my unusual knack to lay them alongside what I believe is the biblical direction."[7]

Shuttlesworth's more formal education at Selma University and Alabama State University consisted of a few more courses in religion (in part because that subject was not his major). For the rest of his life, he remained suspicious of esoteric interpretations that strayed away from what he deemed the plain and pure reading of Scripture.

As founder and president of the ACMHR, Shuttlesworth had served as the master of ceremonies for the Birmingham mass meetings since their inception in June 1956. Shuttlesworth founded the ACMHR in response to the NACCP being outlawed in Alabama. While Shuttlesworth rarely gave formal speeches and sermons, during the 1963 mass meetings (for which we have records) his off-the-cuff remarks (strategy announcements, recollections of the day's events, and humorous stories) often morphed into poignant impromptu homilies. Scholars of black preaching, particularly folk preaching, do not restrict sermons to either one genre or occasion. That

7. Manis, *Fire You Can't Put Out*, 42.

31

is, often one might be moved to preach sermons whether fully prepared or scheduled to do so or not. Literary scholar Dolan Hubbard has noted,

> The black oral tradition utilizes the structure that has become associated with improvisation and jazz but that we know more appropriately can be attributed to the sermon. This structure reflects the elasticity of African American culture and the African continuum.[8]

Many of Shuttlesworth's mass meeting remarks of 1963 reflected this "elasticity" of which Hubbard speaks. The bold Baptist preacher was conversant in improvisational oratory, which according to scholars on homiletics, such as the renowned Henry Mitchell, is the bread and butter of black preaching. Even when a black preacher delivers a prepared sermon, he or she must leave room for the Spirit to move and the congregation to respond, which will invariably lead to unplanned yet stirring and stimulating insights. The spirit-infused antiphonal relationship between preacher and congregation produces a culturally empowering gospel message shaped by "combined memory and narrative improvisation."[9] These elements, *combined memory* and *narrative improvisation*, compose pathways to rhetorical invention in black preaching, pathways that are, within the African American church tradition, every bit as salient as exegetical Bible study or researching theological works.

In his classic work *The Oratory of Negro Leaders: 1900–1968*, Marcus Boulware makes the following observations about Shuttlesworth:

> The Alabama leader and orator is a tremendous "off-the-cuff" speaker in what, if done formally, would be called a "question-and-answer period." . . . While his speeches may lack some of the sonority and resonance of ancient oratory, his extemporaneous messages surge with enough fervor to rouse his audience to action . . . Mr. Shuttlesworth can play on the emotions of listeners at a meeting in a manner similar to Heifetz bowing and fingering the strings of a violin.[10]

Boulware's structured assessment of Shuttlesworth's informal but efficacious style comes curiously close to a spontaneous remark the preacher made regarding his voice during the April 22, 1963 mass meeting:

8. Hubbard, *Sermon and the African American Imagination*, 7–8.

9. Mitchell, *Black Preaching*, 20.

10. Boulware, *Oratory of Negro*, 216–17.

> You can't hear? You hear that? Well, I can raise my voice, you know. They say the difference between a preacher and a politician is that a preacher starts low and ends high and a politician starts high and ends low.[11]

Boulware also cites C. K. Steele Sr., who was "an effective speaker and leader" of the Tallahassee movement. Steele's assessment of the Shuttlesworth's vocal style echoes the sentiments expressed in the above quote:

> He starts with a low tone of voice that soon rises to a high pitch. He seems to have a gift for catchy sentences. For an example, when referring to Bull Connor, former police commissioner of Birmingham, Fred Shuttlesworth remarked, "We have taken the Bull out of old *Bull* Connor and made a steer of him." He has kept the Alabama movement alive by the slogan, "The Movement Must Move."[12]

As was and is the case with most seasoned orators, be they politicians or preachers, Shuttlesworth understood the power of a turn of phrase to turn the tide of his audience's beliefs, opinions, or actions. He likewise knew that depending on the rhetorical situation, when orators raise their voices they can raise the persuasive stakes. Emoting through one's voice is not exclusively emotional, simply a matter of unvarnished pathos. The preacher's voice can demonstrate his enthusiasm and conviction, enliven and elucidate the sermon, and move as well as mobilize the audience.

THE IMPROVISATIONAL POETICS AND HERMENEUTICS OF BLACK PROPHETIC PREACHING

Taken together, Boulware, Steele, and Shuttlesworth acknowledge the linguistic interplay between preacher and audience, a relationship that illuminates the indelible link between sound and meaning in African American preaching. James Henry Harris, a professor of practical theology and authority on homiletics, explains:

> The nexus between the oral and the aural is always a part of the existential present and contributes to the meaning of the message in the mind of the hearer. The spoken word has power; what you

---

11. Shuttlesworth, Presiding remarks, April 22 (Holmes, transcript).

12. Boullware, *Oratory of Negro Leaders*, 216.

hear is indeed what you get. This means that African American preaching is often as acoustical as it is semantic.[13]

In other words, *how* something is said (style and in this case sound) equates with *what* is said. One well-circulated folk story about a brilliant but dispassionate young black preacher candidate ends with this wise old deacon's review and counsel: "Put some fire in you sermon or put your sermon in the fire."

However, the verbal dexterity Shuttlesworth and other African American preachers demonstrated includes more than pitch or projection, accomplished more than just warming up and wooing the audience. One conclusion that can be drawn from Harris's observation above is that interpreting the Scripture is, within the African American oral tradition, often indivisible from performing the Scripture. Reading, speaking, and hearing may be separate acts but are not viewed as such when questions of spiritual or political salvation are at stake.

A company of scholars of black rhetoric and preaching, including Henry Mitchell, William Pipes, Geneva Smitherman, John Rickford, Keith Gilyard, and Kirt Wilson, have noted that African American linguistic play is serious business, even when the African American orator appears, as was often the case during the mass meetings, to be joking. Throughout the bittersweet history of Africans' experience in America, humor has operated as an indispensable rhetorical device—one that not only provides catharsis for the black auditors but further functions as a sane and sophisticated form of critiquing the powers that be. One need only glance at a few genres of African American expressive culture—proverbs, slave narratives, and folktales—to illustrate this point.

More significantly still, the black preacher communicates on multiple levels of pathos, as Henry Mitchell argues, through his or her own use of tone, rhythm, repetition, role playing, and storytelling. As it was for Shuttlesworth, this practice is an acknowledgement of at once individual style and a larger African American sermonic tradition, one that values the rational but venerates the passionate. However, I am hardly referring to passion for its own sake or raw emotionality. Rather, the passion captured in the poetics of African American preaching calls upon the past culture of African American forefathers and foremothers as routes to challenging the dominant culture that both marginalizes black experience and minimizes black expression as merely emotional release. That Shuttlesworth could

13. Harris, *Word Made Plain*, 78.

"play on the emotions of his listeners," as Boulware notes, should not diminish one's appreciation for his substantive content, therefore.

According to Aristotle, pathos is an indispensable component of rhetoric. In book 2 of *The Art of Rhetoric,* he argued that passionate, unlettered orators would likely sound more reasonable to the masses than formally trained ones. Whereas the lettered orators persuaded others using structured and intricate reasoning, the unpolished orators persuaded their audience with "what they know" and "what more nearly concerns the audience."[14] Perhaps Aristotle partly referred to those orators' experiential connection to the audience. For my purposes, Aristotle's observation may suggest an avenue for analyzing Boulware's exploration of "combined memory and narrative improvisation" in black preaching. That is, obviously a black preacher makes use of tropes, narratives, arguments, and other forms of cultural language that resonated with African American church members. Furthermore, Shuttlesworth's playing on his listeners' emotions should not be viewed in the same manipulative light with which Socrates condemned the sophists. Shuttlesworth moved the masses who attended these meetings to an end they held in common, rather than one that would benefit only him. On the other hand, one might associate Susan Jarratt's revisionist reading of the sophists with Shuttlesworth's mass meeting rhetoric: fragmented narratives may give us insights into to the rhetorical and other cultural values of marginalized groups as well as how mainstream discourses might be critiqued.[15]

In other words, African American preaching style affords observers with one of multiple examples of how verbal performance can serve a hermeneutical function. Mitchell observes:

> Just as the New Hermeneutic of Ebeling and others has sought to recapture vital messages of Luther and the reformation for the benefit of their descendants, so must the Black hermeneutic seek to look into the message of the Black past and see what Black ancestors could be saying to Black people today.[16]

Mitchell reminds us that the New Hermeneutic dispensed with any assumption that hermeneutics consists of culturally detached and objective strategies of interpretation. These strategies were both entrenched in a particular milieu and provided a legacy for the people of that culture.

14. Aristotle, *Art of Rhetoric*, 289.

15. Jarratt, *Rereading the Sophists*, ch. 3.

16. Mitchell, *Black Preaching*, 19.

Preaching provides such a legacy for African Americans, as it dispenses with Eurocentric notions that privilege textual interpretation over oral performance. Thomas Hoyt Jr., a professor of New Testament hermeneutics, concurs. He argues that African Americans had to refashion Eurocentric principles of biblical interpretation, like the critical-historical method, to meet their particular and pressing sociopolitical needs. In order to accomplish this, African American preachers set about reimagining biblical stories drawing upon the black oral tradition.[17] In other words, biblical interpretation was facilitated through rhetorical imagination. James Henry Harris expresses a similar sentiment:

> Preaching style is not the antithesis of content but a corollary or constituent element of the content and hermeneutics (theory) of preaching. If the task of hermeneutics is to bridge the distance between text and interpreter (or listener), the orality and gestures of the preacher often contribute to the effectiveness of preaching.[18]

It is difficult to overemphasize Harris's point about the preacher's "orality and gestures." In the black church, sermons, songs, and shouts from the minster and congregation become the packaging for which all knowledge is delivered, understood, and evaluated. Existential, social, political, and philosophical issues are tethered to the ceremonial practices of the black church and filtered particularly through preaching. Black preaching packages pragmatic or practical knowledge. As a result, sermons often move from private matters of personal moral choice to public, indeed prophetic, matters of social justice. During times of great local and national crisis, like the civil rights movement, the homiletic focus shifted substantially from microvirtues to macrovalues. One would be hard pressed, therefore, not only to draw hard and fast distinctions between black preaching and hermeneutics (or rhetoric and philosophy) but also to restrictively definine the genre of the African American sermon itself. Of course, there are commonly accepted elements of the black sermon. Not every speech act is a sermon any more than any piece of African American music is jazz. But like jazz, as I noted by citing Dolan Hubbard earlier, the African American sermon commands a level of artistic and creative "elasticity." And like jazz, the interaction between audience (congregants) and performers (preachers) influences the duration and direction of the performance. While the

17. Hoyt, "Interpreting Biblical Scholarship," 24–26.

18. Harris, *Word Made Plain*, 77.

black sermon has been a celebrated form of communication religiously and culturally, black congregants, particularly during times of struggle, expected to find a prophetic word from the Lord whenever their pastors opened their mouths.

Within African American expressive culture broadly and black preaching particularly, style rarely takes a backseat to substance. This is not to say that African American sermons or other forms of black rhetoric should be confined to the "decorous," as cultural critic Vorris Nunley has well argued. Instead, the poetics of black preaching are intimately intertwined with the philosophy, politics, and social critique that such discourse conveys. Or, as George Shulman argues, poetic language is a part of the vernacular of the American prophetic language. Black preachers use style (oral and gestural according to Harris) to interpret the Bible for the congregation as well as to enable the congregation to interpret and interrogate the real world, not exclusively in a holier-than-thou sense, but as citizens passionate about social justice. In short, black preaching blurs at most, or complicates at the very least, the lines between style and substance, the sacred and the secular.

Therefore Shulman's contention that the prophetic language that characterized the civil rights movement was more about poetry and rhetoric than it was about philosophy needs to be modified. Hermeneutics is to philosophy what preaching is to prophecy. As a species of philosophy, black hermeneutics often overlaps with black preaching, so that distinctions between the "production and reception" of knowledge relevant to the African American struggle are not always easily made (See Steven Mailloux). This is not to say that African American approaches to socially conscious hermeneutics and homiletics are without limitation. Scholars such as Thomas Hoyt suggest that black clergy have allowed their own cultural presuppositions to entrap them in the same exegetical pitfalls as their white counterparts. Biblical proof-texting to substantiate extremist views constitutes one example. However, the African American oral tradition commands and demands that the telling and hearing, reading, and interpreting of the Scripture ultimately lead to liberation and equality.

PREACHING THE HELL OUT OF EARTH:
THE PROPHETIC POETICS OF SOCIAL JUSTICE RHETORIC

Like many other African American rhetors, therefore, Shuttlesworth offers literalist readings of Bible doctrines infused with the prophetic rhetoric of social justice; these readings distinguish him from conservative Christian fundamentalists whom Sharon Crowley and Cornel West critique in their respective books *Toward a Civil Discourse* and *Democracy Matters*. While Shuttlesworth advocated many of the strict moral codes of the Religious Right, and, more significantly, their apocalyptic sense of a literal Day of Judgment, his biblicist-inspired political vision, unlike those of Pat Robertson, Tim La Haye, and the late Jerry Falwell, concentrated more on the material state of the disenfranchised than on personal, moral standing. To apply West's terms, Shuttlesworth's Christian rhetoric was "prophetic" rather than "Constantinian." For West, the former type of Christian orator challenges the status quo, in keeping with the minor prophets who boldly critiqued oppressive displays of politics and religion, whereas the latter type of Christian rhetor, like the Roman emperor Constantine did, uses religion to appease the political status quo and reinforce the standing of the wealthy. West spotlights the civil rights movement as a premiere forum for the practice of prophetic Christianity. While he does not mention Shuttlesworth specifically, based on the criteria West sets forth, Shuttlesworth more than qualifies as a prophetic Christian. The following selection is taken from Shuttlesworth's sixth annual presidential address to the Alabama Christian Movement for Human Rights. In June 1962, he proclaimed that

> Babylon of old was warned by the prophets; but having become drunk off power and pride, and thinking that her powerful army and wonderful Swinging Gardens would sway the future, she did not heed the voice of God when He said . . . "Behold, I am against thee, O thou most proud, saith the Lord God of hosts: for thy day is come, the time that I will visit thee. And the most proud shall stumble and fall and none shall raise up: and I shall kindle a fire in his cities, and it shall devour all around him" (Jeremiah 50:31–32). Truly Babylon, which had "been a golden cup in the Lord's hand" a chance to unify the world and lead men into the ideals of brotherhood and justice . . . Can we discern any difference in today's Birmingham and yesterday's Babylon? . . . Babylon became mad and was destroyed. Alabama and Birmingham have become drunk off the wine of the southern way of life, and have become mad with power. Not willing to sober themselves with the vitality of Twentieth-Century light, they persist in 1860 standards.[19]

19. Shuttlesworth, Sixth Presidential Address, in Houck and Dixon, eds., *Rhetoric, Religion*, 465–66.

In this speech, Shuttlesworth deployed commonplace curses associated with prophetic rhetoric: denouncing secular pride, condemning stubborn rejection of God's message, and proclaiming the certainty of judgment. Shuttlesworth additionally focused on a racial, regional, and social repentance, drawn from a rudimentary reading of Scripture often associated with the strident moral dictums of the Religious Right. However, his reading was not constrained by these dictums. Shuttlesworth's fundamentalist objections against personal sin didn't diminish or dilute his prophetic convictions against larger, weightier injustices perpetuated in the public sphere. That is to say, the microvirtues of piety and purity neither replaced nor overshadowed the macrovalues of social justice and inclusive democracy. In fact, for Shuttlesworth the prophetic voice was neither mainly nor exclusively defined as *foretelling* (the principal narrative strategy for the Religious Right). Prophecy was about *forth-telling*, or bold and brazen proclamations against the precepts, principles, and practices of the status quo. This valiant stance would also win approval from West, as he invokes the classical Greek descriptor *parrhesia*[20] to characterize the frank speech of civil rights heroes and heroines.

As a result, not only did Shuttlesworth use the poetics of the black sermon to communicate informal messages for, from, and about his people, he further revised and reinvented the structure, style, and tone of mainstream discourses whenever they were deployed to disenfranchise black Americans. Shuttlesworth most likely knew that the southern white ruling class would continue to manipulate language for its own social, economic, and political benefit. This is perhaps why he amended the initialism KKK from Ku Klux Klan to King, Kennedy, and Khrushchev, as a refrain during the mass meetings. This initialism provides one example of Shuttlesworth's informal yet intentional use of anaphora and alliteration to critique the many methods southern whites employed to defer the rights of blacks by privileging and ordering a particular narrative chronology.

Perhaps by reworking KKK as an initialism Shuttlesworth may have signaled his grasp of the apocalyptic story line, which fundamentalists often deem an essential component of a prophetic narrative. According to Andrew Manis, the apocalyptic has functioned as a narrative element in the South since the Civil War. The coming of the end became a refrain in southern Baptist rhetoric during both World Wars and the legislative battles surrounding civil rights. Shuttlesworth's likely recognition of the

20. West, *Democracy Matters*, 209–11.

apocalyptic narrative places him within a larger rhetorical universe that includes King, Kennedy, Khrushchev, and the Klan. All four spoke, to greater or lesser degrees, at one time or another, deploying apocalyptic language, including cataclysmic tropes, like fire, to depict possible end-of-days story lines. The Klan believed that the push towards desegregation would lead to miscegenation, Roman Catholic religious domination, Jewish economic control, social anarchy, and ultimately a divine curse. For Kennedy and Khrushchev, the apocalypse could entail nuclear annihilation that might result from a full-out war between the USA and the USSR. For King, the world could end physically, but more importantly, spiritually, through the triple threats of racism, militarism, and poverty.

Of course, the Klan, as an extremist group, rejected any person or idea supporting civil rights, Roman Catholicism, and Communism. They considered all of these ideologies as varying manifestations of godlessness. The same could be said to some degree of southern Protestant clergy, including black ministers: King 's father did not initially want to vote for Kennedy because he was Roman Catholic—or Dixiecrat politicians. Similarly, northern politicians of both major parties reverently rejected Communism and, at the very least and on the whole, had strong reservations about civil rights legislation—and, before Kennedy was nominated and elected, about a Roman Catholic presidency. Shuttlesworth shrewdly rejected the core substance of Klan exclusivist religious rhetoric while retrieving and revising their sense of the apocalyptic. The civilized world would end if the race problem were not addressed in terms of social integration and full democratic inclusion.

Shuttlesworth was able to reject the Klan's racism and religious bigotry while remaining rooted in what Andrew Manis would view as the worldview of southern American civil religion. American civil religion fuses "patriotism and piety."[21] For the most part, white and black southerners saw a seamless connection between fierce patriotism, strict morality, and allegiance to their region. However, more progressive black preachers, such as Shuttlesworth, would add the inclusion of African Americans in the democratic process as an indispensable component of American civil religion.

Therefore the civility of American civil religion could be achieved only through an unrelenting critique of official and unofficial expressions

21. Manis, *Southern Civil Religion*, 13–14.

of white dominance and discrimination. Shuttlesworth advanced his case in poetic terms during a mass meeting on April 25, 1963:

> But segregation has a way of making folks leave off certain things in order to get at certain points. I said that the unwritten rule has been that if the mob don't stop the Negroes, the police can. And if the police can't, the courts will, and that's exactly what they trying to do now . . . And we, the Negroes, have learned that we substitute another m for m: marshals for mob.[22]

With the last sentence, Shuttlesworth concisely exposed a central ideological tension within the civil rights movement: federal sovereignty (represented by the marshals) versus southern anarchy (represented by the mob). The citation also dredges up images of school integration battles, such as the fight to get James Meredith enrolled into the University of Mississippi as well as Shuttlesworth's effort to get his own children into Phillips High School. Shuttlesworth's stylistic yet substantive critique of white narrative privilege, through the alliteration (King, Kennedy and Khrushchev), redeemed the original initialism from the fanatically antiblack, anti–Roman Catholic, and anti-Communist destructive readings circulating in American culture to reconstructive reinterpretations that at once call upon and critique the prejudicial categories that Klan rhetoric constructed.

THE POETICS OF AFRICAN AMERICAN PATRIOTISM

Like the NAACP and the Southern Christian Leadership Conference (SCLC), Shuttlesworth similarly refashioned the anti-Communistic rhetoric that Hoover's FBI and southern white racists spread against the movement into a recurring message that actually favored civil rights. By arranging *Khrushchev* to represent the third letter in his initialism, Shuttlesworth may have demonstrated some understanding of the network of intersections among domestic policies, international public relations, global economics, religious bigotry, racism, and colonialism. Nevertheless, Shuttlesworth strove to describe the domestic civil rights movement as a microcosm of the global battle for freedom and justice. His remarks from the April 25th mass meeting illuminate this point:

22. Shuttlesworth, Presiding remarks, April 25th (Holmes transcript).

Now, I've have always believed that it's not in Cuba where this thing
is going to be won. It's not in Caracas, Venezuela, Bogota, Columbia. You are in the focal point of history, right here tonight.[23]

Seeing the civil rights movement as a smaller yet salient manifesta-
tion of the larger international struggle for freedom was not a new to the
Birmingham crusade. Martin Luther King Jr. and other civil rights notables
had been discussing intersections between global policies and domestic
racial politics since the 1950s. This would only make sense given the in-
roads into American race relations that Communists tried to make during
the 1930s and '40s, in particular against egregious examples of southern
American racism like the Scottsboro case.

As a native southern Protestant, Shuttlesworth surely knew the culturally engrained reservations that southern whites held about what they
deemed the triple threats to individual liberty: Communism, Roman
Catholicism, and civil rights. Consequently, white southerners sought to
squeeze all of these story lines into one narrative box with international
concerns holding the preeminent place while Shuttlesworth, as the above
quotes suggest, reshuffled the story lines in the box, affording the African
American struggle the place of social and political priority. Further, southern and northern politicians were more inclined to address racial injustices
at home that had been exposed on the global stage.

Shuttlesworth also knew that most efforts at ensuring African American political and social rights had been maligned as Communistic plots. To
be sure, by at least the 1920s, white southerners thought that Communists'
subversive ideas would appeal to their black counterparts, and some of these
fears were justified. For example, "in Birmingham, Alabama, the industrial center of the South, black and red became inextricably intertwined."[24]
Shuttlesworth understood that many people of color, including a large
contingent in Alabama during the Depression, had been attracted to the
Communist Party's promises of racial equality. By 1945, "the Soviet Union
had exploited racial discord in the United States to attempt to discredit its
claims to world stewardship."[25] By 1947, President Harry Truman, liberal
and progressive Democrats, as well as moderate Republicans, began to
incorporate rhetoric that included the theme of civil rights, primarily in
response to the Soviet challenge, but partly to walk the political tightrope

23. Ibid.
24. Woods, *Black Struggle*, 19.
25. Pauley, "Truman and the NACCP," 225.

of winning northern black votes on the one hand and appeasing conservative Republican and southern Democratic senators on the other. The fundamentalist country preacher knew, as the above remarks on Cuba suggest, that the America's political response to civil rights would ultimately be about what was profitable economically and pragmatic internationally rather than about what was moral, ethical, or even legal nationally. In other words, the hypocrisy of American democracy was and sometimes is to fight for international freedoms before and often instead of domestic freedoms.

On the other hand, by juxtaposing Khrushchev with Kennedy and King, Shuttlesworth forged a subtle yet subversive space for redrawing the boundaries of patriotic civil rights discourse. As Jeff Woods has noted, several civil rights leaders knew that by dissociating themselves from the relatively few Marxists among the movement, they were losing some of the most fervent volunteers. However, the "Red Scare,"[26] not to mention the support from white liberal political establishment black leaders sought, demanded such distancing. Shuttlesworth's inclusion of Khrushchev, then, though admittedly a part of the larger comic-critical strategy he solicited with the entire initialism, invited, indeed demanded a consideration of which elements of Marxist ideology were redeemable for prophetically and poetically critiquing American racism.

Shuttlesworth's use of King, Kennedy, and Khrushchev reflected what Kenneth Burke considers the rhetoric of cooperation.[27] For Burke, the rhetoric that encompasses and produces authentic persuasion must be born of antagonism. To say that there were multiple antagonisms that existed among the individuals, ideologies, and institutions represented by Shuttlesworth's initialism would be an understatement. King and Kennedy were not allies joined at the hip for civil rights. As an officer in the SCLC and participant in civil rights activities beyond Birmingham, Shuttlesworth possessed firsthand knowledge of what David Niven styled Kennedy's "glacial change"[28] approach to civil rights. A firm believer that the Reconstruction had been a failure, Kennedy was initially convinced that changes in race relations should, as Niven argues, take their course naturally. Such an approach would inevitably put King at odds with the Kennedy administration, especially since King saw the 1960s as a critical moment; this conviction would preclude any notion of gradualism when it came to racial justice.

26. Woods, *Black Struggle*, 10.
27. Burke, *Rhetoric of Motives*, 102.
28. Niven, *Politics of Injustice*, 36–38.

Kennedy's reticence to act during a civil rights crisis, such as during the violence that accompanied the Freedom Rides of 1961, greatly disturbed King and Shuttlesworth, who put his life directly on the line by preaching about the Freedom Rides weeks before the event, by dispatching members of his congregation to pick up Freedom Riders from a Birmingham bus station to take them to hospitals, and by allowing some of the riders to stay in his home. For this last act, Birmingham police officers stood outside of Shuttlesworth's house threatening to arrest him for holding an interracial gathering in his home.

Nevertheless, Shuttlesworth reflected bravado several times during the mass meetings that belied a close political alliance with the Kennedys, one that allowed him the familiarity to call them by their first names. Though his audience would have recognized these moves as humorous staging to some extent, the political stakes entailed in civil rights, not to mention the alliances made with the Kennedys, could not be taken lightly. In fact, Shuttlesworth did talk to Robert Kennedy on a number of occasions. The day after the Freedom Riders were brutally attacked in Birmingham, for example, Shuttlesworth talked with the attorney general over the phone several times. Moreover, despite the criticisms that prominent civil rights leaders, including Roy Wilkins, Martin Luther King Jr., James Farmer, and Julian Bond leveled against John Kennedy for his compromises with the South before and after being elected president, the more widely circulated narrative among African Americans depicted Kennedy as a fierce proponent of civil rights. David Niven concurs, when he notes that Shuttlesworth

> was particularly vociferous in his condemnation of Republicans and celebration of Kennedy. When Shuttlesworth's services were visited by white Birmingham police officers . . . Shuttlesworth would point to the men and say, these men "voted for Nixon, along with the other white people." While in Shuttlesworth's thinking Eisenhower "never did nothing for the Negroes in the eight years he was there," the Kennedys were lionized . . . In the aftermath of the Freedom Rides, Reverend Shuttlesworth shouted to his parishioners, "We thank Jack, Bob, and God," for progress in civil rights.[29]

Later "in a 1963 Louis Harris poll, African Americans were asked who had done the most for civil rights. The top three answers were the NAACP,

29. Ibid., 168.

Martin Luther King Jr., and John F. Kennedy."[30] For Nick Bryant, Kennedy's window dressing practices of inviting black people to White House parties and appointing them to high-profile but ineffectual positions projected an image of civil rights success by "association."[31] Unfortunately, being seen with black people was a dismal substitute for incorporating progressive policies to help them. Still, Shuttlesworth's anti-Republican remarks illustrate the gradual shift of black support to the Democratic Party. This shift began with Franklin Roosevelt, gained momentum during Kennedy's presidency, and would peak during Lyndon Johnson's administration.

While the Freedom Rides exemplified the uneasy alliance that was developing between the Kennedys and King, this event further exposed the unacknowledged link between segregationists and Communists exploiting African Americans. In his fifth annual presidential address to the ACMHR, Shuttlesworth opined:

> We have been victims of police negligence, police oppression, and mob violence. All this in Alabama, U.S.A. Small wonder then that some people are asking the facetious question, is this United States or Russia? In testimony on the witness stand, Commissioner Connor, who signed two state warrants against me charging me with conspiracy, testified that I and the little group of students who were trying to catch a bus, formed a mob; and that in effect there were two mobs. Is the commissioner trying to fool the intelligent white people of this community? He certainly isn't fooling the Negroes! Is a man a mobster simply because he seeks, in a lawful and Christian way, his rights? And why weren't the police on the scene before men with lead pipes and other weapons beat defenseless Negroes and Whites onto the ground? And why didn't the police arrest these men? Will the KKK rule Alabama in the twentieth century?[32]

That Shuttlesworth once again equated the Klan with Communists would be highly offensive to segregationists. Preserving the racial caste system was not only necessary to maintain the southern way of life, but doing so also represented a heroic gesture of patriotism. For southern segregationists, those who challenged the enshrined norms of the status quo—be they white northerners seeking to integrate interstate bus travel, or southern-born blacks demanding integrated lunch counters—were either

30. Ibid., 171

31. Bryant, *Bystander*, 161

32. Shuttlesworth, Fifth Annual Presidential Address, 1961.

influenced by Communists or might as well have been. Shuttlesworth reinterpreted southern resistances to integration, refashioning the narrative so that African Americans seeking justice and the white Americans that aided them were actually the patriotic ones. Bull Connor's testimony against Shuttlesworth and the Freedom Riders on the one hand and his failure to protect them from mob violence on the other demonstrated that status-quo segregation cut against the grain of law and order.

In fact, Shuttlesworth went on in that presidential address to explain why blacks would be utterly offended by the widely circulated myth that in seeking civil rights they were merely Communist dupes:

> Negroes do not need a communist to tell them what their rights are. Our hearts are not impressed by the dogmas of Karl Marx and Lenin; Negroes loathe Kruschev [sic] and his tactics; we are wild about that Galilean stranger who taught us to love even those who bomb our homes and dash our brains onto the ground.[33]

By mentioning three famous leaders associated with Communism, Shuttlesworth demonstrated his nuanced knowledge of the shadings of this ideology. As a result, he and other people of color could not be persuaded to join a radical movement that they knew well and, consequently, despised. While it was a well-circulated fact that Communists tried to woo African Americans to their cause with promises of social and economic equality, Shuttlesworth argued that African Americans were discerning enough to recognize such efforts as mere tactics. Black Americans vying for civil rights were not looking for tactics; they longed for an ideology that could be incorporated into a lifestyle and parlayed into meaningful civic engagement.

The dismissive tone with which Shuttlesworth claimed that "the Klan has given way" to the more formidable forces of civil rights, Communism, and a Roman Catholic presidency also encompassed critical idealism. Shuttlesworth was well aware of the Klan's militant determination and terrorist tactics, especially in light of what they considered damnable religious and patriotic heresies (they saw an inseparable link between the two), beginning with *Brown v Board of Education*. Just two years after and largely because of the *Brown* decision, the Klan claimed a membership of two hundred thousand. As a result, the seemingly caviler way in which Shuttlesworth dismissed the Klan's significance should not leave the impression that he underestimated either their danger or influence; rather in comparison to

33. Ibid.

the constellation of social, economic, political, and legal forces represented by his initialism, the Klan was well on its way to being marginalized. More significantly, the prophetic genre upon which Shuttlesworth relied included a narrative structure in which evil would be punished and the oppressed vindicated.

The antagonist cooperation illustrated by Shuttlesworth's remarks was played out differently through Kennedy's relationship with Khrushchev. Like other informed Americans, Shuttlesworth was aware of the near cataclysmic misses represented by the Berlin negotiations and the Cuban missile crisis. Each event could have led to a nuclear disaster. As a private citizen, Shuttlesworth could not have known how close the country actually came, but the threat of mutual nuclear annihilation was a part of the international consciousness during the time. A less apparent subtext, but one that Shuttlesworth was well aware of, was Kennedy's and Khrushchev's respective, contested narratives of freedom, narratives aimed at people of color internationally. As Khrushchev saw it, the USSR fought heroically to save the people of Asia, Africa, and Latin America from the clutches of colonialism, which capitalism, he argued, fostered. For Kennedy, conversely, peoples of color across the world must be liberated in some cases and protected in others from the stranglehold of Communism, which would choke off individual freedoms.

While Shuttlesworth and other civil rights leaders criticized soviet Communists for stifling individual freedoms, they likewise castigated American capitalists for failing to, initially in some cases or consistently in others, secure black citizens' said freedoms. Both Kennedy and Khrushchev believed that the other's narrative, if played out, would lead to apocalyptic destructions internationally. In contrast, as Shuttlesworth's initialism suggests, either the Communist or capitalist narrative, unchecked by the civil rights narrative, would hasten the apocalypse.

Curiously, then, Khrushchev's atheism, Kennedy's Roman Catholicism, overshadowed by his pragmatic politics, and Shuttlesworth's prophetic African American Christianity collided within their respective constellations of apocalyptic rhetorics. These included, among other moves, averting what each envisioned as the cosmic chaos that would ensue if their sociopolitical worldview was not accepted. "Vision," then emerges as significant trope in the narrative of the apocalyptic. Greatly influenced by the cosmic visions from the prophetic biblical books of Daniel, Ezekiel, and especially Revelation, current right wing fundamentalists believe they have acquired the divinely sanctioned view of Scripture, which, in turn, validates their conservative political and social visions for the nation and world. The Klan drew upon these books to construct their exclusionary vision. African American prophetic rhetoric, conversely, from David Walker onward, contains a pervasive current of apocalyptic language compelling white America to envision the curse that would befall the nation if racism endured.

As Shuttlesworth envisaged by redressing the ideological import derived from the letters *KKK*, we may envision, perhaps beyond his original comic-critical intent, readdressing the racialized, classed, and globalized dogmas that inform contemporary national and international rhetorics of social justice. The colorblind rhetoric that the former enslaver supreme court justice John Marshall Harlan espoused in 1896 and that Kennedy promoted in 1963 alone could neither liberate nor empower people of color. According to Nick Bryant, Kennedy would, by the summer of 1963, practically abandon his notion that the Reconstruction trounced on southern sovereignty and thus should affect the pace of his civil rights program. He came to recognize, with head and heart, the pervasive culturally ensconced evil of segregation.[34] What Kennedy did not and perhaps could not fully grasp is that for white southerners democratic privileges were skin deep, the exclusive province of Anglo-Saxons. Kennedy's political rhetoric specifically and 1960s rhetoric generally could stand to be further scrutinized through the lens of the critical theory of whiteness studies.

Not surprisingly, color (or to a considerable extent the colors black and red) had come to signify the central social and political dilemmas for post–World War II America. Racist color consciousness coupled with conscious obsession with red-baiting not only constituted the pillars upon which southern white supremacy stood but, moreover, normalized the acceptance of white American privilege regardless of region. Given the age-old and widely circulated negative theological associations with black and red as signifiers, the trope of vision would play itself out in canonizing a raced, classed, and gendered orthodoxy in the South. Any and all departures from this holy social vision constituted more than heresy; the digressions represented clear plot lines in the apocalyptic narrative.

This chapter has introduced Fred Shuttlesworth's revised use of the initialism KKK as rhetorical device rooted in the poetics, hermeneutics, and, most significantly, prophecy intertwined within the black preaching

---

34. Bryant, *Bystander*, ch. 22.

tradition. Using this initialism enabled Shuttlesworth to describe poetically both African Americans' critique of sociopolitical injustices and their undying patriotism amid the civil rights struggle.

However, did the rhetoric of the Birmingham mass meetings need to extend beyond the clergy? Certainly the potential for its effectiveness ranged beyond the preacher's voice and church walls. But could the Birmingham crusade use authentic and authoritative voices from the pew as well as from the pulpit? In the next chapter, one controversial movement leader will answer these questions.

3

"Do You Want to Be Free?"

James Bevel, Black Prophetic Rhetoric,
and Grassroots Agency

"One is the force of complacency, made up of many Negroes who have lived so long in the midst of this dark and desolate night of oppression that they've given up in the struggle for freedom, and they've adjusted to segregation. Made up of another group of Negroes that because they have gained a degree of academic and economic security and because they profit by segregation that they have become insensitive to the problems of the masses of people."[1]

—Martin Luther King Jr.

"If the people move, then the leaders can move."[2]

—Roy Wilkins, NAACP

The last chapter discussed how Fred Shuttlesworth made use of formal and informal presidential rhetoric that tows the line between poetics and hermeneutics. This chapter turns to James Bevel. Particularly, I contend

1. April 22nd, 1963 Mass meeting (Holmes transcript).
2. April 25th, 1963, Mass meeting (Holmes transcript).

that Bevel's mass meeting speech of April 12th, 1963, lays the groundwork for a grassroots prophetic rhetoric of mobilization whereby the black masses could recognize and exercise sociopolitical expression and agency with or without ministerial leadership. From at least the mid-nineteenth century, African Americans were accustomed to following dynamic leaders in their often religiously infused sociopolitical movements. Many of these leaders were Moses archetypes.[3] By the time of the civil rights movement of the 1950s and '60s, getting African Americans as a group to act independently of that type of leadership was a formidable task, although there were moments where this did happen. The Nashville Student Movement and the Student Nonviolent Coordinating Committee (SNCC) represent two stellar examples. Historically, there had always been black individuals among the masses who would stand up and speak out against institutional injustices. However, many others believed that such expressive autonomy was above the rhetorical pay grade of the black rank and file. That the Birmingham campaign and most mass movements among African Americans were entrenched in the patriarchal, top-down, ministerial leadership of the black church hindered many laypersons from even considering speaking truth to power.

This dilemma draws me to rhetorical strategies of James Bevel, sit-in pioneer, SCLC Field Secretary, and architect of the controversial but ultimately successful Birmingham Children's Campaign. Foreshadowing the black liberation theology of the late 1960s,[4] James Bevel's April 12th mass meeting speech, delivered during King's first night of imprisonment in Birmingham, expands the concept of God's kingdom beyond eschatological (heavenly) considerations and addresses real-life institutional injustices. Unlike the current discourses of the Religious Right, Bevel's rhetoric made use of biblical tropes like the kingdom as a way of empowering the marginalized black masses to enter into conversations held in the public sphere without trying to regulate them. Perhaps more significantly, Bevel's speech called his audience to the quality of autonomy and agency that has characterized a range of exceptional individual black orators from the eighteenth century to the present.

---

3. See Moses, *Black Messiahs and Uncle Toms* for a solid survey of this type of leadership.

4. See Cone, *Black Theology of Liberation*, 33 and 132–33.

SETTING FOR BEVEL'S APRIL 12TH SPEECH

The leaders of the Birmingham campaign did not agree on every issue related to civil rights. As one might imagine, there were differences of opinion as to how to execute an effective protest that would remain Christian and patriotic. King actually welcomed divergent voices around him. With his skill in Hegelian synthesis, King had a long-standing practice of encouraging strident disagreement on strategies for a particular demonstration only to chime in the final moments with a thoughtful synthesis. During the weeks of the Birmingham campaign of 1963, these reflective strategy sessions became fewer. Fred Shuttlesworth, who had been formally fighting for African American rights in Birmingham since 1956, had invited King's SCLC to help but clearly saw the campaign as his. While his most pronounced conflict with King would emerge towards the end of the campaign, Shuttlesworth never lost the sense that God had called and ordained him to lead black Birmingham to freedom.

To clarify, the issue was not whether the campaign should be patriotic. All of King's lieutenants and Shuttlesworth believed that to varying degrees. The issue was not even whether to use mass demonstration. Obviously all bought into that decision. Rather, what would be the nature of these demonstrations? Where should the demonstrators strike? How often? How assertively? Who should participate? This last question became a constant source of irritation as the ranks of volunteers increasingly thinned. Of course all of black Birmingham did not support the campaign, especially at the beginning. From the popular and conservative pastor J. L. Ware to the highly successful businessman A. G. Gaston to the average black resident, support for the campaign as well as its path to victory remained unclear. Obviously, recruiting from the upper echelons of black Birmingham presented a problem. Even when the black upper class in other southern states sympathized with the goals of a particular civil rights demonstration, they—like many whites—might support the cause through anonymous donations. After all, many of the African American well-to-do wouldn't want to risk losing the semblance of the American dream they had managed to scrounge up despite racism. African Americans hailing from the working class constituted the likely recruits for this or any other civil rights campaigns, because paradoxically they had nothing and everything to lose at the same time. However as frustrations about blatant racism in Birmingham had been brewing for years, the boiling point of mid-1963 dissuaded many of Birmingham blacks of all classes from participating. The tide of

African Americans calling for self-defense against state-sanctioned brutality had been rising across the nation. Listening to the rhetoric of Malcolm X and others that dominant society considered militant, some people of color sought to organize for self-defense; others would impulsively explode riot style if pushed too far. Black Birmingham was not exempt from these feelings.

In sum, relative uncertainty about strategy, many individuals' respective self-interest, and increasing fear of black retaliatory violence resulted in waning interest in the campaign. While the SCLC and ACMHR had a clear strategy of targeted boycotts and marches (which was known as "Project C" for "Confrontation," as the April and May phase of the Birmingham movement came to be called), the leaders nevertheless met several challenges shortly after beginning. In addition to resistance from the conservative segment of the black community and internal disagreements, Project C was losing volunteers. Many of those who volunteered were filling up the jails, but there was not enough money to bail them out. Before this thirty-eight-day campaign ended some 3,400 participants had gone to jail, including two thousand students.

And the clock was ticking. With an increasing sense that the Birmingham campaign might be unraveling, King convened a strategy meeting on April 12th. At the same time, support from the larger African American community was waning; the white press was routinely burying coverage of the demonstrations. Sensing that his lieutenants were discouraged and knowing that he did not want Birmingham to become another Albany, Georgia, where the chief of police had detained the demonstrators without brutalizing them, King retreated into another room, changed into his marching clothes of a work shirt and blue jeans and returned to the room where the meeting was being held. According to Andrew Young, King stated that he didn't know what to do but that something had to be done. He then walked out the door and led an impromptu march that resulted in his arrest. Abernathy joined King in jail. Later that day, Shuttlesworth was arrested. With the national leader of the civil rights movement, his chief lieutenant, and the de facto head of the Birmingham campaign in jail, what would happen to Project C? More immediate, however, was the question of who would deliver the mass meeting sermon that night.

The second question may seem to significantly trail the first in importance. However, the mass meetings generally and mass meeting speeches particularly were essential for informing, instructing, inspiring, and mobilizing movement participants. Given the highly Christianized culture of black and white southerners, one would expect the mass meeting to be structured like a church service. As Wyatt Walker observes, these meetings were church services replete with raised hymns, earnest prayers, and stirring messages that resembled sermons in almost every respect.[5] All were welcome to testify, but not everyone could preach or *bring the word*. As spontaneous, creative, and, to some degree, free as the southern black worship experience was, an underlying form existed, a structured spontaneity. And the pastor's message, which had to be imbued with African American language, custom, culture, and worldview, constituted a critical element in that form. Through the sermon the preacher served as counselor, teacher, community leader, and spiritual advisor. The local pastors would in most cases had already established this multifaceted relationship with the congregation through the pulpit, but more importantly, though their everyday encounters with congregants, such as weddings, funerals, and hospital visitations. In other words, the local pastors had an ethos that came in handy at the mass meetings.

The southern black church was also quite invested in the periodic, often seasonal revival meeting in addition to Sunday services. Designed to win the sinner and the wayward or inactive Christian, the revival was a special series of services lasting for several consecutive days to a few weeks. Summer months were the most popular times for the less politically oriented revival, but depending on how pressing the reason, the revival could happen at any time of the year and with frequency. As historian David Chappell, among other scholars, has noted, civil right mass meetings were essentially revivals.[6] The overtly evangelical tone of mass meeting messages infused these gatherings with the same or (in the case of crisis moments like April 12th) more spiritual fervor and devotion, for even given the sociopolitical challenges, only God could "make a way out of no way." While Martin Luther King Jr. especially and Ralph Abernathy secondarily were considered headliners at the mass meetings, any preacher delivering the main message was accorded the status of the guest preacher at a revival. The congregants believed that God sent all preachers, but that the revival preacher was called for exigent times.

On April 12th, 1963, when Martin Luther King Jr., Ralph Abernathy, and Fred Shuttlesworth were jailed (or, as the faithful would opine,

5. Walker, *"Somebody's Calling My Name,"* 184.

6. Chappell, *Stone of Hope,* 94.

"providentially hindered" from attending the mass meeting), the attendees needed the guest pastor to offer a special word from the Lord—a word of courage and conviction, so that audience members could continue to participate in the movement, but also to convey a word of comfort because of the three missing figureheads. As I noted earlier, the mass meetings, like a typical Sunday or revival service, included singing (or raising several hymns), prayer, testimonies (either congregants recounting God's intervention in their lives or short sermons from one of the pastors present), and the main message. Announcements would also likely constitute a part of the Baptist service, though not necessarily a sacred part. Because of the sociopolitical nature of the mass meetings, however, announcements were integral for reviewing or debriefing the day's events as well as planning for the coming day. Announcements could come before or following the main message. All of these elements were present during the April 12th meeting.

Someone would introduce the guest pastor or main speaker. On this night Andrew Young, a prominent lieutenant in King's SCLC, did the honors. Young introduced Bevel to this mass meeting crowd as a young man with little hair. Young used this good-natured teasing in a lighthearted fashion to offset the anxiety Bevel faced in Mississippi and to emphasize his practical wisdom, or what the Greeks would call *phronesis*. As we observed earlier, and will in great detail later, it was not unusual for mass meeting leaders and participants to use humor especially during the more stressful times. Even this night, with the Birmingham campaign in jeopardy and King, Abernathy, and Shuttlesworth jailed, mass meeting attendees found several opportunities to laugh before, during, and after the main message. As an SCLC field secretary and copresident of the Nashville Student Movement, Bevel had worked in support of civil rights all over the South, most notably during the Nashville sit-ins and the Freedom Rides. It is therefore no wonder why Young told the audience that the number of battle scars Bevel received during movement would bring anybody close to God.

Obviously, this was a crucial moment of rhetorical exigency and possibly a turning point for the movement. The SCLC had very recently arrived in Birmingham to assist Fred Shuttlesworth's organization. Now King, the leader of the SCLC and the national civil rights movement—a movement that seemed to be on the wane—was in jail. This was also Good Friday, the Friday before Easter, the holiday that celebrates the resurrection of Christ. Significant of course to all Christians, this Easter held a special place for Birmingham blacks. As an act of protest, movement leaders instructed black parishioners not to shop for Easter clothes. Since, according to Wyatt Walker, many southern black churchgoers customarily bought new Easter outfits whether or not they could afford them, neglecting to at this time would cause the white merchants, who usually didn't hire blacks, to feel the economic pinch. Although most movement participants were willing to make this sacrifice and more, some could not help but feel a bit disheartened. More significant than the act of forgoing such an important aspect of the yearly celebration, the fact that the Easter holiday signified new life at a time the movement might be dying was telling.

BEVEL'S SPEECH

Nevertheless, Bevel handled this speech with gravitas. He began by complimenting his audience—a traditional, ceremonial gesture with particular traction in the black church and for visiting pastors. On the face of the speech, he seemed to diminish his own ethos by claiming that his oration would not teach his auditors anything because they had heard from excellent ministers—especially King and Abernathy. Further, Bevel noted that the audience appeared to be relatively prosperous and showed good taste by wearing "good clothes and fine hats"[7] Indirectly, Bevel appeared to be setting up the purpose of his speech: to persuade rather than inform his auditors about their respective roles as active and independent citizens within "the kingdom of God." Indeed, Bevel views his own participation in the movement to be so frenetic that going to jail would offer him a much-needed vacation from helping to promote the "campaign for the kingdom of God."

Bevel's discussion of the kingdom of God was incisive. Depending on one's theological perspective, the kingdom of God could refer to God's reign in heaven and the Christian's hope to ascend there after death. By another interpretation, the kingdom of God refers to spreading God's rule upon the earth—a potentially frightening prospect to be sure when one thinks of the crusades in the Middle East or, more relevant to this reflection, how the Ku Klux Klan justified their promotion of white supremacy. For current times, campaigning for the Kingdom of God conjures up images of the Religious Right's attempts to transform American democracy into a theocracy, from Jerry Falwell's Moral Majority during the 1980s to the Tea Party's religiously inflected xenophobia. However, in African American religious thought, the

7. Bevel, Speech mass meeting (Holmes, transcript).

sacred and the secular—in this case, heavenly hope and anticipation of a better life on earth—are intertwined. They are intertwined not merely or particularly in terms of what is now called the prosperity gospel, but instead because black people of faith sought and expected to receive justice on earth as an harbinger to receiving peace in heaven. In fact, the Minor Prophets of the Old Testament were critical of wealthy individuals who were neither charitable nor interested in promoting social justice. Black leaders from David Walker to Martin Luther King Jr. routinely criticized white racists Christians as hypocrites, misguided, or both. White religionists couldn't expect to go to heaven if they were giving their black brothers and sisters hell on earth.

So Bevel's appropriation of the kingdom of God represented more than a response to the racism of the 1960s. This reference locates Bevel's speech in a larger narrative going back to slavery: that God wants his oppressed people to be free and will spread his rule to bring about this transition. This is why James Cone and Vincent Wimbush, among others, have argued that associating the black struggle with the exodus constituted not only a historically accurate correlation but also a theologically sound one. If the children of Israel had been oppressed under Egyptian rule according the Bible narrative, then certainly people of color under slavery and later segregation were a type of oppressed Israel. Hence, the substance of the trope "kingdom of God" functioned as a major plot component throughout Bevel's speech, calling upon the biblical narrative of God's ultimate sovereignty on earth and a present-day political narrative in which God's people (civil rights workers) will expand God's reign of justice by liberating the oppressed.

Still while most African American southerners embraced the exodus narrative for slavery, the way in which they applied this narrative to segregation depended on a number of factors. One of these factors was the black person's economic status. If one were as wealthy as A. G. Gaston (Birmingham's richest black resident during the time) or a poor laborer or domestic (a significant number in Bevel's audience), juxtaposing the black struggle in Birmingham with the Old Testament Israelite fight for freedom might seem either impractical or inspiring. Bevel assumed that a part his audience accepted the trope of campaigning for the kingdom of God as analogous to the Birmingham struggle, and he sought to convince those who didn't.

Spreading the kingdom of God and the liberation that results from doing so became the basis for the question that would frame Bevel's speech.

In typical ministerial fashion, Bevel took his subject from a biblical text. In John chapter 5, Jesus asked a man who had been sick for thirty-eight years, "Do you want to be healed?" That this man was reclining next to a pool of water, which was legendarily a source for healing dramatized Jesus's question. Bevel spiritualized and applied Jesus's question to his audience, arguing that they were sickened by their current sociopolitical status. African American church members from slavery onward often spiritualized biblical texts. Doing so served at least two purposes. Spiritualizing texts was a symbolic means by which black people of faith from slavery to segregation shrouded part or all of their intentions from white oppressors. More significantly for rhetoricians interested in narrative theory, activism, or movement history, spiritualizing allowed a seamless continuity between the biblical past and African Americans' present. Ironically, spiritualizing allowed them to embody in their time biblical events from the past.[8] Oppressed people, blacks being chief among them, were not the only group that spiritualized texts. However, given the heinous crimes they faced in America and other parts of the diaspora, spiritualizing was rhetorically and existentially necessary.

As a result, the connection Bevel drew between the physically sick man in his Bible text to the social, psychological, and spiritual sickness that infected Birmingham fell within a well-established tradition in black preaching rhetoric. Therefore this move strengthened his claim that segregation could mar the dignity of the human body or the "temple of God." Segregation could further minimize what was "sacred" and "beautiful"[9] in each of them. State-sanctioned racism—the social ill of which Bevel spoke—was pervasive and contributed to all of the nation's ills. Many, though clearly not all, of Birmingham blacks evinced this sickness whenever they accepted their second-class citizenship and refused to do anything about it. Birmingham whites who perpetuated the system of black disenfranchisement were also sick. Similar to Frederick Douglass's claim that slavery dehumanized the enslaved and enslaver,[10] Bevel's vision presented no one as immune from this social sickness, even claiming that some of the preachers who participated in the Birmingham movement might be inhibited by the debilitating disease of passively accepting racism. To be sure, the sickness of segregation extended to "this church" and could be found right in "this

8. For an incisive analysis of this idea, see Miller, *King's Biblical Epic*, ch. 6.

9. Bevel, Speech (Holmes transcript).

10. See Douglass, *Narrative in the Life*.

pulpit."[11] Bevel would return to this theme of the sickness of segregation spreading to the pulpit. Since African American preachers were historically sociopolitical and spiritual leaders rolled up into one, Bevel's claim was both disturbing and insightful. If black preachers could be corrupted or otherwise marred by segregation, then what hope remained for the average parishioner? If preachers ceased speaking with authority, could any congregant be expected to exercise the agency to speak out against injustice? Perhaps this is one reason why Bevel surmises that as a sickness, segregation had "destroyed the best that is within us."[12] Virtually no one, including preachers like Bevel, was immune to giving in to segregation and giving up on their freedom.

Throughout his speech, Bevel linked the sickness of segregation to foolishness, lack of insight, lack of knowledge, apathy, but, mostly, a failure to exercise agency. The disease of segregation had for the most part afflicted whites with first three symptoms, while blacks, his primary audience, had been afflicted chiefly with the latter two. White people could not or in some cases chose not to notice racist structures that undergirded their privilege and progress. By 1963, these carefully constructed structures had been shrouded under seemingly innocuous abstractions such as custom, tradition, and the southern way of life. The average white Birmingham resident might not begin to perceive the horrors his black counterpart faced until the demonstrations brought them to light. And even then, local whites could easily scapegoat black demonstrators as local troublemakers or outside agitators. Even sympathetic white residents could no more understand the intricacies of these struggles than any man could empathize with a woman's birthing pains. By themselves, even white allies to the movement could neither advance black progress nor ensure the exercise of black independence.

All the political, social, and psychological challenges Birmingham blacks faced could be traced back to the social ills of slavery and segregation, which Bevel argued "would make anybody sick."[13] For a brief moment in the speech, therefore, Bevel seemed to be not only empathizing with some black people's less than full commitment to the Birmingham campaign but excusing others as too sick to participate as well. However, this observation contrasted with the overriding thrust of the speech, namely, that black Birmingham possessed the agency to better their lot. Bevel then shrewdly illus-

---

11. Bevel, Speech (Holmes transcript).

12. Ibid.

13. Ibid.

trated the ironic psychological payoff his people might gain from passively accepting segregation or remaining sick. He recounted a personal anecdote about his grandmother, who from the time he was four to the time he was seven feigned sicknesses. Why? Bevel said that his grandmother enjoyed favors that were extended to the sick, including being brought fruit and being excused for not keeping her house clean. Similarly, some blacks wanted the sickness of segregation to continue because then they would not have to compete in the "arena of life";[14] they could tether themselves to a spirit of mediocrity and, more to the point, not have to test the proposition that all people were created equal. For Bevel, this theopolitical narrative evoked in the notion of the kingdom of God, was largely disrupted by spiritual ignorance and sickness. The speech challenged repeatedly the epistemologies that have led to, among other things, black people opposing civil rights and fear of exercising those rights. While Bevel empathized with other African Americans sickened by segregation, he nevertheless reserved a substantial amount of his criticisms for blacks who failed to exercise their God-given right for personal and, by extension, political agency:

> They don't want to get well. No, no . . . we don't want get well. Well a lot of Negroes right in town tonight . . . [T]hey want to labor under segregation, for, you see, to remove the valley of segregation is to put all men into the arena of life. And there are a lot of Negro men who don't want to get out there in that arena. For out there in the arena of life it means that we have to compete with everybody.[15]

The question, "Do you want to be healed?" functioned as the central refrain throughout his speech. From the outset, Bevel interchanged the word "free" for "healed," transforming the question to "Do you want to be free?" The second question is actually not a different question but is at once a spiritualizing and contemporizing of the first question. Exchanging or interchanging words of a song or in Scripture represents a form of spiritualizing, which I alluded to earlier. Vincent Wimbush traces this rhetorical orientation to the syncretism that characterized West African religions.[16] One of the only ways that the newly imported Africans could truly embrace their oppressors' religion was to refashion the rituals, customs, and language so that it more closely resembled the religions of the motherland. So

14. Ibid.
15. Ibid.
16. Wimbush, "Bible and African Americans," 85.

Bevel enacted an entrenched discursive tradition when, during this speech, he vacillated from "Do you want to be healed?" to "Do you want to be free?"[17] Indeed, the congregation for this very mass meeting, as was routinely practiced during other mass meetings and demonstrations, engaged in a similar semantic exchange while they sang. For example, "I woke up this morning with my mind set on Jesus" became "I woke this morning with my mind set on freedom."[18]

The adaptive rhetorical traditions rooted in African American cultural history empowered Bevel's audience to weather the political storms of mainstream southern politics. Neither government-sanctioned racism nor economic limitations, nor conservative, gradualist politics that some black clergy embraced were substantive reasons for rank-and-file blacks failing to move forward in obtaining their civil rights. Bevel conceded that he once was afraid of Bull Connor, associating Birmingham's commissioner of public safety with the legendary outlaw Jesse James. However, Bevel came to conclude that Connor could not prevent African Americans from exercising their democratic right to protest. Bevel's comparing Connor to Jesse James struck a chord with his audience, for by 1963 Connor had achieved almost iconic status. During an *Eyes on the Prize* interview, Fred Shuttlesworth spoke to the irony of appointing someone as public safety commissioner who was so "unsafe."[19] Connor was not only a virulent racist rabidly committed to segregation, but also an effective speaker in his own right. Before entering politics, Connor gained some notoriety as a radio announcer calling baseball games. The terse yet colorful and somewhat melodramatic cadences that characterized his radio speech took on a strident, pseudoreasonable tone when he publicly addressed the issue of segregation. His vociferous words were backed up with aggressive and rash action, even in the eyes of some Birmingham whites. While Connor lost considerable public confidence when he was voted out with other commissioners and replaced by a mayor and city council, he remained a formidable opponent, as he refused to step down as public safety commissioner. His impulsive, shoot-from-the-hip persona inspired his supporters but freighted his political opponents, terrified many blacks, and transformed Connor into the

17. Bevel, Speech (Holmes transcript).
18. Birmingham mass meeting, April 12, 1963 (Holmes transcript).
19. Else and Vecchione, prods., *Eyes on the Prize*, vol. 2.

perfect villain for the drama of the Birmingham campaign. Still Bevel insisted that "Bull Connor doesn't have it in his power to free the Negroes."[20]

Since Connor personified the seemingly insurmountable political forces supporting segregation, Bevel's claim that Connor wields no real power over black volition represented the first critical turning point in the speech: Birmingham's black citizens had control over aspects of their lives that they believed the government did.

In a related albeit more personal and directly economic vein, Bevel argued that even the possibility of losing a job shouldn't deter blacks from demonstrating. Since God fed "the ants and the roaches, the bedbugs and cockroaches,"[21] he would surely feed his people that were trying to advance the kingdom of God by seeking freedom. Bevel's reference to God's care for natural creatures would most likely conjure up for his listeners the gospel song "His Eye Is on the Sparrow," a song that had circulated in the African American church for decades and had become a trope for God's care and protection through the most difficult times. The lyrics for this song are based on Matt 6, in which Jesus encouraged his listeners not to fret about basic necessities like clothing and food because God's reign, providence, and care extended to the "lilies of the field" and the "birds of the air."[22]

Interestingly, even though Bevel was a minister—as were the major leaders of the Birmingham campaign—he reserved his strongest criticisms for white and black clergy, who were unquestionably sanctioned as leaders in many southern communities. He indirectly criticized black clergy who were indifferent or opposed to the civil rights movement. He and his audience could have had in mind African American pastors like the prominent J. L. Ware, who preferred a gradual, law-and-order approach to African American progress, as opposed to direct action.[23] Obviously, Ware was not alone in this belief. Law and order versus direct action was becoming a major source of tactical disagreement by 1963. The NAACP, the SCLC, and the SNCC all sought legal sanction for their cause as one ultimate goal. However, these organizations differed about the means by which to attain this goal—the NAACP adhering to legal means almost exclusively, the SNCC preferring direct action, and the SCLC, under King, seeking a synthesis of the two.

20. Bevel, Speech (Holmes transcript).

21. Ibid.

22. Matt 6:26–30.

23. Eskew, *But for Birmingham*, 260.

Bevel also disapproved of white clergy who supported segregation. He referred to one prosegregration pastor as representing white clerics who are "good speakers" and "good liars too."[24] High-sounding oratory, even in the name of God, that failed to speak truth to power was deceptive discourse. Bevel's criticism recalls how rhetoric has been critiqued for being manipulative, morally bankrupt discourse from Plato's accounting of Socrates's dialogues on the sophists to modern and postmodern skepticism about finding a single, unalloyed truth in politics. Bevel castigated black and white ministers who lacked conviction about ensuring the rights of African Americans as a means for expanding the kingdom of God. However, the brunt of Bevel's claim about the sickness and foolishness caused by segregation was directed at Birmingham's black community not depending upon leaders of any background or quality to achieve and sustain their freedom.

Echoing the grassroots sentiments that informed the Freedom Rides, the sit-ins, and the founding of SNCC, Bevel extended the central theme of the kingdom of God to the immediate leadership crisis during this campaign. Birmingham authorities, Bevel said, believed that throwing Martin Luther King Jr. in jail would stop the movement. He also commented on the Birmingham Police Department's surveillance of the mass meetings through the presence of recording devices and police detectives, as if this well-entrenched practice would have further intimidated Bevel's audience. What these officials missed or misunderstood, however, was that the leader of the Birmingham campaign was God. Without a doubt, just as African Americans had historically unearthed continuities between the exodus and slavery, the Easter narrative continued to play out in the Birmingham campaign. White Birmingham officials failed to grasp this point. Just as Pontus Pilate could not curtail the resurrection by crucifying Christ, Bevel contended, so Birmingham officials could not halt the ascent of African American freedom by jailing King or Shuttlesworth.

Embracing their quest for freedom as a campaign for the kingdom of God, which is, therefore, controlled by him, could ideally empower each member of Bevel's audience to realize her own sociopolitical independence. Throughout the entire speech, Bevel alluded to the formidable challenge of trying to do civil rights work in Mississippi. But as he neared his climatic conclusion, Bevel offered four examples of heroism that black Mississippians demonstrated that should dislodge his Birmingham audience out of their state of indecision. The first incident occurred in Ruleville,

24. Bevel, Speech (Holmes transcript).

Mississippi, where two black girls were shot—one in the leg and another in the head. The very next night, when some racist white Mississippians assumed that they had likely frightened the local black community away, they instead witnessed a mass meeting with standing room only. Bevel mentioned elderly African American women in another southern town who despite threats to their safety, marched downtown. What Bevel did not mention, but he and some in his audience would likely understand, was that authentic grassroots participation represented a challenge to sexism in mainstream society and the civil rights movement. Given their majority standing in most southern black churches, it was a foregone conclusion that women would participate in demonstrations. However, male leaders of the movement preferred to regulate sisters to office work and other traditional, mainly domestic, roles. These traditional practices prompted Ella Baker[25] to found SNCC to encourage the students to re-envision the civil rights movement in grassroots terms, terms readily accepted by students like Bevel's wife and a leader of the Nashville sit-in movement, Diane Nash. Fannie Lou Hamer, a resident of Ruleville, also began participating in the movement at this time. Hamer eventually rose up against racism, sexism, and classism to become the vice president of the Freedom Democratic Party of Mississippi, a biracial coalition that would challenge the legitimacy of official Mississippi delegation at the 1964 Democratic convention.[26]

Bevel inserted his own experience driving along a lonely Mississippi road on Thanksgiving as the third example of black heroism. Acting alone, a racist motorist shot at Bevel but only shattered his window. Both the white driver and Bevel stopped their cars. Bevel jumped out and asked the driver why he shot at him. Upon hearing the question, the drive curiously sped off. Granted that many, if not most, southern racists of the time did their dirt cowardly and covertly, shielded by crowds, night shadows, or white sheets. Still, both Bevel's spontaneous courage and the driver's sudden flight illuminated Bevel's point about the lengths black Birmingham might have to take to achieve their freedom. And just as Bevel declared "Blessed be the name of the Lord"[27] upon reentering his car, his audience would have to acknowledge how God could empower their own sense of agency.

The fourth example Bevel used the audience would readily recognize. James Meredith had enrolled as the first black student in the University of

---

25. See Ransby, *Ella Baker*, ch. 8.

26. For a comprehensive rhetorical biography, see Brooks, *Voice That Could Stir*.

27. Bevel, Speech (Holmes transcript).

Mississippi. Everyone in Bevel's audience knew that this tremendous victory came with a firestorm of controversy, from Mississippi governor Ross Barnett blocking Meredith's initial entrance George Wallace–style to subsequent riots on campus in which many were injured and a foreign journalist killed, to a politically pragmatic President Kennedy reluctantly federalizing troops to keep the peace in Oxford, Mississippi. Perhaps none in Bevel's audience would be privy to the political grandstanding and cowardly compromising that went on behind closed doors between Governor Barnett and President Kennedy. What they did know, even without having all the details, was that Meredith's courageous move resulted in numerous death threats against him. Bevel described Barnett's use of sheriffs, highway patrol officers, and hoodlums as conspiring to keep Meredith out of the university. Bevel dramatized these threats by ascribing personal qualities to a bullet. He argues that while whites were accustomed to blacks "bowing"[28] or submitting to injustice because of a bullet, Meredith was not to be swayed from his determined course. This anthropomorphic transforming of the bullet into a living being recalled one of the many rhetorical techniques black preachers employed to enliven their sermons and thereby persuade their audiences. Another rhetorical trope used in the African American church was to contemporize not just biblical narratives, but to highlight specific persons or portions within that narrative. When Bevel speaks of Meredith not "bowing" to segregation, his audience would recognize the three Hebrew boys who, during Jewish captivity in Babylon, refused to bow down to pagan gods. Just like Meredith they were threatened, but in their case they were placed in a fiery furnace. According to the story, the three Israelite boys came out of the furnace unscathed because an angel had been in the furnace with them. Bevel adapted this last element to dramatize Meredith's arrival on the University of Mississippi campus after a riot incited by white students: When Meredith came on campus, it appeared to be two men and one looked like the son (angel) of God. The thrust of Bevel's four examples was clear: if his audience would boldly and sacrificially demonstrate to advance God's kingdom, He would protect them.

Bevel buttressed his argument about God-infused individual liberty by emphasizing how becoming free involved sacrificial yet direct and doable acts, rather than complex understandings. He did not get his courage from eating chicken; "he got in the jailhouse."[29] On the surface, "chicken"

28. Ibid.
29. Ibid.

may signify the basic provisions his audience were afraid of losing when they joined the movement. But because the audience laughed, Bevel may also have been playing on the stereotype about African Americans loving chicken. Often black preachers, comedians, and other black performers made light of stereotypes to both diminish their potency and take control of them. The second comparison is even more telling. Bevel didn't acquire his dignity in the "seminary"; he "got it on the picket line."[30] Bevel and his audience recognized that Jim Crow segregation had often blocked African Americans from a quality education. Further, while most blacks valued education, given its impracticality for the menial jobs that most of them acquired as well as the ways in which mainstream education was used to demean black bodies and cultural knowledge, many remained suspicious of book learning alone, preferring instead a synthesis between what was learned in the schoolhouses, the church houses and their parents' houses. Such a merging of sanctioned and unsanctioned, formal and informal sources would likely ensure that black knowledge remained practical rather than merely theoretical, spiritual rather than just cognitive, liberating rather than conformist. As proud as the older members of Bevel's audience might have been of him for obtaining a seminary education, they knew, like Bevel alluded to earlier, that seminar graduates could lie too, that aspects of their education did not necessarily ring true for black religionists, particularly in regard to the struggle for human dignity.

As a result, even if the majority of his audience members were deprived of formal education and economic independence, there was one natural motion that could advance the Birmingham movement and assert their agency: they could get up and walk. Many of Bevel's intended audience, like the sick man in the gospel narrative, were waiting for some miracle or *voodoo*. By pairing these supernatural acts, Bevel illustrated the range of African American ritual healing and divine intervention. Miracles were rooted in Westernized religion, while *voodoo* was situated in African spirituality across the African diaspora.[31]

Curiously the ultimate sign of spiritual wellness as well as psychological and political liberation was a radical counterculture consciousness and conduct that some black and white people might likely deem foolish:

> We enjoy, some of us, not being responsible. Some of us don't want
> get well you see because to get well is to have courage; to have

30. Ibid.

31. See Murphy, *Working the Spirit*.

courage is to act like a fool in the face of violence; to have courage is to stand up and tell the truth in spite of what happens to you. But a lot of us are not willing to get well. We don't want to stand high and put our heads up high and tell the truth.[32]

Appropriating the descriptor of the right kind of "fool" probably refers to Pauline theology: "I am a fool for Christ."[33] And since earlier in the speech, Bevel called segregation "foolish," this brand of foolishness should be considered qualitatively different, as it represented one's commitment to and willingness to sacrifice for Christ. Moreover, the radical counterculture rhetoric that Bevel espoused sought to redraw the boundaries of authorized knowledge and status quo politics, so as to compel his audience to a fearless activism:

> Now all the newspapers, and all the television cameras, and all the white policemen sitting up wondering what you going to do. Because they wondering too, whether you're going to be free . . . [T]hey're just here tonight just trying to find out whether you want to be free or not. And I don't care what they do. They can bring guns, and tanks, and little mics and everything and if you answer the question and said, "Yes we want be free," there's nothing they can do about it.[34]

Once they decided to exercise grassroots agency through moving their lips and feet, none of the threats that Bevel enumerated during the speech could ultimately stop the Birmingham campaign—neither the physical violence represented by guns nor the discursive violence that could be wrought through print, audio, and visual media.

Notwithstanding the liberating necessity of African Americans adapting westernized religion and education, what was needed to participate in the Birmingham campaign was the more natural and universal act of walking. The act of walking was ritualistically reenacted within the church walls in many ways. Borrowing from protestant revivalism, at the end of every mass meeting service, the last speaker invited people to join the campaign by walking down the aisle. More often than not, the songs sung during the mass meetings conveyed a syncopated rhythm that sounded like footsteps. During this particular mass meeting, the congregation improvised the words "walk, walk," to punctuate the song "This Little Light of Mine."

32. Bevel, Speech (Holmes transcript).

33. 1 Cor 4:10.

34. Bevel, Speech (Holmes transcript).

Another song addressed the need for black mobility more directly, "Got on My Traveling Shoes."[35] As Gary Selby notes in his book on Martin Luther King Jr.,[36] walking is a rhetorical act through which a social movement creates a narrative. True, the civil rights demonstrations from Montgomery to Birmingham expanded the definition of democratic protest. As profound as these historic marches were, they also constituted a fresh way to look at rhetorical theories of narrative, from Walter Fisher's narrative rationality to Steven Mailloux's narrative as a component of rhetorical hermeneutics. For Fisher, what we call "rational" or "reasonable" is constructed by personal or communal narratives.[37] What is rationally true to us must ring true with our experience and hold fidelity to that experience. Aside from the more historically pervasive influence of Western African syncretism and eclecticism of black religious culture that scholars like Wimbush examines, narrative rationality partly explains why people of color could carve out a religion of freedom from one that was used to oppress them. For Mailloux, narrative constitutes one of the components of rhetorical hermeneutics, a theory by which one ascertains the "production and reception" of a communicative event within an historical context.[38] In other words, we can't understand the Birmingham campaign—and arguably the broader civil rights movement—without interpreting the rhetorical significance of the Birmingham marches. Still further, we can analyze Bevel's call for walking as a part of what Geneva Smitherman calls "narrative sequencing." Narrative sequencing speaks to how stories appeal to black audiences within black spaces. Smitherman considers "preaching" and "testifying"[39] as one form of narrative sequencing. Consequently, these church-inspired rhetorical rituals practiced within the mass meetings, and the physical actions—like marching—that grew out of them, could be included in the larger story about the African American freedom struggle.

Black bodies walking in protest suggests a hermeneutical lens to examine rhetoric and agency. Though it is clear that African Americans in Birmingham did not need economic status or higher education to start marching, beginning to do so could set them on the journey to achieving the American dream for them and their children, and to attain levels

35. Mass meeting, April 12th, 1963 (Holmes transcript).

36. Selby, *Rhetoric of Freedom*, ch. 7.

37. Fisher, *Human Communication*, ch. 7.

38. Mailloux, *Disciplinary Identities*, ch. 2.

39. Smitherman, *Talkin and Testifyin*, 150–55.

of success that they never imagined. Toward the end of his speech, Bevel raised a series of questions that speak to and, perhaps beyond, his audience's greatest aspirations of what an integrated Birmingham might look like:

> Do the fathers here want their children to be free in this town? Do you want to walk downtown with your head up? Aren't you tired of being exploited and walked on by some white trash? Are you tired of that? Do you want some of the jobs that you been locked out of? Do you want that? Do you want to be the policeman yourself so you can stop beating folks over the head? Do you want to work downtown in the city hall yourself? Do you want that? Do you want your son to stop being convicted and put in the electric chair for raping somebody they had never seen? Do you want to be treated like a child of God like you are? Do you want that? Then get up and start walking.[40]

In this rich, robust conclusion, Bevel returned to the central theme with which he began: segregation had been psychologically, socially, and politically debilitating to Birmingham's black citizens, and only they could act to heal themselves. The series of questions, apparently rhetorical by design, began with a focus on black children. Bevel envisioned a possible future for his audience's children, a future in which they would not have to migrate from the South. Actively seeking freedom would ensure Bevel's audience the dignity "to walk downtown,"[41] their heads held high. Experiencing true democracy and exercising authentic agency meant that blacks need not avert their gaze as they stepped to the side to let a white person pass—a widespread southern custom. While controversial and arguably bigoted, Bevel's comment about no longer "being exploited and walked on by some white trash"[42] spoke to the uneasy relationship between race and class in Birmingham. While many African Americans were marked by their poverty, they were primarily marginalized because of their race. Wealthy African Americans all over the South, like Birmingham's A. G. Gaston, were relatively shielded from the economic stings of segregation but could not venture beyond the social and political boundaries white society had set up. Even some white southerners of the lowest economic class could dismiss Gaston as a nigger.

40. Bevel, Speech (Holmes transcript).
41. Ibid.
42. Ibid.

Bevel's next question addressed broadly the jobs his audience "had been locked out of."[43] This question further exposed the interconnection between racism and economics. From slavery to segregation, racial oppression was largely about money. With his next two questions, Bevel listed specific jobs, working as a police officer or in the Birmingham city hall. But the open-ended nature of the question about "walking downtown with your head up" can be connected to the symbolic nature of marching. Historically, African Americans bore witness to the simple yet profound nature of walking to take them where they needed to go. Hundreds of the enslaved used their legs to escape to freedom individually or though collective efforts like the Underground Railroad. Folk of color in Baton Rouge, Louisiana, and Montgomery, Alabama, had brought bus companies to their economic knees by walking in dignity rather than riding in shame. The first step to African Americans realizing not only economic security but the self-actualization and pride that comes from good jobs was to literally to start walking.

Bevel's questions about his audience working for the Birmingham Police Department and city hall underscored the ultimate claim of the civil rights movement: true justice included black citizens being able to fully integrate into the mainstream. To the eyes of segregationists or other interested in maintaining the status quo, civil rights activists seemed to be anti-establishment and even anarchist. Opponents of the movement advanced this idea despite herculean efforts on the part of African Americans from Montgomery to Selma not only to express allegiance to Old Glory but to carry the flag during marches. So Bevel's queries about the potential for his black audience to work as police officers and in city hall would have struck a nerve with them. To say that police brutality had been rampant in the South was an understatement. Many police officers in Birmingham and elsewhere in Dixie had beaten and brutalized black bodies into submission, often with impunity. Much of this abuse took place under the guise of the officer exercising his duty. Police brutality was also entrenched in racist ideological and biblical proof-texting: take the assumption that blacks were heirs to the mark of Cain and the curse of Ham and therefore needed to be controlled lest their savage natures be unleashed. No wonder Bevel's questions included the assumption that when some of audience members became police officers they would not be capriciously beating people over the head. Likewise, city hall signified the lengths to which white officials

43. Ibid.

70

would go to disenfranchise black citizens. City hall conjured up images of qualifying tests for voting such as being asked to interpret a section of the state constitution to the satisfaction of the city clerk or estimating the number of bubbles in a bar of soap or jellybeans in a large jar. Bevel's question implies that given that position, African Americans would never discriminate against or brutalize voters in the ways they had been.

The question about African American males being falsely accused of rape cut to the heart of racism and the unreasonable horrors that could result from it. The idea of black men being sentenced for sex crimes unjustly was a common occurrence for Bevel's audience. When the alleged infraction involved a black man making advances at a white woman, all bets were off. Rumors and hints of impropriety had sent black men and boys to their deaths, through both illegal and so-called legal means. This audience would recall the most publicized but hardly uncommon instance of this practice: the murder of fourteen-year-old Emmett Till in 1955. Till had been visiting his family in Mississippi from Chicago. After bragging to some local boys that he had a white girlfriend up north and upon being dared to go into a nearby store and speak to the white female proprietor, Till entered the store and, after purchasing some candy, either wolf whistled at the woman or said "Bye, baby." The woman's husband and brother-in-law murdered Till in such a brutal fashion that Till's corpse, later displayed from his open casket in newspapers across the nation, stirred an international outrage and arguably contributed to the inception of the modern civil rights movement. While commenting upon the atrocity of the Till murder, Fred Shuttlesworth expressed a sentiment that many African Americans shared. Who knew how many hundreds of black boys, killed like Till, remained undiscovered in southern backwoods?[44] So Bevel's query about a black son going to "the electric chair for raping somebody they had never seen"[45] carried decided traction and force.

The last rhetorical question offered a fitting crescendo because it circled back to Bevel's original argument that his audience already possessed all the dignity and agency that they needed to act autonomously as citizens of the kingdom of God: "Do you want to be treated like a child of God like you are?"[46] No matter how long and hard white oppressors used religion to dehumanize African Americans, black Christians had learned to flip the

44. Else and Vecchione, prods., *Eyes on the Prize*, vol. 1.
45. Bevel, Speech (Holmes transcript).
46. Ibid.

script, and, through leaders like Bevel, to collectively transform their angst and anger into, to borrow from King, "a spiritual anvil that would wear out many a physical hammer." Like democracy, capitalism, and other ideologies associated with the nation that had abused them, African Americans, like other marginalized people, chose to recast, reconfigure, and re-create religion from a force that dominated to one that delivered them. Much of this may be related to a culturally informed penchant for constructing rhetorical commonplaces, including honing in on narratives, tropes, maxims, proverbs, and idioms (to name a few) that are liberating.

Within this last series of questions we have just examined, Bevel repeatedly inserted the question, "Do you want that?" This question served as a refrain, rose from the text and returned to the central question of black agency and accountability: "Do you want to be free?" Bevel was arguing for more than an up-by-your-bootstraps radical individualist agency that today's neoconservatives tout. Bevel was calling his audience to something much larger than any one individual in his audience achieving the American dream. Bevel was calling these black congregants to a communal sense of sociopolitical agency. And through his own rhetorical performance, not to mention those of other mass meeting rhetors, Bevel enacted a ministerial, rhetorical authority that respects and will, if need be, step aside for the masses.

Clearly Bevel's plea was for neither the elimination nor marginalization of ministerial leadership. In fact, at the critical moment of the Birmingham campaign, the black masses would look to clerical leadership that understood its role and rhetoric as simultaneously sacred and secular. As the next chapter suggests, Ralph Abernathy saw himself and preached as one called to religiously inspire the people to be sure, but to critically instruct them as well.

4

Between Prophecy and Pedagogy

Ralph Abernathy's Rhetoric of Instruction and Critique

"He was the kind of preacher who could reach anybody in a congregation. And he had a simplistic way of explaining everything in minute detail to the fact that even children could understand it. [H]e had a philosophy that if you are an effective speaker, what you say must be simple enough for everybody to comprehend, or else you're not a good speaker. [I]f you are going to communicate with people, it's got to be that kind of communication, and yet it can be profound."[1]

—Juanita Abernathy, Widow of Ralph Abernathy

This chapter focuses on Ralph Abernathy's May 3rd mass meeting speech. Often marginalized in civil rights history as merely King's second-in-command, Abernathy was an extraordinary leader and orator for critical moments during the civil rights movement—from its canonized inception in Montgomery to his assumption of the mantle of leadership of the Southern Christian Leadership Conference (SCLC) following King's assassination. While Abernathy arguably would never reach the widely touted rhetorical heights that King scaled, he was hardly insignificant as

1. Interview with the author, June 2009.

73

an orator. Indeed, as his May 3rd speech will illustrate, Abernathy communicated why African American religious oratory proffers a sociopolitically and intellectually potent critique of mainstream discourses like newspapers and history books. Further, while such an ambitious rhetorical agenda may not have been Abernathy's intent in this speech, I am suggesting that he had mastered the black sermonic tradition, which in raw or refined forms has inspirational, instructional, and critical promise. In other words, Abernathy stands in long line of black preachers who in instructing their congregations in sacred and secular matters also taught larger American society in ways that could be classified as prophetic.

On one level this claim is similar to an argument that Karen Rowe makes about some forms of religious oratory, from medieval times to the eighteenth century. Religious orations that were characterized as informative often served a persuasive function as well. Rowe advances this claim in part to critique the compartmentalizing of eighteenth-century rhetoric into distinct aims.[2] That a rhetor could be informative and persuasive at the same time was not just an academic exercise for African American preachers. Just as black music represented a cacophony of seemingly discordant sounds, structures, and styles that worked harmoniously to a desired effect, so black preaching (often but not always prophetic at its core) instructed African Americans to honor their culture, understand mainstream ideas, and prepare themselves to function within larger society. Particularly during segregation, but even currently, the church house has served and serves as a schoolhouse, cultural community center, and political meeting place. Historian Wilson Fallin Jr. suggests that Alabama has a particular fertile history when it comes to black churches providing their own schools to make up for neglect that institutional white racism produced.

Given this history one should not be entirely surprised that during the May 3rd mass meeting, Abernathy and his auditors fulfilled more than an austere, devotional role one might expect from a church assembly, even one with an ostensible political agenda like the mass meetings. Approximately one month old, the Birmingham campaign was losing volunteers and momentum. James Bevel, considered by many on King's staff to be radical, erratic, and a little irrational,[3] had recommended that the leadership enlist

---

2. Rowe, "Painted Sermons," 296–98.

3. Bevel actually welcomed the accusations that he was a bit crazy. See Branch, *Pillar of Fire*, 54.

school-age children as marchers. With the memory of SCLC's failure in Albany, Georgia, still fresh on his mind, King reluctantly agreed.

They began marching on May 2nd, some according to plan, other children rushing to join their counterparts literally at the last minute. Without question, some of these young people did not take the cause for which they were marching seriously, but the leaders of the campaign, Birmingham's white status quo, the nation, and the world did. Most understandably fear best characterized their parents' state of mind. Most southern black parents had taught their children about the racism within the justice system. As John Lewis remarked concerning his volunteering for the Freedom Rides, most black parents exhorted their children to conform to the straightjacket traditions of the Jim Crow system so as to stay out of jail at any cost.[4] The southern judicial system treated blacks unjustly, often elevating minor offenses to major ones. Even when African Americans deliberately or inadvertently violated a taboo like failing to exercise the appropriate deference to a white person they might be legally detained or, worse, fall victim to vigilante violence. To face the prospect of jail head-on, as these school-age movement volunteers were doing, would be to pull the tail of a lion.

That lion was a divided city government. The mostly white electorate had voted in a mayor and city council to replace the city commissioners among whom the infamous Eugene "Bull" Connor was numbered. As Connor had refused to grant even the smallest concession to the proponents of civil rights, he certainly would not give quarter to his political opponents, even though they shared similar segregationist sentiments. For instance, Martin Luther King Jr. characterized Birmingham's new mayor, Albert Boutwell, as a man who affirmed segregation with a softer tone than did Connor. Their commitment to that ideology, however, was identical.

Into the fray of a faltering civil rights movement and a fractured city government marched hundreds of young people, many of whom were not yet old enough to drive. Before day's end on May 2nd hundreds of these students were arrested, a significant portion of them ironically transported to jail in school buses. Weighing heavily on the minds of the audience of the mass meeting on May 2nd was, what would happen to their sons and daughters or nieces and nephews in the Birmingham jail? Surely the Birmingham campaign needed to advance, but how would the children be protected in jail? Another wave of students marched on May 3rd, 1963. Yet

4. Else and Vecchione, prods., *Eyes on the Prize*, vol. 3.

this time before some were arrested, many would face the horrific, dangerous, and practically unspeakable indignity of fire cannons and snarling police dogs.

The audience of the mass meetings for both nights needed information, comfort for that moment, and hope for the future. Curiously, the spirited music and rousing homilies and speeches peppered with humor that characterized earlier mass meetings were a part of the May 2nd and May 3rd meetings. By the time Abernathy mounted the pulpit on each of these occasions, the audience was more than ready to receive his trademark irreverent humor, his unvarnished yet poignant critique of Birmingham officials, and his folksy delivery. However, the critical difference—and the issue that drives this chapter within the context of this book—is how Abernathy asserted his ethos: combining the roles of black folk preacher, cultural pedagogue, and sociopolitical prophet. Stylistically, he called upon the conventions of an African American country preacher, dispensing wisdom, wit, and biblical exposition in low cadences and penetrating imagery. To the white reporters and police officers present, Abernathy functioned as a teacher by presenting, preserving, and promoting black culture, setting and keeping the record straight. Also, for his white and black auditors, Abernathy offered a prophetic critique of those who would distort the patriotic legacy of African Americans and deprive these citizens of color of their rights. Scores of black ministers before Abernathy combined the roles of preacher, pedagogue, and prophet. The Old Testament prophets themselves insisted on their listeners preserving the biblical doctrines or teachings that promoted social justice and held government officials accountable for ignoring cries of injustice.

Abernathy's May 3rd speech illustrates how Birmingham mass meeting rhetoric ironically empowered black preachers and parishioners to meet the sociopolitical demands of standard American English often using nonstandard or vernacular rhetorical strategies. Abernathy's well-established role as preacher preserved his spiritual and cultural authority before black congregants, while his roles as pedagogue and prophet projected a rational and critical ethos before the white police officers and reporters present. For African American churchgoers, these roles were usually inseparable. From slavery through segregation, black audiences had grown accustomed to a preacher invoking positions of pedagogue and prophet both to tell *their story* and contend for the relevance of African Americans' struggle for justice. The blacks attending the May 3rd meeting were likely no different.

Perhaps these combined roles evolved from the West African Griot, who functioned as a storyteller and guardian of truth.[5] On the other hand, given the venerable and indispensable tradition of African Americans teaching about their culture outside of mainstream venues, including churches, one might call Abernathy a "phronimos" or pedagogue of practical wisdom, as Vorris L. Nunley employs the term.[6]

HEARING ABERNATHY AND KING:
STYLISTIC CONTRASTS AND CRITICAL CONTEXTS

Abernathy's rhetorical achievements during his May 3rd speech can be better understood by comparing his homiletic style to Martin Luther King's. However, as Nunley cogently argues in *Keepin' It Hushed*, acute analyses of black rhetorical style should entail richer theoretical understanding of its substantive dimensions. Otherwise, we remain focused on stylistic ornamentation for the sake of being "decorous." This is not my intention here. Rather, I want to briefly reflect on King's and Abernathy's respective styles to unearth larger, mostly Eurocentric assumptions regarding what gets legitimized as complex, intricate, or sophisticated discourse. While conceding his and King's rhetorical aptitude ("Both of us could give a good rousing speech when it was required"), Abernathy articulated some clear contrasts as well:

> I had come from the country, and my speeches and sermons were usually delivered in simpler language than his and were full of folk sayings and anecdotes from the world of rural Alabama. Martin, on the other hand was more the city dweller and the academic, who drew his illustrations and language from books, though he knew the dramatic impact of quoting an old spiritual in the midst of a learned discourse on scripture.[7]

Abernathy suggested, among other ideas, that his style might connect with a larger segment of the audience that attended the mass meetings and other civil rights rallies better than would King's. Further, while ostensibly applauding King's command of standardized texts, Abernathy offered a backhanded compliment to his own approach when he said that King

5. For an original discussion of how the Griot figure can bridge civil rights and contemporary African American rhetoric, see Banks, *Digital Griots*, chapter 4.

6. Nunley, *Keepin' It Hushed*, ch. 5.

7. Abernathy, *Walls Came Tumbling Down*, 189–90.

recognized the value of peppering his learned scholarly reflections with the lyrical force of the spirituals. As a number of rhetors and rhetoricians have attested, the spirituals illuminate and demonstrate the rich efficacy of African American folkways of knowing and communicating.

Richard Lischer offers a useful contrast between King and Abernathy's respective oral performances during the mass meetings that occurred in Selma, Alabama:

> As a speaker, Abernathy was everything King was not: homespun, down-to-earth, a master of mimicry, uproariously funny. No one had mastered the Lowndes County vernacular as Abernathy had, and no one could warm and charm a crowd as Abernathy could.[8]

Lischer, like others who study civil rights rhetoric, highlights the respective features present in King's and Abernathy's oratorical styles as marking possible educational differences between the two. Lischer views Abernathy as an effective orator; nevertheless, one might interpret his effectiveness as limited to the realm of entertainment, rather than the informative, to pathos instead of logos.

However, as I observed in the chapter on Shuttlesworth, Aristotle considered pathos to be central to the rhetorical enterprise. Pathos played to a common sensibility with which a community could identify, rather than excessive emotionality commonly associated with fundamentalist religion and sophistic rhetoric. Even though Abernathy had been preaching for fifteen years and held a master's degree at the time of the Birmingham campaign, neither white people in his audience nor many scholars of rhetoric today would consider him a formally trained orator. Perhaps Abernathy, like many other southern black preachers of the time, did not wish to convey the air of an academic, but he communicated common knowledge and shared experiences to his black congregants in a way that epitomized the rhetorical reasoning fundamental to Aristotle's enthymeme. Like the Jews during the Holocaust, African Americans had learned to question economic, religious, scientific, and sociopolitical arguments that directly or indirectly promoted their inferiority, no matter how elaborately reasoned.

Hence, Abernathy's folksy style likely increased, rather than diminished, his power as a rhetor. Like a long line of black preachers who blended, to borrow from Geneva Smitherman, "the sacred and secular,"[9] Abernathy

---

8. Lischer, *Preacher King*, 255.
9. Smitherman, *Talkin and Testifyin*, 88–90.

capitalized upon the poetics of African American Vernacular English to rationally synthesize biblical and sociopolitical ideas. Yet scant attention to the scattered displays of Abernathy's rhetoric in rhetorical texts, documentaries, standard histories, and popular culture has led to little substantive analysis.

In *Stride toward Freedom,* King praised Abernathy as an effective orator and versatile movement leader:

> Ralph's slow movement and slow, easy talk were deceptive. For he was an indefatigable worker and a sound thinker, possessed of a fertile mind. As a speaker, he was persuasive and dynamic, with a gift of laughing people into positive action. When things became languid around the mass meetings, Ralph Abernathy infused his audiences with new life and ardor.[10]

King's commendation of Abernathy echoes Aristotle's praise of the emotive rhetor. Of the qualities that King ascribed to Abernathy, "sound thinker" and "dynamic" are rarely mentioned in standard histories or rhetorical treatments of the movement. Both qualities suggest a deliberation one might need to counter Birmingham's dominant and oppressive narrative. However, these qualities take a backseat to Abernathy's humor. Nevertheless, even the persuasive effects of Abernathy's humor have been generally underplayed—that he, as King noted, had a penchant for "laughing people into positive action."[11]

Gary Selby, among few rhetorical scholars, has examined Abernathy's persuasive use of humor. Drawing on four speeches delivered in Albany, Georgia, and Birmingham, Alabama, Selby argues that Abernathy's oratory represents a rhetorical use of humor known as the "burlesque."[12] In contrast to the comic frame that Kenneth Burke and other rhetoricians describe and that Selby claims King employed in many of his mass meeting speeches, the burlesque encompasses a use of language that is far more critical of one's opponents than that of the comic frame. Several mass meeting rhetors, including Fred Shuttlesworth, used humor as well, and just as King and Abernathy recognized, humor did not diminish the seriousness of their messages. Taken together, King's and Selby's respective characterization of Abernathy will bolster my overall argument about him functioning as a preacher, prophet, and teacher.

10. King, *Stride toward Freedom,* 74.

11. Ibid., 74.

12. Selby, "Scoffing at the Enemy," 134.

SYNOPSES OF KING'S AND ABERNATHY'S
MAY 3RD SPEECHES

The horrors of dogs and water hoses unleashed upon school-age children on May 3rd, 1963, presented King and Abernathy with a critical moment for the Birmingham campaign and the larger civil rights movement. While other prominent leaders spoke, most mass meeting crowds considered King and Abernathy headliners. Throughout the history of these worship-service-style political rallies from Montgomery to Memphis, Abernathy usually preceded King. Yet on some occasions, significantly so for the purpose of this chapter, Abernathy's speech followed King's. Abernathy's following King on this decisive occasion afforded him a unique place of significance before the white reporters; his words were the last they heard, even though they may have chosen not to record them.[13]

Both King's and Abernathy's respective May 3rd speeches captured the devout yet critical patriotism integral to the civil rights movement. Both speeches stressed the movement participants' undying love for the principles of democracy and unyielding insistence that those principles be truly applied to all. While each oration addressed current affairs and history, King's speech focused on the former and Abernathy's concentrated on the latter.

King's speech reviewed the goals of the Birmingham movement within a broad international context. He endeavored to link this critical moment of Birmingham officials' abuse of school-age children with the spirit of the times. He began by contrasting the unprecedented horrors of the moment (represented by dogs and water hoses) with a pragmatic yet transcendent force of nonviolent resistance, a soul force that could "wear out"[14] any human type. Nonviolent resistance, even in this extreme case, emerged as not only the most spiritual choice but also the most reasonable. In fact, he connected the spiritual and the rational using an example about himself and his brother taking a road trip on winding highway, where many inconsiderate drivers in the oncoming traffic "were forgetting to dim their lights."[15]

---

13. During a 2005 interview, C. Herbert Oliver told me that the cameras, which had been focused on King, were turned off when Abernathy rose to speak. However, the police reports, according to the well-established procedure of monitoring the mass meetings, summarize Abernathy's speech along with the other speakers present that night (Birmingham Police Report, May 7, 1963).

14. King, Speech at Mass Meeting, in Towns, comp., "We Want Our Freedom," 148.

15. Ibid.

Growing weary of this dangerous insensitivity, King's brother, A.D., was tempted to respond in kind. King dissuaded his brother by exhorting him that someone "has to have sense on this highway."[16] Failing to respond in a nonretaliatory way would lead to mutual destruction, similar to the "eye-for- an-eye philosophy" that would render "everybody blind."[17]

Since the mass meetings were strategic planning sessions as well as spiritual assemblies, King often reminded crowds of the overarching goals of the entire movement. These goals, which varied only slightly from city to city, included (1) desegregation of public facilities, (2) equal employment opportunities, (3) immediate release of movement participants from prison, and (4) the appointment of a biracial committee to work with the mayor on race relations. With his trademark penchant for Hegelian synthesis, King intertwined an expanded discussion of these goals with an analysis of constitutional principles and global politics that underscored the timeliness of the Birmingham campaign. The slow pace of desegregation in schools and other public facilities was comparable to standing at the shores "of history trying to hold the tides back."[18] Birmingham officials should not have viewed movement members' requests for a speedy response to integration and fair employment as a Communist plot. The international tides flowing for human rights in Africa and Asia suggested otherwise. The demands for political parity in the form of a biracial committee and the willingness of the demonstrators to be jailed represented the best in the democratic tradition of protest.

With the discussion of the jailed (mostly school-age) protestors, King closed his speech by circling back to the theme of the pragmatic spirituality of their timely cause. King transformed jail into a spiritual haven, a place where "you can meditate a little."[19] King recycled this idea through many of his better-known speeches. Further, practically and productively, "you can get a lot of things done that you need to do."[20] King referred to his own jailhouse experiences of catching up with his reading and completing writing projects. As school-age children seized the time by protesting at the risk of being jailed, King urged his listeners that were on the fence about participating in the movement to make an immediate commitment. They

16. Ibid.
17. Ibid., 147.
18. Ibid., 149.
19. Ibid., 150.
20. Ibid.

should remember, that they only had a minute "just sixty seconds in it, but eternity is in"[21] that short time.

Abernathy's speech underscored why black people's track record in building America justified their aspirations in Birmingham. He directly complimented King's rhetorical abilities while indirectly affirming his own right to speak:

> And whenever we hear from the prophet (*Uh huh*),[22] and he speaks as he has spoken tonight (*Amen, Yes*), I feel that nobody else ought to attempt to speak. (*Yes, Amen*) But [*Laughter and scattered applause*]—we ought to really go home [*More laughter*] with that message burning in our hearts. But in spite of that, I do have a little lesson [*Laughter and applause*] that I want to say (*Well, Say it*) because it is on my mind (*Well, Say it now*), and it is on my heart.[23]

Abernathy's tone conveyed his trademark humor, indicated partly by the audience's passionate response, while the content set up the cognitive and affective value of his ethos in a way that writing might not.

The body of the speech introduced two interrelated narratives, ostensibly designed to get and keep the record straight about the African American struggle for civil rights. One narrative I refer to as *made history* and the other I refer to as *making history*. African Americans made history through enslaved and segregated labor—"Who was it that cleared the new ground?"[24]—as well as military service, from the first casualty of the American Revolutionary War to the soldiers who shed their "red blood" with their "white brothers"[25] on the beaches of Normandy. They were making history during the Birmingham campaign by expanding the borders of freedom. Abernathy likened this history in the making to a biblical epic, one that starts with the children of Israel crossing the Red Sea out of slavery (signifying segregation) and ends with an heavenly scene encompassing numbers that "no man could number" (signifying full democratic participation on the part of Birmingham's black citizens). In fact, black democratic participation might begin to reach apocalyptic proportions the very

---

21. Ibid., 151.

22. To illustrate the rhetorical force of call-and-response, I transcribed the audience's responses during Abernathy's speech. I've placed the verbal responses within parenthesis, and the nonverbal reactions, like laughter and applause, are bracketed.

23. Abernathy, Speech, mass meeting (Holmes transcript).

24. Ibid.

25. Ibid.

next day. As James Bevel dubbed May 3rd "D" (Demonstration) Day, and King's speech predicted that May 4th would be "Double D-Day," Abernathy referred to the coming morrow as "V" (Victory) Day. The connection Abernathy forged between history and current affairs amended the standard historical account about black people locally and nationally. While Abernathy noted alliances that had been made with northern civil rights leaders and that could be made with Washington politicians, the force of his authority partly lay in his ability to tell the story of the black masses using their idiom.

HEARING ABERNATHY:
A TEACHER IN A CLASS OF HIS OWN

Abernathy's musings on the past through his people's vernacular lays one foundation for my argument regarding how he performed as a folk preacher, prophet, and pedagogue. In his May 2nd speech Abernathy claimed that he "speaks with authority," an explicit allusion to Christ in the Synoptic Gospels. Like Christ, Abernathy set the efficacy of his words against what Royster and Williams call "officialized"[26] discourses of that day. Abernathy adopted the persona of Christ to frame his ethos as a teacher, depicting his speech as a "lesson" that the reporters had "to get." One citation from the May 3rd speech highlights this point:

> The Negro came to the United States of America in sixteen hundred and nineteen. (*Amen, Talk*) Now we have a lot of reporters here tonight (Amen), a lot of photographers here. [*Laughter*] They're standing in the back, down front. The city detectives are here and everybody (*Yes*), and I want them to hear me tonight. [*Laughter and sustained applause*] We came here in sixteen hundred and nineteen. (*Amen, Yes sir*) Now read any history book you want to read [*Laughter*], and you won't find it stated any better than that. [*More laughter*] I know my lesson. [*Laughter and sustained applause*][27]

Later in the speech, Abernathy returned to the now well-known date of 1619 and names his source: Lerone Bennett's now classic African American history *Before the Mayflower*. Abernathy's skepticism about "any book you want to read" was not leveled at all written histories, therefore, but

26. Royster and Williams, "History in Spaces Left."
27. Abernathy, Speech (Holmes transcript).

only at the ones that white Americans produced, which marginalized the African American experience.

Abernathy's humorous skepticism resonated with his southern black audience, and his taunting of white reporters was particularly strategic. Gene Roberts and Gene Klibanoff have observed that southern liberal white reporters were slow in getting around to writing about the civil rights struggle, and when they did, they seemed more concerned about defending the South from northern criticisms. This initial lack of front-page focus for the movement was perhaps the most formidable challenge that the SCLC faced. On the heels of a virtual failure in Albany, Georgia, King, Abernathy, and the SCLC needed mass publicity to succeed in Birmingham—publicity that both the local white papers, the *Birmingham Herald* and the *Birmingham News,* and the black-owned and -edited *Birmingham World* resisted giving.[28]

Moreover, in challenging the reporters and police detectives with a revisionist lesson, Abernathy shaped the conditions under which narratives for, about, and by African Americans were received, perceived, produced, expressed and even silenced. To put the matter differently, Abernathy positioned his oral performance over the white reporters' written performances (newspapers and standard histories for instance), inviting us to reconsider the power of African American oral traditions and theoretical expositions of orality and literacy. For Abernathy, his down-home rhetoric was not only a legitimate form of communication, but within this particular pedagogical arena (the mass meetings), it was also a form more fitting than were standardized ones: "If these reporters didn't get that, they never will get the message."[29]

Through this medium, Abernathy established his authority to speak using both mainstream democratic and marginalized African American religious traditions. The following two citations bear out this observation:

> I talked today with Los Angeles, California. (Amen, Talk) I talked this day (*Talk now*) with Nashville, Tennessee. I talked this day with New York City. (*Amen*) I talked this day with Washington DC. (All right) [*Applause*] But I want you to know that they are looking to Birmingham (*Amen*) because you started something. (*That's right*) Roy Wilkins said, "Ralph, tell 'em that we're behind them all the way." (*All right*) We got a straight line to the White

28. Roberts and Klibanoff, *Race Beat*, 306–7.
29. Abernathy, Speech (Holmes transcript).

House. (Yes, Talk to us) And we're gonna talk with the White House. (Amen) We wanna hear from the White House. (Amen) If Bull Connor will not do it, Governor Wallace won't do it, then Bob Kennedy will. [Laughter and much sustained applause][30]

By mentioning his ready access to a wide array of people and places, Abernathy positioned himself as a spokesperson for a movement that had captured the consciousness of the nation. The movement had arrested the notice of citizens north and south, east and west. It had moved other civil rights leaders and, more importantly, the attorney general and the White House to begin acting on behalf of the nation's long disenfranchised citizens of color. By declaring that the inaction of local or state officials in Alabama ultimately would not likely prevent the White House from acting, Abernathy dismantled the state sovereignty justification for perpetuating segregation. Still, within the same context, Abernathy saw fit to announce unequivocally his right to speak for other African Americans:

> But these reporters don't believe me. [*Laughter*] They think that I'm just a rabble rouser and an agitator. (*Amen*) But I speak with every Negro in Sixteenth Street backing me up tonight. (*Yes*) [*Applause*] I speak with every Negro in Birmingham who is in his right mind backing me up tonight. [*Applause*][31]

This citation suggests that Abernathy did not seize nor did the white establishment grant him the right to speak for his people. Rather, he earned this right by experiencing the struggle with them.

Therefore, Abernathy unsettled the hold white Birmingham officials believed they had on the discourses of justice, equality, and political access. And Abernathy's discursive challenges to the standard record places his rhetoric within a larger African American rhetorical tradition against white society controlling, compromising or commercializing black language and narrative. These efforts at monitoring African American expression ranged from well-intentioned efforts by abolitionists who wrote prefaces to slave narratives and wealthy sponsors of the Harlem Renaissance to ill-conceived racist characterizations by those who produced the minstrel shows and films, such as *Birth of a Nation*. My recovery of the Birmingham mass meeting speeches suggests, not only a missing piece of the rhetorical narratives

30. Ibid.
31. Ibid.

written about this site, but, more significantly, it challenges the official written record of what went on in that site: the police surveillance reports.

Since police reports were traditionally considered a detached genre of writing, they would be deemed a more objective account of the mass meetings than even the newspapers, not only for contemporaries of Abernathy, but also for scholars studying these rallies. Granted, these reports were and are invaluable primary sources for gathering facts, particularly due to the scarcity of audio recordings of the meetings. However, given the sophisticated communicative dynamics of the black church tradition and my argument about Abernathy's oral performance as prophet, preacher, and teacher, these reports would be insufficient for reconstructing the rhetorical narratives of these meetings. Put another way, the presence of the police detectives in the mass meetings and the reports they later wrote did not necessarily alter the rhetorical strategies, arguments, and narratives that mass meeting rhetors, such as Abernathy, used. In fact, when the Birmingham mass meeting rhetors mentioned the detectives, they did so by selectively and strategically incorporating these detectives' presence and perspectives within the traditional rhetorical frame of African American call-and-response.

In other words, the detectives played appointed roles in the "antiphonal call-and-response ritual,"[32] a ritual primarily concerned with the communicative give-and-take among preacher, sermon, and intended audience, yet on a secondary level, between the preacher and an unintended, hostile, absent or even imagined audience. Rooted in West African notions of communal consciousness, epistemology, politics, aesthetics, music, and rhetoric, the African American call-and-response tradition encompasses more than the verbal and bodily feedback between the preacher and the pews. Rather the sermon, or any discourse that entered into its topical purview, including the police reports, became a shared rhetorical and literacy event, instead of a static, authoritative text. To be sure, the call-and-response event persuaded, inspired and entertained, but further instructed, created, and critiqued knowledge and shaped worldviews. Call-and-response constituted one salient means by which the African American church became a revolving and evolving site of piety, polemics, and pedagogy. Rhetors and auditors change positions and postures at a moment's notice. In this sense, the church transforms into neither a preacher/teacher-centered nor congregation/student-centered space but becomes a moment-centered one. Hence

32. LaRue, *Heart of Black Preaching*, 11.

the, newspapers and police reports lost their hegemonic moorings within the communally discursive seas of call-and- response. As black preachers had historically revised biblical narratives like the exodus to assign the role of Pharaoh to a white oppressor, mass meeting orators sometimes assigned white detectives and reporters staged roles in the mass meeting drama. On this occasion, Abernathy deliberatively transformed the surveillance reports and newspaper articles into written versions of the congregation's verbal feedback.

Abernathy's counterhegemonic critique of written records of the Birmingham movement, whether mainstream newspapers or police re-ports, was situated within a larger paradigm in which the events that were deemed authoritative accounts of history and contemporary events were turned on their heads, but not simply because these accounts were writ-ten. These mainstream accounts fell short whenever they failed to consider diverse narratives and narrators, especially when said narrators were telling their stories. Abernathy clarified this point when he discussed the irony of African American patriotism:

> But he remained faithful to this land. (*That's right*) He fought in every war. (*Amen*) Write it down. [*Laughter*] . . . Whether it was on that . . . Sunday morning at Pearl Harbor (*Amen*) or on the beach at Normandy (*Amen, Talk*), black boys, black fathers (*Amen*) gave their red blood, along with their white brothers (*Amen*), to preserve this nation. (*Amen*) All the way from Boston Commons, when Crispus Attucks, a black man (*Amen, Yes*), was the first one—write it down you all don't know it. I want you to get it. [*Laughter and applause*] A black man was the first one to give his red blood (*That's right*) in an effort to bring this nation in to being. (*Yes, Amen*) Ever since then, Negroes have been rising and falling (*Amen*), blundering and stumbling (*Amen*), mistreated, neglected, and dejected, (*Amen*) but still singing from the bottom of their hearts, "God bless America" (*Amen*), "the land that I love." (Amen) "Stand beside her and guide her" (*Amen*) "with the light from above. From the mountain to the prairies" (*Yeah*)" to the oceans white with foam" (*Say it, Say it*), "God bless America, my home sweet home." (*Yeah*)[33]

Through this exchange, black listeners could affirm and white observ-ers might understand Abernathy's countermainstream views of patriotism and the traditional narratives that had been used to order these views. For

---

33. Abernathy, Speech (Holmes transcript).

Abernathy, African Americans' relationship to America involved critical loyalty. One climatic moment in the May 3rd speech captures this tension:

> I was in New York City the other night, and I told them that the Negroes of Birmingham are not going back to Africa. (*All right*) Our ancestors came from Africa but we didn't come from there. (*Amen*) But until the Englishman goes back to England (*All right, Amen*), until the Italian goes back to Italy, until the German goes back to Germany (*Amen*), the Mexican goes back to Mexico (Amen, Talk), the Frenchman goes back to France (*Amen*), and the white man gives the country back to the Indians . . . [*Laughter and much sustained applause*][34]

In this passage, Abernathy deftly linked critical citizenship, as well as rhetorical and political agency, to the contentious issue of the sovereignty of space. Who really belongs to the land? Within the context of this remark, Abernathy had already discounted the black nationalists' notion that most African Americans wanted to return to Africa. Abernathy introduced this point because he and his audience realized, though he did not mention directly, that many white persons, particularly white supremacists such as the Klan, agreed with the black nationalists about separating the races. But by pointing out that everyone was displaced from their native land, albeit by voluntary immigration or by forced transport (both of which he mentioned earlier in the speech), Abernathy complicated the American Slave and Ellis Island narratives. The only group that could lay claim to native geographical sovereignty, insofar as the U.S. was concerned, would be Native Americans. The rest of us are visitors. Hence, if black people didn't belong here, white people didn't either.

Moreover, the passage exposes the restricted territorialism that racial discrimination often inspired. For some racists, blacks belonged in Africa; for others, they belonged in the South. Abernathy offered a humorous, indirect, yet poignant critique of the racism that partly fueled the great migrations when he noted:

> For as Martin Luther King has said in his famous speech, "we want all of our freedom." (*Yes sir*) And we want it here (*Yeah, Yes sir*), not in Chicago. (*Yeah*) I was up there the other day and almost froze to death. [*Laughter*] It's too cold up there.[35]

34. Ibid.
35. Ibid.

From pragmatic voices, like Booker T. Washington to more militant ones, like Robert Williams, countless southern-born people of color have argued for their right to remain in that region, while also being guaranteed their civil rights.

Not surprisingly, then, one repeated theme that Ralph Abernathy explored is religiously inspired autonomous rhetorical agency. In his May 2nd speech for example, Abernathy opined:

> I've said it over and over again, and I'll say it again to you tonight that the Supreme Court cannot free the Negro. These white friends who've come to our rescue cannot free us. The NAACP cannot free the Negro; the court cannot free the Negro. The Southern Christian Leadership Conference cannot free the Negro. If the Negro is going to be free, he must free himself.[36]

Such agency addresses why Nunley might call Abernathy a "phronimos."[37] Abernathy communicated practical, relevant, and critical notions related to the African American freedom struggle to be sure. However, Nunley further argues that a black phronimos uses "African American Hush Harbor rhetoric," rather than "African American public podium-auction block rhetoric." The latter approach focuses on discourses that sanitize or downplay the most salient views, needs, and concerns that blacks collectively possess for the sake of mainstream success. Rhetors that use this approach do not necessarily have a slave or sell out mentality. Rather, they seek to project to white society a more "consumable" and tamer notion of blackness. The former approach, African American Hush Harbor rhetoric, infuses all expressive enterprises with *parrhesia*, which means "speaking frankly" and "speaking truth to power."[38] Indeed, *parrhesia* seems practically synonymous to prophecy as I have examined it thus far in this book.

Ultimately African American agency, freedom, epistemology, and expression could not and would not be confined to mainstream written discourses, even though some of those discourses, like the law, seemed to assist blacks in their struggle for authentic democracy. Catherine Prendergast has underscored the folly of assuming that law could sufficiently address the educational, economic, and social marginalization blacks faced through landmarks such as *Brown v. Board of Education*, especially since the legal system rested on privileging literacy as white property.

36. Abernathy, Speech (Holmes transcript).
37. Nunely, *Keepin' It Hushed*, 108.
38. Ibid., 1.

Therefore, the civil rights movement needed more than law; it needed prophetic rhetoric. Abernathy's speech illustrates why. Abernathy would call upon his persuasive humor, insight, and instruction to help ease the tensions that followed that fateful day of May 3rd. On May 12th, two days after a tentative settlement to the demonstrations was reached, the Gaston Motel, where King resided during the Birmingham campaign, and A.D. King's home were bombed. Approximately two thousand five hundred black people rioted near the downtown as a result. Four months and three days later, Thomas Edwin Blanton Jr., Bobby Frank Cherry, and Robert "Dynamite Bob" Chambliss conspired with other Klan members to blow up the Sixteenth Street Baptist Church. The explosion killed four African American girls: Addie Mae Collins, Cynthia Wesley, Carole Robertson, and Denise McNair. King feared that this tragedy might lead to mass rioting worse than what occurred on May 12th. Tragedy did strike in the aftermath of the Sixteenth Street Church bombing, as five fires raged in the African American business section and two black teenagers were shot. King believed that as a result of these escalating tragedies many Americans of both races might consider the civil rights movement a failure and withdraw their support. While King deserves all of the credit he has received for sustaining the movement through this horrific time, Abernathy also played a lion's share in keeping the peace as well. The folksy, prophetic, inspirational and instructional rhetoric that Abernathy used to move Birmingham residents would also encourage people in mass meetings across the nation, including in Selma, Alabama, during SCLC's next great battle: national voting rights legislation.

These first four chapters have demonstrated the rhetorical range of prophetic rhetoric as practiced during the Birmingham mass meetings: from hermeneutics to poetics, from grassroots politics to pedagogy. But another crucial question remains: Is prophetic rhetoric usable only for clergy or formal religionists? Chapter 5 turns to this issue.

5

Minor Prophets and Major Politics

James Farmer, Roy Wilkins, and
the Secular Prophetic Stance

"The words of the prophets are written on subway walls and tenement halls."[1]

—Simon & Garfunkel, "The Sounds of Silence"

So far, this book has advanced the claim that the Birmingham mass meetings of 1963 constitute a site for enriching an understanding particularly of black prophetic discourses and generally of what George Shulman calls the prophetic genre of American politics. I have shown that the oratory various speakers used during these mass meetings textures both the notion of African American rhetoric and American democratic discourses.

This chapter focuses on James Farmer and Roy Wilkins as minor prophets within the panoply of Birmingham mass meeting rhetors. The designation *minor prophets* is taken from the Old Testament, and, as was the case with these individuals, is not meant to diminish the importance of Farmer and Wilkins. Indeed, the minor prophets of the Old Testament were stellar representatives of that rhetorical tradition. Their messages were not minor insofar as larger biblical themes were concerned, but rather, the geographical territories or audiences they addressed tended to be smaller

1. Simon, "Sounds of Silence."

than that of major prophets, including Jeremiah, Daniel, and Ezekiel. Also, because their books of prophecies tended to be briefer than those composed by their major counterparts, Old Testament Minor Prophets typically concentrated on core issues—less on religious rituals and more on social concerns such as justice for the dispossessed and provisions for the poor.

When I refer to James Farmer and Roy Wilkins as *minor prophets,* I have a couple ideas in mind. First, while both hail from Christian backgrounds, neither could be deemed prophets in the way the other mass meeting preachers like King, Abernathy, Shuttlesworth, and Bevel might be. They neither projected the pastoral persona nor deployed most of the commonplaces and communicative techniques associated with black homiletic rhetoric. In fact neither of the organizations they headed was founded or regulated by the black church. Second, New York, the headquarters for both organizations, was geographically and ideologically detached from the South. Both Farmer and Wilkins wielded a national influence in the struggle for black liberation and were numbered among Martin Luther King Jr., Whitney Young, John Lewis, and Dorothy Height as the major movers ("Big Six") of the integrationist civil rights movement.

Yet I refer to Farmer and Wilkins as prophets despite their cosmopolitan secularism. As I have noted, thinkers as varied as David Chappell, Cornel West, and George Shulman have extended the definition of *prophet* beyond religious terrain, instead suggesting that prophets, regardless of their worldviews, speak truth to power at critical times and in significant places. Beyond any dogmatic, doctrinal, or sectarian definition, prophecy is situated within a certain set of cultural contexts. In this chapter, I will use Farmer's mass meeting speech from May 2nd and Wilkins's mass meeting speech from April 25th, 1963, to position them as national civil rights spokespersons and minor prophets within the mass meeting rhetorical tradition.

JAMES FARMER'S RHETORIC
OF HUMAN SPIRITUALITY AND INTERRACIAL UNITY

"I must insist that a demonstration is not a riot."[2]

—James Farmer

2. Farmer, *Freedom When?,* 27.

It would be quite easy for Farmer's May 2nd, 1963, speech to float under the radar of historians and rhetorical scholars. This was the first day of the children's march, so historians might be expected to track the narrative of this controversial experiment that James Bevel had proposed without mentioning Farmer. Historians have also given attention to the rising tempers and lowering morale that evolved from what some considered a desperate move as well as the political infighting in city hall between the newly elected mayor and city council and the ousted city commissioners, especially Bull Connor. Rhetorical scholars, including Richard Lischer, have discussed how King handled this delicate set of conditions, the most pressing being the several children imprisoned after that day of demonstrations. In the last chapter we sketched Abernathy's stellar rhetorical performance as preacher and pedagogue. Obviously, rhetorical scholars have examined King's May 2nd and 3rd speeches, both because of his iconic status, and because of the conditions that surrounded these critical dates. Understandably, then, Farmer's speech given on May 2nd might go virtually ignored. Further, because the mass meetings of April and May 1963 have been underplayed by historians and underexamined by rhetoricians, one might expect a discussion of Farmer's participation in the salient May 2nd meeting to appear as a footnote, if at all.

Farmer was born in Marshall, Texas, and as the son of a father who was an exceptional academic and preacher, one might have expected Farmer to follow one of those paths. The young Farmer did attend seminary, but he never practiced ministry, at least not in any traditional sense, though he one time referred to himself as a "jack-leg preacher" to establish his authority in an argument he was having with someone about the need for religion to be socially relevant and racially inclusive. Both Farmer's seminary training and self-designation as a "jack-leg preacher" are pertinent to this chapter. "Jack-leg preacher" was a derogatory designation for a preacher who didn't measure up in some way. Typically it had reference to pastors who didn't practice what they preached morally, but the term "jack-leg" could also refer to a parson who lacked either education or the call. Since Farmer was educated, his appropriation of this term may refer to his epicurean lifestyle of eating, drinking, and smoking. For my purposes, the designation "jack-leg" highlights Shulman's secularization of the prophetic stance, which is a view that significantly broadens that rhetorical purview of prophecy and those that practice it.

Like the novelist and activist James Baldwin, Farmer was a humanist of the first order who whetted his rhetorical whistle with the Bible. Both initially encountered *nommo* or the spiritual energy, force, and essence of black language through the African American church. Both had preaching fathers (a stepfather in Baldwin's case) who possessed puritanical sensibilities by which the sons could not abide. Both men found it ethically inconsistent for their fathers to rigidly conform to a restrictive moral code while compromising with the restrictions of white racism. Baldwin became disillusioned with the black church largely because the fervor he saw displayed for church rituals and repressive lifestyles were not translated into blacks loving themselves and fighting against the institutionalized, racist dehumanization. Farmer's disillusionment hardened while he was attending seminary. His denomination, the Methodist Episcopal Church North, had compromised on segregation by reestablishing a connection with the Methodist Episcopal Church South. However, blacks, wherever they resided, would belong to the Methodist Central region. This blatant act of institutional racism soured Farmer on organized religion and sparked the flame for his secular prophetic voice. He titled his Howard University thesis "A Critical Analysis of the Historical Interrelationship between Religion and Racism." While Farmer had acquired the core of his rhetorical abilities from the black church and retained a belief that this organization could be instrumental in liberating African Americans from segregation's caste system, like Baldwin, Farmer had to leave the church to preach the gospel.

Farmer's prophetic stance remained rooted in but not regulated by religion. In his book *Lay Bare the Heart*, Farmer discussed his intellectual coming of age, which I would also characterize as constituting his first steps in converting from seminary student to secular prophet. His mentors or fathers in the social gospel faith included Melvin Tolson, his Wiley College debate coach; Howard Thurman, the renowned black Christian mystic, theologian, philosopher, and Howard University Seminary professor; and V. F. Calverton, a celebrated Marxist literary critic who found the customs of segregation barbaric. When Calverton visited Wiley as a guest lecturer on drama, the undergraduate student Farmer was arrested by more than his critical insights. Calverton was one of the first white men Farmer ever heard critique blacks (in this case regarding a student drama production) without speaking harshly or paternalistically.

From each of these men, Farmer learned unexpected lessons beyond the anticipated ones. A notable poet and English professor, Tolson insisted that Farmer not settle for intellectual mediocrity, even when he could still excel academically while doing so. Instead, Tolson implored the young Farmer to read widely, well beyond the books his professors assigned and "digest" them rather than merely "taste" the words. Thurman, who taught Farmer in a Christian social ethics course, was a major intellectual force in the civil rights movement, shaping the thoughts of future leaders, including Farmer and King. Thurman's lessons extended beyond the halls of Howard; they were conveyed through his nationwide lectures, international travels, and abundant correspondence. From Thurman's Christian social ethics course, Farmer learned about an indivisible relationship that could be forged between spirituality and social justice. Spirituality—not necessarily organized religion—could infuse social movements with a practically unstoppable collective energy and force, as evidenced by Gandhi's widely touted successful campaign against British colonialism.

Indeed, it was through his study of Gandhi that the influences of two of Farmer's mentors (Thurman and Calverton) would intersect. Calverton and Farmer kept in touch after the two met during the drama convention at Wiley. Calverton broadened Farmer's intellectual horizons through suggested readings and rigorous discussions, but it was through Calverton's and Thurman's respective interpretations of Gandhi that Farmer began apprehending an uneasy reconciliation between spirituality and social justice. Whereas the theologian and mystic Thurman characterized Gandhi as an exceptional spiritual leader, the atheist-aesthete Calverton deemed him a shrewd politician. In a related yet surprising vein for Farmer, Calverton was not dismissive of Farmer's interest in spirituality and, to a much lesser extent, religion and their relationships to racism at worst and social progress at best. Farmer summarizes the overall impact that Calverton and Thurman had on him when he notes,

> One was a sensual, hedonistic, atheistic iconoclast; the other an icon—spiritual, theistic, moralistic. One was dedicated to the things of the mind, with the spirit thrown in; the other was dominated by things of the soul, with the mind thrown in. Neither would accept any dichotomy between mind and spirit.[3]

Farmer's secular prophetic voice blended chords of collegiate debate, mystic contemplation, social activism, and humanistic skepticism. All of these chords would coalesce into a critical consciousness that demanded

3. Farmer, *Lay Bare*, 142.

that he engage in prophetic critique. Farmer had begun his seminary edu-cation after being drawn to the social gospel. While he remained interested in this movement that attempted to remedy contemporary society's ills through liberal theology and pragmatic philosophy, Farmer was more in-terested in the social rather than in the gospel side of this prescription. He informed his father that he would not be entering the ministry. Instead he would adopt the spiritual yet activist principles of Gandhi's philosophy of nonviolence to stamp out racism.

Farmer began his activist journey as a member of the Quaker-inspired Fellowship of Reconciliation (FOR). Like many white slave abolitionists, the members of FOR addressed social injustices through peaceful, non-confrontational means. When Farmer and a small group of FOR members staged a successful sit-in against a Chicago restaurant that refused to serve African Americans, the leaders of FOR seemed impressed with Farmer's leadership. As a result, the director of FOR, A. J. Muste, agreed to Farmer's request that he form a subgroup that would engage in direct action activi-ties like sit-ins. The founding group formed in 1942 and carried the acro-nym CORE (Committee of Racial Equality). Several months later, other committees of racial equality sprung up in other cities, but remained under the auspices of FOR. Farmer proposed at the annual convention that FOR incorporate sit-ins as a nationwide tactic. However, key members of the organization challenged the peacefulness of this approach. Would not any disruptive direct-action approach, even nonviolent sit-ins, be confronta-tional? Farmer and FOR would agree to disagree on this point and eventu-ally part ways. During the 1940s and '50s, CORE would continue to operate in iterant fashion, without FOR's sanction and, temporarily at least, without Farmer's consistent leadership.

Farmer held brief stints as union representative and as program direc-tor for the NAACP under the leadership of Roy Wilkins. For the latter job, Farmer hit the ground running, crafting numerous proposals concerning how the NAACP could be both more efficient and proactive, which were proposals that, according to Farmer, waited untouched on Wilkins's desk for months. While he believed that he was not taken seriously in his NAACP job, Farmer nevertheless learned some valuable lessons from it. First, he learned that civil rights organizations, while all presumably fighting for black advancement, still vied for prominence and support. Farmer recalled one incident when Martin Luther King Jr. and Ralph Abernathy visited the NAACP headquarters to discuss the SCLC's fundraising approach. Before

King and Abernathy arrived, Wilkins complained to staffers, including Farmer, that the fundraising the SCLC conducted through church collections at mass meetings was siphoning off money from NAACP membership drives. When the SCLC officers arrived, the conversation that ensued took on merely a veneer of civility. King suggested that SCLC continue to concentrate on raising money through church parishioners' contributions while the NAACP focused on membership drives, which King encouraged. When Wilkins bristled at this suggestion, King, according to Farmer, became visibly irritated. A semblance of a cordial discussion went on a little longer, but by the end of it the representatives of the two organizations parted without achieving an actual resolution.

The second lesson Farmer learned from working at the NAACP is that although he admired the SCLC and NAACP and would continue to work with them in the future, he found both organizations to be ideologically limited in their efforts to achieve social justice for African Americans. The SCLC's focus on black ministers and their church members potentially excluded two important allies in African American fight for freedom: whites and secularists of all races. Undoubtedly, Farmer knew many unchurched whites who financially supported King and the SCLC; nevertheless, he probably wondered how many agnostics or atheists of any race felt comfortable with the strictures imposed by black Protestantism. Farmer would never lose this empathy for those who were motivated by something other than Scripture to serve the cause of racial justice. Later as national director of CORE and on the eve of the Freedom Rides of 1961, Farmer suggested a moment of silence, rather than a word of prayer, which one member of the group had recommended. As for Farmer's view of the NAACP, their exclusive focus on legal redress could not generate the sense of urgency, grassroots enthusiasm, and involvement that direct demonstrations could.

Farmer carried these and other lessons with him when he became national director of the Congress of Racial Equality in 1961. He and the organization had come a long way since 1942. He was no longer the quick-witted, glib twenty-two-year-old who was passionate about fighting for social justice but who lacked a deliberative rationale or a clear sense of personal vocation. Furthermore, the organization was no longer a committee or appendage of the Fellowship of Reconciliation; it was no longer subject to that larger organization's dictates and directions. Still, because of the association with FOR, the newly minted CORE was considered a pioneering organization when it came to direct demonstrations, and Farmer, despite his mere forty-one years, was a seasoned statesman of the civil rights movement. King, while Farmer's junior, had been the nationally recognized head of the civil rights movement since the Montgomery bus boycott, a fact that Farmer and Wilkins resented in their own ways. Nevertheless, King would later publicly commend Farmer and CORE for blazing the trail for direct-action and civil disobedience.

As a result, Farmer approached the podium of the May 2nd mass meeting at Sixth Avenue Baptist Church with a national ethos. The sit-in movement that had spread like wildfire all over the South might have been fanned into flame by the students from North Carolina A&T in 1960, but the spark had come from Farmer and his FOR cohorts in the 1940s. The Nashville Student Movement, under the leadership of Diane Nash, might have continued the Freedom Rides because of the horrific brutality CORE volunteers faced in Alabama, but Farmer's CORE had begun the journey not in Washington DC in 1961 but in 1947, under the FOR with a trip called the Journey of Reconciliation. However, despite Farmer's impeccable credentials as a freedom fighter, he might appear to be a bit of a misfit at the mass meetings. Though the son of a preacher, he was a self-described humanist. The fact that he was from New York was of little ultimate consequence, since the Birmingham campaign was open to and in fact needed help from every willing soul, despite racial, religious, or regional origin. While Farmer had spoken before NACCP and SCLC crowds, his comportment might have distanced him from this southern black Baptist audience. Farmer possessed a booming, commanding voice and spoke with the precision of a big-city news anchor, yet his gestures were stiff and his bearing stoic.

This is not to say that Farmer was not an effective orator stylistically and substantively. His formal studies with Thurman and informal studies with Calverton had planted within him an insatiable, lifelong love for learning and critical thinking. Since his collegiate debate days, he had honed his oratorical and critical thinking skills in promptly advancing and countering points. In fact, he was one of the few mainstream civil rights leaders who not only was willing to debate Malcolm X but was also able to effectively rebut some of the black Muslim minster's one-liners and sound bites. The forensic skills acquired from Tolson not only blossomed in the debates that Farmer had with Malcolm X and others, the point/counterpoint structure informed Farmer's mass meeting speech on May 2nd. After referring to Farmer as "an eloquent speaker" and "finished orator," Marcus Boulware in his classic *The Oratory of Negro Leaders* observed the following about Farmer's rhetorical style and substance:

> His voice has unusual flexibility, range, and a slight vibrato. Farmer is a logician whose language and words are strictly for intellectual debate. Yet, it would be comparatively easy for him to adapt his language and vocabulary in a manner that would arouse the masses on account of his ethical and persuasive appeal. People are convinced that his words and actions are the same thing. With him persuasive oratory has not been imperative, since he has utilized most effectively the medium of militant and intelligent action. Those who have heard him speak know that, as he proceeds, his voice becomes more vibrant and resonant, more convincing and dynamic—the necessary requisites of an orator to drive home his ideas.[4]

Boulware's description of Farmer resonates with Quintilian's depiction of an ideal orator as a "good man speaking well." As significantly, Boulware characterized Farmer as someone who walked the tightrope between classical notions of philosophical deliberation and stylistic craft. Farmer was certainly not a sophist as Plato understood that term, consumed with oratory that pleased or pacified listeners as a means to self-promotion rather than prodding one's listeners to think critically and live ethically. Nor was Farmer so consumed with dialectic analysis that he would avoid moments of strategic rhetorical performance.

Nevertheless, as the fourth speaker for the night and not being a cleric, Farmer found himself in an unenviable position. What would he say after this historically horrific day? His speech was sandwiched between well-regarded preachers who offered the people a buffet of biblical wisdom, sermonic wit, and inspiration. May 2nd was critical moment for the Birmingham campaign, as it was the first time schoolchildren participated in mass in these demonstrations and were, subsequently, arrested. Several preachers spoke that night. King inspired the audience by reminding them of the justice of their cause and the collective sacrifice that must be made to make freedom for all a reality. Abernathy's mass meeting speech encouraged the crowd with his trademark folksy humor, stressing his character, competence, and commitment to the cause. He used himself as a prime example of a leader who was a "damn fool"[5] for Christ, and Shuttlesworth's

4. Boulware, *Oratory of Black Leaders*, 220–21.
5. May 2nd Mass meeting (Holmes transcript).

impromptu remarks, as master of ceremonies, included, as per usual, a curious yet rhetorically effective homiletic blend of exhortations, announcements, anecdotes, summation of strategies, and plans.

Shuttlesworth introduced Farmer in terms commensurate with the latter man's status within the movement. Since much of the success of Farmer's speech would come from the ethos he brought to this mass meeting, Shuttlesworth commended CORE as the organization that "added a new dimension to the civil rights movement."[6] Through the widespread and effective use of nonviolence, CORE had shown itself to be not only "Christian," but "even spiritual."[7] Shuttlesworth's last phrase indirectly, perhaps tacitly, acknowledged CORE's far-reaching appeal to the churched and unchurched. Shuttlesworth then presented Farmer as "the power behind the throne" and the "man on the throne."[8] Farmer was widely recognized as having a powerful influence on bringing people from various stations together. Perhaps not surprisingly, therefore, Farmer's organically structured yet poignant speech was organized around the theme of a spiritual unity that blurred in some cases and transcended in others constructed boundaries. The Birmingham campaign, as Farmer noted early in the speech, had both "inspired people all over the world" and "people all over the nation."[9] In keeping with lessons rhetorical scholars would later learn from Kenneth Burke, Farmer envisioned certain divisions as leading to identification and ultimately, through effective rhetoric, unity. The speech attempted to transcend international, national, regional, institutional, and racial lines by calling upon a pragmatic human spirituality.

Farmer's speech moved right into the ceremonial acknowledgement of Shuttlesworth, King, and Abernathy. He gratefully latched onto Shuttlesworth's compliment that CORE had supplied a needed dimension to the civil rights movement. To thunderous applause, Farmer noted that the Birmingham movement participants had provided "an additional dimension"[10] to the civil rights movement. The democratic demonstrations by and jailing of African Americans in Birmingham had motivated people as far as Africa, who had sent Farmer letters and stood ready to aid the campaign. The theme of the international support for the Birmingham campaign would

6. Ibid.

7. Ibid.

8. Ibid.

9. Farmer, Mass Meeting Speech (Holmes transcript).

10. Ibid.

recur throughout Farmer's speech. International support for the civil rights movement broadly defined was a recurring theme in Martin Luther King Jr.'s speeches as well. Leaders like King and Farmer knew that from FDR to JFK, the federal government did not want America's race problem to cause international embarrassment. During World War II, leaders such as the inimitable A. Phillip Randolph had capitalized upon America's fight against fascism abroad to bring focus to discrimination against blacks within the United States federal government. As a result, certain presidential decisions regarding civil rights, such as Roosevelt's executive orders against federal employment discrimination and even Truman's desegregation of the military, must be seen within a context of not just domestic pressure but also international publicity. This is not to say that no president wanted to make any strides in civil rights, but as Mary Dudziak, among others, has argued, several presidents, including Kennedy, preferred gradual moves towards black rights, so as not to lose white support by appearing to encroach on southern sovereignty. Most politicians north of the Mason-Dixon Line didn't want to appear to be supporting what some had derisively called the "second Reconstruction." For a time, Kennedy himself had accepted the widely touted view that the first Reconstruction was a political failure.

Farmer's globalization of the Birmingham campaign implicitly elevated this civil rights struggle to a human rights struggle. Having framed the Birmingham struggle within the context of international support, Farmer drew further connections between the support that other civil organizations offered to Birmingham and national unity. All of the other mainstream civil rights organizations, including SNCC, the SCLC, CORE, and even the NAACP publicly supported the participants in the Birmingham campaign. Farmer stressed that while Project C was barely one month old, fifty chapters of CORE were already boycotting Woolworth stores within their respective cities because of the racial discrimination practiced locally by that chain store. On the surface, CORE's national decision to boycott Woolworth might seem unfair. However, this choice illuminated and buttressed Farmer's claim about the Birmingham campaign particularly and the civil rights movement generally transcending national boundaries.

Though the selfless acts of Birmingham campaigners, the national civil rights movement gained momentum, and this momentum was contagious. People were so inspired nationally, Farmer, said, that they were "demonstrating in Georgia again" and in "small towns in Alabama," and when the system of Birmingham segregation was toppled, "Mississippi won't be far behind."[11] The dismantling of "Mississippi" segregation would have seemed next to impossible for many southern African Americans to imagine. In fact, many had expressed this level of incredulity when the Birmingham campaign began. After all, Birmingham was reputed as "the most thoroughly segregated southern city." At the start of the speech, Farmer had called Birmingham the "bulwark of segregation" and confessed, while his auditors laughed and applauded, that he had believed that Shuttlesworth and other leaders would "never get" the campaign "off the ground in Birmingham."[12] However, the system of Birmingham segregation appeared to be crumbling, and if there were hope for Birmingham, there was hope for the rest of Alabama. If they could "break the solid wall of segregation in Birmingham," they would eventually "break the wall of segregation throughout Alabama."[13] And if Alabama could be desegregated, Mississippi could too. If there were hope for Mississippi, there was hope for the nation. Ideologies, nefarious or noble, were not confined to region. Neither should support or rejection of various points of view be restricted to a particular territory.

Farmer invoked the unity of the very different civil rights organizations as a microcosm for national unity. There were disagreements among and within civil rights organizations. The very existence of the NAACP, the SCLC, SNCC, CORE, and ACMHR reflected divergent perspectives on how civil rights could be achieved, as well as which strategies, methods, and leadership styles might represent the best mediums for reaching those goals. Unity among civil rights organizations represented an ideal, and like the American ideal of democracy, was perhaps attainable but not yet attained. Be that as it may, Farmer wanted his audience to work with the assumption that all the organizations of the civil rights movement were uniting behind Birmingham campaigners.

Having established the notion of inner-organizational unity within the civil rights movement, Farmer turned to the local and national disunity that racism caused and that marred the ideals of democracy, liberty, and freedom. There were interworking local and national obstacles to the widespread unity that was fomenting behind the Birmingham campaign. Some, such as the Birmingham police detectives, would try to, according

11. Ibid.
12. Ibid.
13. Ibid.

to Farmer, "trip them up"[14] by reporting what was observed in the mass meetings, which supposedly would intimidate and ultimately frighten away some participants. Both the quasi-satirical tone in which Farmer delivered this remark and the raucous laughter that follows reaffirmed two claims that I have made in earlier chapters. First, the regular presence of local police detectives and their surveillance equipment during the mass meetings had become the fodder for a constant stream of jokes rather than pervasive fear among movement participants. Second, mass meeting orators used the detectives as stock players in the rhetorical scene produced for a particular speech as well as within the larger drama of the Birmingham campaign. In this drama, as in all drama, comic relief was a necessary component, and making the police detectives the foils in this freedom drama afforded such relief on several occasions.

This may be why Farmer followed up this needling of the police detectives with a story that illustrated the importance of unity on the local level. A woman was drowning, and a lifeguard reached out trying to save her. From the boat he grabbed at her head, and the woman's wig came off. He then reached to secure her arm, which also came off as it was artificial. Finally, the lifeguard dove into the water, desperately attempting to catch the woman by the leg, discovering that it too was artificial. Frustrated as he emerged and wiping water from his eyes, he shouted, "Lady if you just stick together I can save you."[15] Neither the reference to police detectives' surveillance as incidental and ineffectual nor the story about the drowning woman was shared solely to evoke laughter from the audience. The times were serious as evidenced by the sons and daughters of many in the audience who had been arrested earlier that day. The laughter this night, as it had always been for African Americans during the long history of racism, functioned cathartically, inspirationally, instructionally and, ultimately, persuasively.

Farmer's speech continued to inspire pockets of laughter as he expounded on the national pervasiveness of racism. Discrimination knew no lines, regionally or ideologically. Playing off the distinction between southern de jure racism and northern de facto racism, he developed this contention about the ubiquity of racism by critiquing the well-worked warning that white officials across the South employed concerning "outside agitators." At least since the inception of the civil rights movement, both

14. Ibid.
15. Ibid.

southern moderates and blustering segregationists had spun a narrative that unrest among blacks and whites didn't arise from the southern way of life but instead from outsiders whose presence and activities irritated local blacks and disturbed the collective peace. By the time King and the SCLC came to Birmingham, this canonized narrative had reached fever pitch and was circulated by moderate and hardcore segregationists as well as by some well-respected local black residents such as A. G. Gaston. Yet Farmer, without mentioning blacks who might be complicit in promoting this narrative, critiqued the moniker "outside agitator" as an excuse motivated as much by economics as by any deeply seated southern provincial traditionalism. Farmer then posed a critical question, salient not only to his speech but also to the premise that true democratic protest transcends and traverses geographical boundaries: "Who is an outsider?"[16] Birmingham was one of the industrial centers of the South, so city officials were not worried about outsiders when they encouraged "industries to move into the state,"[17] nor were they flustered about state sovereignty when the federal government sent them monetary subsidies, some of which came from taxpayers who did not reside in Birmingham. This logical inconsistency and ethical duplicity led Farmer to deconstruct the descriptor "outside agitator" by declaring "anybody with us in the fight for freedom is one of us."[18] Since racism knew no geographical boundaries, revolts against it should be neither localized nor carried out by hometown folks exclusively. Or as King often noted, citing Oliver Wendell Holmes, "Injustice anywhere is a threat to justice everywhere."

Antiblack racism had metastasized from the inception of slavery in the United States, spreading contagiously and continuously from south to north, east to west. If the Birmingham campaign specifically and the civil rights movement generally were to be successful, then the advocates of racial justice had to be honest about how pervasively diseased the body politic had become. Farmer recalled for his audience how he owned up to New York racism in the most peculiar space—a Mississippi jail. On the last leg of the Freedom Rides, Farmer and several of his associates had been jailed in Jackson, Mississippi. Farmer resisted the demeaning southern white tradition of a black man being called "boy" by informing his jailers that at forty-one he had long since moved beyond boyhood, and he was

16. Ibid.
17. Ibid.
18. Ibid.

also losing his hair. He also refused to respond with the customary "yes sir" when called. Farmer goes on to recount his jailers' strained efforts to address him respectfully. After calling him "Farmer" for a time, they tried to add mister, but the only remote approximation that split their lips was "Um Farmer."[19] To uproarious laughter, Farmer continues: They asked whether "Um Farmer" could purchase a home anywhere in New York that his money could take him. While he thought of a comeback, his captors posed another question: Could he work anywhere in New York commensurate with his abilities? Farmer did not disclose to his audience what his jailers said after he responded to both questions in the negative, but he was crystal clear about the conclusion that had to be drawn from this encounter: "Anywhere you find people of color, you will find prejudice against colored people."[20]

This reminder that racism literally knew no geographical boundaries moved Farmer to introduce two experiences—one just outside his hometown of Marshall, Texas, and the other in Ruleville, Mississippi. Each exposed the psychological impact of racism on the white race. In a scene that would be quite familiar to his audience, Farmer recalled how when he had been a teenager, he and his father were confronted by a police officer on their way back to Marshall. The police officer demanded to know why Farmer's father was passing through. After being told the purpose for their trip, the officer posed a predictably racist yet conversationally irrelevant question: "Don't you know that we don't allow Negroes in this town after dark?"[21] What gave Farmer and his father pause was not this stock scene of racist exchange that was played out in many southern spaces during this time, but the mental energy such a preoccupation with blacks' comings and goings represented. Farmer followed this scene with a more recent one. While engaging in civil rights activity in Ruleville, Farmer came across an ordinance stating that all blacks should be in their homes with the lights out by midnight. A black family who lived next door to the house where Farmer was staying was paying last respects to a dying relative at 12:30 one night. A police officer knocked on the door demanding that the lights be turned off. Upon finding out why the lights were on, the officer repeated his command laced with curses and a threat about shooting the lights out if they were not turned off. Farmer then commented on the neurotic spillover of racism. White bigots were "staying up late nights wondering what Ne-

19. Ibid.
20. Ibid.
21. Ibid.

groes are doing." As a result, Farmer declared that he "feels sorry" for Bull Connor, who most certainly had "difficulty in sleeping."[22]

White racists ironically crossed geographical boundaries literally and ideologically while irrationally seeking to constrict black mobility physically and economically. To keep blacks in their place meant restricting their movement and achievement. The same racists that demanded black movement in some cases tried to prevent it in other cases. Calls to get out of town by sundown were matched with demands that southern blacks not migrate to the north, leave their sharecropping spaces, or engage in civil rights marches. The racism that characterized the entire nation oozed out of the confines of neurotic minds. Similarly, the unity that should transcend geographical, class, ethnic, and organizational boundaries had to flow from an enlightened mind and be enacted in a particular time and space as civil rights workers and their allies moved critically and continuously.

Thus, from exploring the neurosis of southern white racism Farmer transitioned to the theme of authentic freedom. The participants of the Birmingham campaign had an opportunity to "at long last set this nation free."[23] By disenfranchising African Americans, the southern hegemony had constricted the word *freedom*, forcing it to function impotently as "empty rhetoric and a ritual," rather than evocatively as "a dream, an aspiration, a hope," and "a prayer."[24] Democracy authentically applied to blacks would liberate whites as well. Ironically, it was through their jailhouse experiences that the Birmingham demonstrators (and by extension all civil rights volunteers nationally) could spotlight and enact the authentic meaning of freedom. In other words, their physical imprisonment actually reconfigured the semantic boundaries that bigots nationwide had placed on liberty. This understanding epitomized why direct demonstrations were not only necessary tactically but, more significantly, ideologically. Farmer stressed this idea:

> You are fighting, above all else, to make democracy and freedom mean something. I have never heard the word freedom mean as much as it did when you were singing your song, the song you wrote in jail . . . You have put new meaning by the time you spent

22. Ibid.
23. Ibid.
24. Ibid.

in jail, by the jail food you ate, by your experiences, and by the suffering all of you who were involved in the movement.[25]

Only through deliberation and demonstration could abstractions like "freedom" and "democracy"[26] transform into concrete realities for African Americans. Such a mindset would render jails (actual confining spaces) less intimidating and inhibiting. Because movement participants were fighting for a higher cause, a jail cell, as Martin Luther King Jr. declared on many occasions could be "transformed into a haven of freedom and human dignity."

As Farmer here explored the interdependence of interracial freedom, he targeted a theme that recurred in African American thought from Frederick Douglass to Martin Luther King Jr. When the Daughters of the American Revolution, for example, refused to allow Marian Anderson to sing at Constitutional Hall, they had in essence "forgotten" the American Revolution. However, Marian Anderson singing, "My Country 'Tis of Thee" on the steps of the Lincoln Memorial should have been a cause of patriotic celebration for whites and blacks. Like the civil rights freedom songs, Marian Anderson's singing reflected "her heart and her soul poured into one idea, the idea of freedom and liberty."[27] The nation could achieve the unity that the civil rights movement idealized when all her citizens began to view democracy as an organic and evolving experience rather than a fixed, codified, and exclusive concept.

Farmer closed the speech by citing Langston Hughes's poem "Let America Be America Again." Farmer could have selected fewer more fitting ways to stress how the united efforts of the civil rights movement could lead to authentic freedom for all and thus national unity. Best known for his poetry, Hughes was a premiere cultural critic of the twentieth century, writing plays, short stories, novels, essays, and two lengthy autobiographies. Hughes's literary manifesto, written in 1926, "The Negro Artist and the Racial Mountain," had set the tone for a rhetoric and poetics that blurred the arbitrary lines between art, politics, and racial identity. A relatively lengthy poem for Hughes, "Let American Be America Again," looks at freedom for all as an evolving, contested process rather than a realized fact. While emphasizing the plight of African Americans, the verses also sympathize with "the poor white," "the farmer, bondsman of the soil," and "the worker sold

25. Ibid.
26. Ibid.
27. Ibid.

to the machine."[28] Hughes also explored the unfulfilled dreams of European immigrants and African captives who had yet to realize their aspirations in the U.S.

Farmer's brief citations from Hughes's poem do not refer to race, labor, immigration or captive narratives. Instead, Farmer honed in on verses at the beginning, middle, and end of the poem that implicitly resonated with the above ideas and much more:

> Let America be America again . . .
> The free? Who said free? Not me. Surely not me . . .
> Yes I say it plain, America was never America to me . . .
> I swear . . . America will be.[29]

By ending with Hughes, Farmer employed an artistic way to circle back to his overarching theme of democratic unity. By the time of this speech, Hughes had been writing for four decades, so many in Farmer's audience would have read his poems. Others would have also heard of his extensive national and international travels. Hughes was a Harlem Renaissance artist who had been born in the Midwest but whose art belonged to the world. As he trekked across the globe, his blues and jazz-inflected prose and poetry echoed notes of freedom, justice, equality, and human decency for all. As Hughes had marched for the ideal of global unity through his artistic expression, civil rights workers could achieve actual national unity with their marching feet.

ROY WILKINS: RELIGIOUS PRAGMATIST AND HONORARY MASS MEETING PROPHET

"Roy Wilkins is a package all wrapped up in himself."[30]

—Fred Shuttlesworth

As I alluded to earlier in this chapter, Roy Wilkins might not appear upon first blush to be a candidate for inclusion among those I call *mass meeting prophets*. More than any of the other Big Six leaders representing the civil rights movement, Wilkins, as executive director of the NAACP, seemed

28. Hughes, "Let America."
29. Ibid.
30. Shuttlesworth, April 25th Mass meeting (Holmes transcript).

the closest to both representing mainstream values and reifying the status quo. The NAACP's preference for legal redress and political lobbying above direct demonstration, as well as Wilkins's arrogant and aloof posture, had soured several young activists on the NAACP, including many of those who had been trained by that organization. Nevertheless, Wilkins's speech on April 25th represents a moment when the veteran civil rights leader towed the line between organizational insider and prophetic outsider. Both of the relatively uninhibited communicative spaces represented by the Birmingham mass meetings and the fact that the NAACP had been outlawed in Alabama since 1956 afforded Wilkins the status of an honorary mass meeting prophet. I claim that in this speech, Wilkins borrowed the language of conversion to counter narratives promoting southern white supremacy and state sovereignty. He contended that the generation of African Americans at the time possessed a new insight into and appreciation for their own ethics, culture, and politics. As a result, he argued that blacks should mount a campaign with their words and deeds that could ideally convert white southerners to accept African Americans' sociopolitical expectations.

Moreover, the timing of the speech could not have been more serendipitous. April 25th was the day that Attorney General Robert Kennedy met with Governor George Wallace to try to dissuade him from keeping his pledge to stand at the entrance of the University of Alabama where two black students would try to enroll.[31] The political stakes were high for Project C, and the rhetorical stakes were high for the mass meeting speakers that night—including for Wilkins, the senior leader of the oldest civil rights organization.

The exordium of this speech began in a fairly traditional fashion. He acknowledged Shuttlesworth, King, and Abernathy, calling the last his "good friend." Wilkins then commended his NAACP colleague and the famous attorney, Constance Baker Motley. Wilkins's professional praise of Motley stood in direct contrast to the sexist comments that Shuttlesworth made about women in general as he praised Motley for her particular work in Birmingham. Shuttlesworth said he had formerly thought women could be only "cooks" and "mama." Now there were female "truck drivers," "barbers," and at least one lawyer.[32] Shuttlesworth's praise for Motley's work framed in sexist humor (the audience laughed at the remarks about women's traditional roles) suggests that sexism remained a relatively un-

---

31. Eskew, *But for Birmingham*, 255–56.
32. Shuttlesworth, April 25th, Mass Meeting (Holmes transcript).

questioned practice within the larger civil rights movement and during the Birmingham campaign.

Wilkins also set the tone for the conversion language that peppered the speech when he acknowledged the presence of the police detectives without explicitly referring to them as such:

> I'm glad to be here, and I'm glad you're here, including our guests in the corner. Because in our movement, and this is a great movement that extends everywhere; in our movement, nobody is barred. And in the Christian church, if I understand it correctly, there is room for every repentant sinner. There's a mourners' bench in every church. And those that finally feel the spirit, whether they're thirty or sixty or ninety can come and join.[33]

In this passage, Wilkins aligned himself to the civil rights movement but loosely associated himself with the Christian church. He fully owned up to how inclusive the movement can be by calling it "our"; the Christian church, alternatively, may or may not be something he totally comprehended or, more likely, could account for. However, since much of the civil rights movement was rooted in the rhetorical traditions of the church, some religious language could be applied in radically new and politically relevant ways. Police detectives could and should repent of their unjust treatment of blacks, but as far as Wilkins was likely concerned such a change on the detectives' part may not necessarily be accompanied by increased church attendance or adherence to any other sacred ritual.

Perhaps the shrewdest rhetorical move that Wilkins made in the introduction was the way he positioned himself. In terms of physical performance, he apologized for not being able to "jump around"[34] like Fred Shuttlesworth, who was younger. Expressing humility and one's unworthiness in comparison to the local pastor or preceding speaker has been a frequently performed ceremonial gesture, especially in black churches. However, by mentioning that he was a lot older than Shuttlesworth, Wilkins indirectly established himself as capable of wise counsel. More directly, Wilkins constructed an ethos for this particular occasion by referring to himself as a "visitor" to Alabama and a "guest"[35] of the Alabama Christian Movement for Human Rights and Southern Christian Leadership Conference at the mass meeting. He called himself a visitor, rather

33. Wilkins, Mass Meeting Speech (Holmes transcript).
34. Ibid.
35. Ibid.

than the Executive Director of the NAACP, likely because that organization had been outlawed in Alabama since 1956, which was one factor that had precipitated the founding of the Alabama Christian Movement for Human Rights. The fact that the NAACP continued to work to legalize itself in Alabama did not alter Wilkins's current status in this particular mass meeting. If anything, the continuous legal wrangling to reinstate the NAACP in Alabama caused Wilkins to wonder out loud whether white people, particularly the white jurists who were postponing their decision, were "no smarter than they say"[36] blacks were.

Wilkins's choice to situate himself as visitor laid a persuasive foundation for at least three reasons. First, he preempted the staple and stock charge of being an "outside agitator." Like his audience, Wilkins knew that this charge had routinely applied to anyone, regardless of race, region, or class, who dared to volunteer in the service of advancing civil rights. Many of the NAACP's legal actions over the years had begun with field investigations into southern towns and cities; Wilkins himself had conducted several of these investigations. Indeed, the sixty-one-year-old Wilkins was quite familiar with the charge. However, to position oneself as a visitor at the mass meetings reinforced the narrative of the South being a warm and welcoming place. Second, as a visitor, one held no official status. Wilkins's quasi-satirical intent aside, his refrain from acknowledging his leadership in the infamous NAACP could theoretically set his enemies at ease. The third effect of embracing visitor status was indirect and tacit. If Wilkins's status as executive director was temporarily erased, then ideally so were the rivalries that existed between him and other civil rights leaders, the most famous of whom, Martin Luther King Jr., was in the audience.

Still, visitor or guest status alone would not sufficiently establish Wilkins's credibility within the mass meeting. He had already referred to the people sitting in the corner of the auditorium (the police detectives) as "guests." The concept of southern hospitality extended to and was magnified in the church. A visitor was welcome but didn't wield the rhetorical authority of the pastor, deacons, or resident congregants. As I suggested in the chapter on Bevel, while anyone was allowed at the mass meeting, not everyone was allowed to speak with authority within this venue. Traditionally within black churches even those people who were allowed to testify about what the Lord had done for them did not embody and convey the same teaching clout as the one bringing the sermon for that day. Granted,

36. Ibid.

111

Wilkins was not a preacher. In fact, he could not lay claim to having attended seminary as James Farmer had. According to his autobiography and perhaps unknown to most of his audience that night, Wilkins was skeptical of organized religion, preferring practical, civically engaged, and ethically responsible expressions of faith rather than adherence to sectarian dogma. Like Farmer, he believed that churches could be mobilized as groups of individuals that could advance the cause of civil rights. Core ethical principles rather than church doctrine drove his sense of what he later called in the speech "Christian Humanity."[37] Wilkins further reinforced the idea that he was outside this particular fraternity of preachers when he stated that he was a Methodist, and that no Methodist could "shout or preach like a Baptist."[38] Obviously such a statement could not be quantified and Wilkins meant it to be humorous. Still, his observation echoed how, intentionally or not, the two denominations had rivaled each other for African American members for more than a century, and according to Wilson Fallin Jr., the vast majority of churchgoing blacks in Alabama were Baptist. More pointedly, Wilkins's declaration lowered the rhetorical expectations of his audience. He was neither a preacher nor a Baptist. And he should not be expected to perform with that level of aptitude.

So why should this mass meeting audience listen to this self-proclaimed "visitor" to Birmingham, a Methodist layperson speaking at a Baptist service? Wilkins positioned himself as a "guest of the Alabama Christian Movement for Human Rights and the Southern Christian Leadership Conference."[39] Most listening to Wilkins likely knew that Fred Shuttlesworth had founded the Alabama Christian Movement for Human Rights (ACMHR) in June 1956 in Birmingham after the NACCP was outlawed in the entire state. Martin Luther King Jr. had founded the Southern Christian Leadership Conference (SCLC) in 1957 in Atlanta with a group of ministers from several states. Taken together, the ACMHR and SCLC were more than cosponsors of the Birmingham campaign. Consisting primarily of pastors, the two organizations codified notions of the top-down, cleric leadership of the civil rights movement, a notion that by 1963 was already being questioned by groups like CORE and SNCC. Nevertheless, as a guest of the ACMHR and SCLC, Wilkins was more than speaking for

37. Ibid.
38. Ibid.
39. Ibid.

these organizations; he was also speaking for the preachers, principally Shuttlesworth and King, who would lead them.

As unassuming as Wilkins's exordium appeared in content (appeared because his tone of voice teetered on sarcasm and cynicism), the body of the speech was assertive and arguably surprisingly militant in sections. From the outset, he focused his remarks on white people collectively as African Americans' "greatest tribulation," contending that blacks needed to "lead them."[40] This statement might strike those that knew the interracial history of the NAACP as quite curious. A coalition of whites and blacks had founded the NAACP. As Wilkins rose through the organization's ranks from assistant secretary to editor of the *Crisis* and finally the position as executive director, he knew and remained on friendly terms with prominent whites such as Joel Spingarn, who had held the reins of top leadership. Though Wilkins never stated it, the idea of African Americans needing to "lead" white people can be seen as inverting the trope of the civilized European missionary saving African savages—on the surface from sin but also from their uncivilized cultural practices. Like Farmer, Wilkins inextricably tethered black socioeconomic liberation to white psychological and spiritual salvation, declaring that white people "cannot be free as long as they keep a foot on our neck."[41] However remote the hope, social salvation for the dominant race was real, necessary, and attainable.

The next claim Wilkins made might have stoked his audience's interest more than the first and also constituted one significant idea within the speech. For the most part, whites chose not to or could not understand the self-image and worldview contemporary black Americans possessed. In order to perpetuate ideal narratives about themselves and stereotypical narratives about African Americans, white racists had to refashion alternative, highly contrived plots about the nation and the world. Many of the white officials knew that the narratives they were spinning about white privilege and black pathology might have been untrue. However, according to Wilkins, with the frequent retelling many whites had come to deceive themselves. Often biblical prophets referred to ongoing rebellion against God as having its origin in self-deception. Likewise, during revivals, evangelists often tried to persuade would-be converts by linking the practice of sin to self-deception. Wilkins may or may not have had these ideas in mind. Be that as it may, his seemingly inconspicuous introduction

40. Ibid.
41. Ibid.

somewhat understandably unraveled into a bold renunciation of narratives that perpetuated white hegemonic cultural knowledge, regional economics, and institutional racism overall. Furthermore, while the tone of his voice was sardonic, the range, pitch, and volume hardly varied, and may have been in keeping with the detachment he may have wished to project as a former journalist. Although the body of the speech is loosely structured, as was to be expected, since many orators for the mass meeting delivered impromptu remarks, Wilkins, like a good journalist, wished to demonstrate a command of key facts. This is not to say that all of Wilkins's speech was off the cuff. When Fred Shuttlesworth introduced his senior in the civil rights struggle, he noted that Wilkins had but "one speech."[42] This of course was hyperbole, perhaps to illustrate Wilkins's unshakeable commitment to a core set of democratic values. Wilkins had amassed a stockpile of facts, figures, warrants, and arguments against segregation and for integration after years of lecturing, giving press conferences, legal and political lobbying, and writing.

Wilkins began his revivalist-peppered critique of white narrative privilege by alluding to Alabama governor George Wallace's meeting with Attorney General Robert Kennedy. In keeping with the Kennedy administration's diplomatic, practically hands-off approach to addressing southern institutional racism, the attorney general had come down to Montgomery to see Wallace concerning his inflexible stance in favor of segregated schools. Specifically the governor had announced plans to stand at the entrance of the University of Alabama on the day two black students were scheduled to enroll. The younger Kennedy had been dispatched to Montgomery to dissuade Wallace from this planned course of action. According to their respective press conferences, Kennedy and Wallace had a civil, cordial meeting. Still, Wallace, at least before the cameras, declared that he remained as committed to perpetual segregation as he had declared in his gubernatorial inaugural address a couple months earlier, in January 1963. During that address, Wallace uttered the chilling line that would canonize him within the American imagination: "In the name of the greatest people that have ever trod this earth, I draw the line in the dust and toss the gauntlet before the feet of tyranny, and I say segregation now, segregation tomorrow, segregation forever." Wallace's stubborn segregationist streak moved Wilkins to once again tether, though not chain, his remarks to the language of conversion:

42. Shuttlesworth, April 25th Mass Meeting (Holmes transcript).

114

I hope you'll keep praying for him . . . because he just might be touched. You can't tell. You never can tell. You have demonstrated that if he is not touched, you're going to go ahead doing what you're doing anyway. So you might as well pray for him to be touched. After all, he is the governor of all the people in the state of Alabama.[43]

Notice that while Wilkins does not include himself among those who will pray for Wallace, the governor does need prayer. Wallace needed to change, not where he attended or that he attended church. Wilkins's audience knew that Wallace needed to *repent* for how he mistreated black Alabamans.

Part of Wallace's intransigence about segregation was rooted in a plot line about white southerners paying taxes to a federal government that neither respected their customs nor fairly supported their infrastructure. Wilkins viewed Wallace as regurgitating a common theme articulated by southern politicians, one that portrayed white people from this region as victims of both the federal government and the encroaching civil rights movement. This was why, according to Wilkins, Mississippi and Alabama appeared to favor the filibuster when it advanced the southern way of life but demeaned the process as antidemocratic when it didn't. This was also why both of these states suggested that they were paying more to the federal government in taxes than they were actually getting in subsidies, even though said states obviously needed the money.

For Wilkins, the inverted story line about taxes represented one way white southerners promoted state sovereignty, regionalism, and racism. Wilkins offered detailed mathematical calculations to repudiate these claims. Mississippi and Alabama respectively paid twenty-five cents and thirty seven cents in taxes for every dollar they received from the federal government. In contrast, New Jersey and New York respectively paid $2.33 and $1.75 in taxes for every dollar these states received in federal support. Wilkins landed a rhetorical jab against southern regional pride when he concluded that "New Jersey was supporting Mississippi," and "New York was supporting Alabama."[44] The latter observation was particularly arresting for at least three reasons: First, Wilkins was from New York, and for that reason could likely be assigned the stock label of outside agitator. Second, Wilkins was the head of the NAACP, which had been outlawed in Alabama

43. Wilkins, Mass Meeting Speech (Holmes transcript).
44. Ibid.

and efforts were being made to outlaw the organization in other places in the South. Third, Wilkins as black man stood in and up for the black southerners who were accused of not paying taxes. Yet despite all these levels of marginalization, Wilkins, as a "visitor" to the South and a "guest" of the SCLC and the ACMHR, commanded facts that authorized his ethos and countered the southern narrative about federal neglect, regional interference, and African American financial irresponsibility. One abiding stereotype about African Americans has been that they were prone to laziness. Assuming that black southerners as a group did not have the money to pay taxes represented one version of this myth.

Wilkins's detailed number crunching about tax burdens may appear tedious and dry upon first glance. However, such fine details provided a rational and persuasive repudiation to the myth of southern white benevolence towards blacks residing in that region. Wilkins argued that

> Now they keep telling me that you don't pay taxes and you ought to be happy and satisfied because the white people pay taxes. And if they give you a tumbled-down school you ought to say "Thank you," because that's a gift of the white people. And you don't help to buy your school because you don't pay taxes. Now that's a big fat lie. You know every time you buy a package of cigarettes you pay taxes, and every time you buy anything in the store you pay taxes, and every time you pay rent you pay taxes. You know you pay taxes from the day you're born until the day you die. Whether you're black, white, gray or green, or who you are, that's one thing you can't dodge, the taxes.[45]

Here, Wilkins offered a critique that is more epistemic than economic. The critique was largely economic. The benefit and bane of capitalism was and is an economy controlled by the rich but driven by the middle class and poor. No matter how financially destitute, most will pay some form of taxes and, hence, contribute to the economy. However, at its core, Wilkins's critique is about how racist ideology was and is constructed, a worldview that elevates hegemonic rule over existential reality. What black southerners knew to be true had to be subsumed under recycled propaganda about them being the quintessential beggars who should never be choosers. Notwithstanding the tax breaks that had mostly favored wealthy white people, Wilkins argued that taxes, in principle and general practice, transcended race and class, no matter how interconnected those categories

45. Ibid.

might have operated within the South. Because these southern status quo narratives were about maintaining a normative myth rather than advancing democratic truth, they often contained glaring contradictions. Wilkins illustrated how ironically Mississippi poked fissures in their narrative about black residents not paying their share of taxes.

To counter the reality of black disenfranchisement, the infamous White Citizens Council had produced a film asserting that African Americans owned three hundred thousand homes. Since every homeowner paid taxes, how could one claim, as Wilkins pointed out, that blacks did not contribute? Further, the hypocritical irony of the White Citizens Council producing such a film would likely not have been lost on Wilkins's audience. The White Citizens Council, which was founded in 1954 in Mississippi, had fanned out across the South like an ideological tornado. The White Citizens Council was a highbrow, white-collar brand of the Ku Klux Klan, and their weapons of choice were economic coercion and political intimidation. Black or white residents who challenged the southern racial caste system would feel this group's economic pinch or, in some case, strangle.

Wilkins mounted historical and current international lines of attack against another plot line that the white southerners' status quo used to promote black pathology: Most juvenile delinquents are African Americans. This myth was so pervasive, Wilkins noted, that even many white liberals across the nation perpetuated it:

> Yet if you listen to the white people in Alabama, or Mississippi, or New York, or New Jersey, they look at you and they say, "Yes, you know I believe in equality but why don't you people do something about juvenile delinquency?"[46]

Bigoted views about black criminality crisscrossed regions and ideological bents. Presumably the white northerners and southerners that Wilkins addressed in this passage were somewhat open-minded, as they desired to help African Americans. But Wilkins had already countered their racist assumptions on two fronts. First, he discussed a home for juvenile delinquents that was open for business in Philadelphia in 1824. Since most blacks were enslaved, then the majority race of the residents of this home was likely white—though Wilkins didn't explicitly say so. Instead, he engaged in indirect insult, a form of signifying, when he observed that this

---

46. Ibid.

home "might have been for some other color."[47] Second, while conceding that the scope of the juvenile delinquency problem affected people of color during his time, Wilkins offered a global analysis of youth crime. Youth delinquency extended to the borders of Japan, Sweden, France, England, and Moscow; Wilkins cited news reports to that effect. The rhetorical impact of these news reports extended beyond the stories themselves. Perhaps Wilkins employed the reports to stress how silly it was to restrict any form of human frailty to one group, particularly since within the context of the civil rights movement, juvenile delinquency had impacted America's enemies (Russia) and friends (Japan).

Wilkins then briefly tackled the so-called problem of pervasive illegitimacy among African Americans. While the black community should face actual instances of this challenge head-on, Wilkins observed that "there are a lot of people who have children out of wedlock who are not colored."[48] More to the point, whites who were so inclined likely had the resources to cover up out-of-wedlock pregnancies. Unwanted pregnancies in the black community, just like other presumed social ills, were not solely about ethics; they were also about economics.

The speech then winnowed out from juvenile crime and perceived familial dysfunction to the crime rate, particularly in predominantly black regions like Washington DC. Crime was out of control in the nation's capital, so the narrative went, and of course black residents, as 53 percent of the population, were to blame. Teasing out the historical argument he used about young black criminals, Wilkins played a rhetorical game of bait and switch. He presented a few equally disturbing yet seemingly contemporary descriptions of crime, and then revealed the dates these events actually took place, followed by how few African Americans were a part of the population during those respective historical moments. Wilkins summarized:

> Now in 1858, the Negroes were one-fifth of the population, so who was creating the crime rate then? And on 1920, the Negroes were less than one-fourth of the population, so who was committing the crimes then? And in 1940, they were less than one-third of the population when they were talking about making the streets safe for women. So somebody must have been committing the crime. Maybe it was a zombie . . . You know, might have been a ghost.[49]

47. Ibid.
48. Ibid.
49. Ibid.

Using his trademark snarky sarcasm and signifying, as he had earlier, as well as a few well-placed rhetorical questions, Wilkins demonstrated that the high crime rate in the nation's capital had more to do with the complex interplay among history, region, and sociology than contrived, reductive, and racist assumptions regarding genetic interconnections between race (blackness) and immorality. Intended or not, Wilkins's mention of "ghosts" inverted the racist narrative about black people as spooks. That many whites, some from the North but mostly from the South, blindly believed that African Americans packed the crime statistics meant that they desperately needed to be converted to a new point of view, a point of view to which Wilkins was all too ready to persuade them.

Wilkins adopted the temporary journey back to Washington DC's past to return to a major theme that times have changed. Part of the tenacity about clinging to a fanciful antiblack narrative evolved not only from flawed, deliberated yet distorted knowledge, but it also stemmed from the inability to reconcile this fractured understanding with the new Negro living in a new world. Perhaps more than any other region in the nation, the South was for the most part frozen in the 1950s, with that decade's emphasis on status quo conservatism, zealous religiosity, and cult-like patriotism. To accept that blacks had changed, white southerners would have to reject more than the nostalgic sentiments associated with the past; they would have to reject a white supremacist, regional, nationalist worldview. The new Negro became an embodied metonymy of a changing world, nation, South and, ultimately, community, and family.

Wilkins then returned to an idea recycled by twentieth-century human rights leaders from Gandhi to MLK: in the end, change cannot be legislated. A person "is free from the inside, not from the outside."[50] Without mentioning him, Wilkins here echoed and inverted Frederick Douglass's notion that you could be a slave in form without being a slave in fact. Southern whites had been so manacled to and by segregation that some black southerners might, even in that new age, remain psychologically tethered to this system as well. This was why Wilkins wanted his audience to keep in mind the larger issues that civil right gains represented:

> You know it isn't a question really of whether you sit in at a certain lunch counter or not, whether you have actually won that or not today. That'll come. The real question and the real job was getting into your hearts that you belonged at that lunch counter, that you

50. Ibid.

had a right to be there. And that nobody had the right to tell you
to ride on the tail end of the bus.[51]

For someone such as Wilkins, known as and criticized for being a
stickler for legal redress when it came to advancing civil rights, the above
passage represents an astonishing concession. African Americans believing
the facts that they truly belonged to this nation based on natural rights,
Scripture, or the Constitution, were ultimately more significant than exercising their rights. To cite the prophet Jeremiah, Wilkins seemed to be
suggesting that law had to be "written on the hearts"[52] of not just white
racists but black freedom seekers as well. In short, the emergence of the
new Negro meant the ushering in of a new covenant. And while Wilkins
does not explicitly refer to the prophet, this analysis, indeed the speech as a
whole, still falls within the jeremiad tradition.

African Americans fully embracing their collective sense of worth as
citizens, like the legal and political landmarks that favored their cause, had
been a long, arduous process, a journey that Wilkins believed people of
color had nearly completed:

> We were free from the outside one hundred years ago. The Eman-
> cipation Proclamation made us free from the outside. We had the
> status of citizens, but we were not citizens because we didn't be-
> lieve in ourselves. Well today we do. Today, under the inspiration
> of great leadership, some of which you hear about, some of which
> you don't, leadership in our churches, leadership in our organiza-
> tions, leadership stretching all the way from Wilmington, North
> Carolina, to El Paso, Texas, and from Miami, Florida, up to Seattle,
> Washington.[53]

Of course Wilkins's first observation is not historically accurate. The
Emancipation Proclamation was a controversial wartime measure that
President Lincoln signed that freed enslaved persons only in states that
rebelled against the Union. It would take the Thirteenth, Fourteenth, and
Fifteenth Amendments, the latter two ratified after Lincoln's death, to be-
stow a legal status on people of color that would remain tenuous at best.
Still, Wilkins's overall point was a poignant one. Since slavery, blacks had
arrived at a higher state of sociopolitical consciousness, and leaders from
various regions and out of varying organizational traditions had facilitated

51. Ibid.
52. Jer 31:31–34.
53. Wilkins, Mass Meeting Speech (Holmes transcript).

this journey. What his audience could easily deduce after this last statement was that leadership within the civil rights movement was restricted neither to the church in the South nor to the NAACP in the North. For a man like Roy Wilkins, who likely believed that every other civil rights organization was beholden to the NAACP, this is an arresting admission.

Similar to Farmer, Wilkins emphasized that at this critical moment the Birmingham campaign represented the heart and hub of the rest of the movement. Ironically, the unity that transcended geography (and all the civil rights organizations) grew out of a particular region—Birmingham. This was why NAACP chapters from Des Moines to Greensboro to the Bronx were talking about Birmingham. One could liken Wilkins's gesture here to the spread of prophetic rhetoric within the Old Testament and evangelistic rhetoric in the New Testament, particularly in the book of Acts. According to Calvin Woods, one of Fred Shuttlesworth's lieutenants, the Birmingham campaign was comparable to the start and spread of the early church in the book of Acts.[54]

The gospel of democracy that mass meeting rhetors Woods, Bevel, Shuttlesworth, Abernathy, and King shared in Birmingham would fan out into the rest of the nation. Like the message that so consumed Jeremiah the prophet, and like the Spirit that lit on the tongues of Jesus's twelve disciples, a fervent and deliberative energy characterized the Birmingham campaign, one that could be confined to neither one city, individual, or institution. Whether or not Wilkins was fully invested in these doctrines, they and the rest of the speech nonetheless solidified his position as an honorary mass meeting prophet. Perhaps, more precisely, how could he or any true believer in and devotee to civil rights be considered an outsider to any part of that struggle?

> You know, there aren't any state lines. There aren't organizational lines. I didn't come down here to see about you, because you were with me up there . . . This is the magic feeling of freedom that runs from heart to heart and city to city and state to state. There are no boundaries—no color boundaries and no geographical boundaries. And when we get through with our job, our country's going to be a better country.[55]

Wilkins then attempted to reconcile the tensions he set up at the beginning of the speech. When the aspirations of the civil rights movement

54. Woods interview with this author (Holmes transcript).
55. Wilkins, Mass Meeting Speech (Holmes transcript).

are fully realized, white people would no longer be African Americans' "greatest tribulation," for ideally all would look beyond the "boundaries of color."[56] Given Wilkins's investment in legal discourse and the fight for comprehensive civil rights legislation that would ensue later that year, he may be referring to the ideology of color blindness—but not necessarily. Racial boundaries—like the geographical boundaries that he also called his listeners to rise above—will always exist and will entail certain levels of existential and communal investment. Nevertheless, for the sake of something higher (be that something divine, democratic or pragmatic), one can navigate the shifting, rough, and murky terrains of race and geographical space.

Like many other African Americans, Wilkins related on a personal level to the conflation of ethnic and geographical identifications within the civil rights movement. In his autobiography, *Standing Fast,* he recalled the long -term influences that growing up in St. Paul, Minnesota, had on his worldview:

> In time, life in the warm little house on Galtier Street undid the damage that a forbidding home and a dour father had worked on me in St. Louis. My father had made the journey halfway up the Mississippi before his spirit failed him. I could come up nearly as far up the Mississippi I could travel. The river still connected me to Holly Springs, but throughout my childhood, the South and its way with race were safely behind me. St. Paul was a sturdy melting pot full of Swedes and Germans, French, Irish, and Jews . . . The city had drawn Uncle Sam up from the Mississippi, and unlike my mother and father, he and Aunt Elizabeth had put down strong roots and prospered.[57]

As Wilkins matured, he still preferred living in the North and maintained a fundamental faith in the melting pot, but over the years his travels nationally and internationally left him with little doubt that racism manifested itself differently yet decisively across regions, seesawing between de jure and de facto formulations. However, many blacks still maintained a spiritual connection to the South, whether or not they were born there, regardless of whether or not they personally experienced slavery or segregation. Within the collective African American consciousness, they had, to cite Langston Hughes, "known rivers," and one of those rivers was the

56. Ibid.
57. Wilkins, *Standing Fast,* 22.

Mississippi. The Mississippi came to signify and epitomize everything that could be paradoxically brutal and beautiful about the South particularly and the U.S. generally.

In the tradition of the prophets of Israel and Judah, and in keeping with what Cornel West calls "prophetic religion," Wilkins's speech returned to the theme of speaking truth to political power. He reintroduced the discussion on Robert Kennedy; however, this time Wilkins analyzed the ethics and pragmatics of the attorney general's job. Given that the younger Kennedy's job description ranged from fighting organized crime to making sure corporations played fair, it was a shame that he had to come down to Alabama to negotiate rights for African Americans that the founding documents already guaranteed them. The tendency of southern politicians to ignore the Constitution and the Declaration of Independence when it came to black citizens had become an international embarrassment, one Wilkins could personally attest to when he was visiting Europe during the James Meredith crisis. Italian, French, Swiss, and German people had approached Wilkins in a state of horrified incredulity as they wondered how Governor Ross Barnett could justify keeping Meredith out of the University of Mississippi. Because of the racial unrest in the South, waves of distrust about America's democratic integrity began to spread across Europe, waves that had rippled to east Africa and west Africa, southeast Asia, and ultimately in the corridors of the United Nations. It had been approximately fifteen years since Harry Truman, as the first president to address the NAACP convention, had discussed the international problems that domestic racism might cause. Still the segregationist stances taken by Mississippi governor Ross Barnett and Alabama governor George Wallace were still being perpetuated based on a distorted view of state sovereignty that southern politicians clung to since they stormed out of the 1948 Democratic convention to form the Dixiecrats.

Notwithstanding all of the resistance that southern politicians mounted against black southerners exercising their constitutional rights, Wilkins did not want the attorney general to give his people special treatment. Instead, Wilkins called Kennedy to stand as an impartial arbiter, a legal referee to make sure that southern politicians adhered to federal law, and that no racist constituent "throws a brick or one of those rabbit punches"[58] while African Americans were peacefully demonstrating.

58. Wilkins, Mass Meeting speech (Holmes transcript).

Wilkins was convinced that Bobby Kennedy would do just that. Despite the Kennedy administration's gradualist approach to civil rights—not to mention Bobby Kennedy's own reticence about openly criticizing Governor Wallace—Wilkins was confident that the attorney general would do right by black citizens. In fact, in one of his few explicit references to religion, Wilkins addressed Bobby's personal faith. According to Wilkins, the younger Kennedy had gained a reputation for being the most earnest Roman Catholic among his family members. The rash racism against civil rights workers that had recently marred Mississippi and Alabama contradicted "his conception of religion and religious justice."[59] Wilkins argued that Kennedy's faith had instilled within him an understated fortitude and toughness that would eventually lead him to take a stand on civil rights. With this observation about Kennedy, Wilkins once again highlighted the potential benefit that religion can have on politics when used progressively, critically, and justly.

Wilkins's speech closes on the note that African Americans were bright, bold, and determined enough to do their part, if the government did theirs. Young African Americans who had enrolled in previously all-white southern schools had already excelled. Momentum and the "power"[60] of the Birmingham campaign, its leaders, and even the NAACP (outside of Alabama) were on the right side of an historical tilt and international trend towards social justice, ethnic inclusion, and political empowerment. This is perhaps why Wilkins was inspired to return to the conversion, revivalist language with which he began. He spoke of the "old-time religion,"[61] remarking:

> This is the fire that runs from heart to heart. This is what makes you feel good when you go home. Makes you feel good when you get up in the morning. Makes you able to take on anything the day brings forth.[62]

For Wilkins, the "old-time religion" of blacks was no different than the new thinking embodied by African Americans who opposed southern, status quo racism. Wilkins's take on the old-time religion was relational

---

59. Ibid.
60. Ibid.
61. Ibid.
62. Ibid.

rather than doctrinal, active rather than passive, and assertive rather than accepting.

This chapter has argued that James Farmer and Roy Wilkins functioned as secular prophets during their respective Birmingham mass meeting speeches. For Farmer, this involved deploying a rhetoric that was rooted in religion yet regulated by broader, more inclusive notions of human spirituality. For Wilkins, exercising a secular prophetic stance was only loosely tethered to institutional religion, even though his comments were peppered with the language of conversion. Instead, American and global citizens were obligated to excavate those core prophetic values that promoted freedom, justice, and fair play. Or as the minor prophet Micah surmised, "What does the Lord require? To do justly, love mercy and walk humbly . . ."

6

Between Prophecy and the Presidency

King, Obama, and the Contested Legacies
of the Civil Rights Movement

"The true test of the American ideal is whether we are able to recognize our
failings and then rise together to meet the challenges of our time.
Whether we allow ourselves to be shaped by events and history,
or whether we act to shape them."[1]

—Barack Obama

"And the politicians don't know anything except to say the same old words."[2]

—Roy Wilkins, Executive Director, NAACP

"Why didn't you wait, and give the new government time to act? All I have to say
is that we've been waiting long enough."[3]

—Martin Luther King Jr.

1. Obama, "Knox College," 144.
2. April 25th, 1963 Mass Meeting (Holmes transcript).
3. April 22nd, 1963 Mass Meeting (Holmes transcript).

"We have heard from the prophet tonight. (*Amen*) And whenever we hear from the prophet (*Uh huh*), and he speaks as he has spoken tonight (*Amen, Yes*), I feel that nobody else ought to attempt to speak."[4]

—Ralph Abernathy

Throughout this book, I have wrestled with, though in no way claimed to resolve, the age-old tension between religion and politics. Arguably, the founding fathers, Thomas Jefferson's vacillation between the natural rights and cultural inferiority of the African notwithstanding, could not have wildly imagined a black president. Nor could the founders likely have foreseen the spectacle we as a nation have made of religion in the name of politics. Or is it the other way around?

In this chapter I claim that divergent reactions to Obama's presidency collide with mythical memories of King and, as a result, have unearthed racial tensions and clouded the prophetic legacies of the civil rights movement. In other words, the Obama presidency, as well as his association with King and with past presidents, may serve as a case study for why American society may not be as postracial as many assume. And as the mass meeting oratory of 1963 Birmingham critiqued and thereby expanded the standard narrative of mid twentieth-century progressive democracy, even a preliminary analysis of selections from King's and Obama's rhetoric may force us to challenge the viability of twenty-first-century colorblind and religiously inclusive narratives. Therefore, this chapter begins by examining contemporary views of King's legacy and how they have shaped current understandings of Obama as the first black president. Next, I will analyze King's "I Have a Dream" speech and Senator Obama's March 2007 speech commemorating the forty-second anniversary of the Selma campaign. These speeches are pivotal for at least three reasons. First, each speech is associated with landmark legislation, the Civil Rights Act of 1964 and the Voting Rights Act of 1965, which have respectively canonized the civil rights movement as a once-for-all success. Second, these speeches were given on the brink of and arguably contribute to King's and Obama's ascendencies to national status: King as a national prophet and Obama as national politician. Third, the speeches illustrate how their respective roles as prophet and politician and the legacy of the civil rights movement get muddled.

4. May 3rd, 1963, Mass Meeting (Holmes transcript).

The chapter will then consider a few of President Obama's race speeches that, for the most part, appear to straddle the fence between political and prophetic rhetoric, but actually barely reach the level of "transformationist" rhetoric. In this context, "transformationist" or transformative *rhetoric* would ideally originate from and promote the "egalitarian politics of SNCC"[5] for contemporary times. I close the chapter with an examination of President Obama's speech commemorating the fiftieth anniversary of the Selma campaign.

THE KING LEGACY, MEMORABLE PRESIDENTS, AND THE RISE OF OBAMA

A *Saturday Night Live* skit depicts Martin Luther King Jr. visiting President Obama in a dream the evening following the second inauguration. President Obama's astonishment at meeting the civil rights icon quickly turns to a barrage of questions about how King would evaluate the country and Obama. In keeping with the show's trademark irreverent humor, King responds with digressive, trivial, and bawdy comments about Beyoncé's beauty; he excuses her lip-synching during the second inaugural; and he notes how unflattering he found the first lady's new hairstyle. Sensing Obama's consternation with his refusal to engage in substantive dialogue, King jokes, "Today is my day off—Martin Luther King Day." Mildly irritated with his inability to get straight answers, Obama hears a hastily departing King nebulously commend him, then remark, "I got to go visit Cornel West and tell him to take it down about thirty notches." Like a range of popular-culture depictions of the civil rights movement, from the spate of 1990s feature films to the biting satire of the serial cartoon *Boondocks*, true-life efforts to live up to King's legacy, including the national holiday, are enmeshed in what Kirt Wilson calls "the promises and perils of sentimental memory."[6] It is more convenient to speculate about what King might have done, as long as this does not shatter our fragile view of him, democracy, and our role in transforming it.

In 1964, during a BBC interview, King was asked when America might elect a black president. Unlike Robert Kennedy, who had predicted forty years from that time, King envisaged twenty-five years. While some people, then and now might deem King's idealism as naively unrealistic,

5. Marable, *Black Leadership*, xv.
6. Wilson, "Rhetoric and Race," 20.

others know better. King evolved significantly as a thinker and leader from 1955 to 1968, so one could hardly restrict his idealism to the pie-in-the-sky variety. King was not so heavenly minded that he was no earthly good. His belief that America could elect a black president by 1989 reflected his profound understanding of the nation's unfinished narrative. This country and its capital were built upon the backs of enslaved blacks. Thus, the nation would remain restless until the remainder of the story was told—from building the White House to occupying it. Provocative to be sure, King's prediction was more about what was inevitable rather than how immediate. Part of his genius lay in King's ability to see—indeed, prophesy about—the narrative that others could not. In a similar vein, the ranges of reactions to Obama's presidency illuminated layers of unfinished, unresolved, and perhaps irresolvable national narratives.

Obama's association with King became both a blessing and a burden, for him and the nation. True, Obama alluded to King in his rhetoric numerous times—the most symbolic comparison perhaps being Obama's swearing on King's Bible during the second inaugural. Indeed, Lincoln's and King's Bibles paired at the second inauguration functioned as tropes that appeared to legitimize Obama's presidency and suggested that the narrative of racial harmony might have been nearing resolution. As Lincoln's presidency and King's sociopolitical prophecy were linked to liberation in songs like "Battle Hymn of the Republic," Obama's second term would have ideally taken the high road, where all Americans aspired to see "the glory of the Lord." Even as it harkened back to Lincoln and King by making use of their Bibles, Obama's symbolic gesture at the second inauguration hardly signified that Americans follow the tenets of one or any religion. Rather, the gesture sought to inspire all Americans to experience a sense of belonging, self-actualization, and perhaps vocational purpose that some have found in religion practiced freely, progressively, or prophetically.

To an extent, therefore, comparing Obama to King signified a broader, nationwide impulse to complete an unresolved narrative about the frayed yet intertwining roles of race, religion, politics, and rhetoric. One problem equating the former president to MLK is that no one could live up to King's iconic status, including King himself. The scores of scholarly and popular histories on King spotlight the richness of his thought, while many of the online and other media (right- and left-leaning) interpretations of these histories on the whole represent an obsession to make King someone that he was not and would not have wanted to be. Among the many questions

I have, therefore, is, how might cultural narratives comparing King with Obama, or those contesting King's legacy inform or be informed by what George Shulman calls "prophetic idiom"?

Obama's road to and occupation of the White House evokes thoughts of Emerson's representative man, a morality play, and an R&B song. As a result, perhaps more than any other individual, much of the praise and blame directed towards former president Obama entailed contrasting him to other historical greats. Ironically, he was disliked for being too conservative and too liberal at the same time—the political equivalent to being a Muslim and radical Christian, I suppose. And during the speech announcing his candidacy, then-senator Obama began linking himself to Lincoln. Despite his well-earned reputation as one of the most charismatic leaders in history, Obama was despised for not governing like Roosevelt or Reagan. To some extent, comparing Obama to other presidents was not only fair but appropriate. Obama shares Reagan's enthusiasm for a type of American exceptionalism but for different reasons. As Roosevelt did, Obama believes government should play a role in helping the economically marginalized. Indeed, Obama's main quibble with the iconic Reagan focused on the limits of individualism. Both celebrated individual initiative. But for Obama individualism should not isolate or insulate us from the economic struggles of our fellow citizens.

Some progressives expected Obama to be the new FDR when it came to domestic issues. Nationally syndicated progressive radio talk show host Thom Hartman routinely criticized Obama for not being as fearless as FDR. Several times during Obama's first term, Hartman suggested that the president confront the wealthy and the politicians that represent them the way FDR did in speech at Madison Square Garden on October 31st, 1936. During that address, FDR said: "I should like to have it said of my first Administration that in it the forces of selfishness and of lust for power met their match. I should like to have it said of my second Administration that in it these forces met their master."[7] Hartman's criticism illustrates that even the most progressive thinkers concerning class can remain clueless when it comes to race. If Obama had not been temperamentally inclined to avoid such grandstanding, perhaps he would have been strategically inclined as the first black president.

Obama's relentless zeal for bipartisan consensus during his first term did evoke memories of Lincoln. Obviously race has colored most narratives

7. Roosevelt, speech, para 22.

comparing Obama to any president, especially Lincoln. The great, albeit reluctant, emancipator of enslaved blacks could never have dreamt of a black man occupying his office, given Lincoln's own racist sensibilities. Obama's rise to the White House was the stuff that epics are made of—a truth much stranger than fiction. Obama's first election elevated the optimism King articulated in the "I Have a Dream" speech beyond the confines of this nation's wildest dreams.

In short, many wanted to remake Obama and his polices into their respective notions of the ideal president. Some in the now defunct Occupy movement desired to remake him into a radical Roosevelt, who wasn't radical when it came to black interests. A. Phillip Randolph proved that. A segment of the Tea Party longed to remake Obama into a sainted Ronald Reagan, who obviously wasn't a saint, but who also was not the champion of fiscal conservatism he has been reinvented as. Reagan raised the debt ceiling numerous times. And the Occupy and Tea Party movements wanted Obama to be the Martin Luther King Jr. that they've re-created in their respective ways. For the Left that was the revolutionary King, consumed with antiwar and anticapitalist ideas, and incidentally Christian; for the Right that was a sanitized King, so obsessed with integration and a colorblind society that his politics were actually conservative. Both sides ignored how nuanced King's thought was; both sides tended to miss or minimize the complexity of race and the subtle and—for many Tea Party members—not so subtle manifestations of racism. Postracial does not equal postracism.

Some deemed the almost fanatical resistance to Obama as ironclad proof that the country is not truly colorblind, and in fact remains virulently racist. Mainstream society, so the argument might continue, was paying only lip service to this grand democratic notion of racial inclusion. Or that racial inclusion was fine as far as it goes, if it doesn't go too far, like to the White House, for instance. The psychology behind the racial politics of this country suggests that some fears (from urban riots to the extreme of racial Armageddon) are deep-seated, which is why driving and dying while black remain ubiquitous current events.

In Obama's case, denial surrounding the not so subtle racial antipathy against him was coupled with an even less subtle religious bigotry. To be other by virtue of being black is bad enough. To be black and presumed Muslim shoved Obama's otherness from bad to worse. During both terms of his presidency, Obama met unprecedented resistance to his policies, several of which originated in conservative thinking. While I would hardly discount legitimate reasons for having contested Obama's policies, the depth and breadth of these criticisms may speak to a larger cultural phenomenon, one in which the ideals of democracy clashed with the realities of a rapidly changing world.

No matter how moderate to conservative his policies, no matter how colorblind we claim to be in a postracial America, a goodly number of Americans feared the change represented by Obama's ascendancy: a seismic cultural shift to the *other*. Long before Obama became president, there was a noticeable ethnic demographic shift in America, one in which Anglo-Americans were rapidly becoming the minority. This fact coupled with the circulation of anti–affirmative action rhetoric since the 1980s practically ensured that Obama's presidency would be challenged from the outset.

This is not to say that none of Obama's polices has contributed to his persona of otherness. His executive order on immigration also had right-leaning citizens screaming that he had gone too far and left-leaning constituents saying that he had not gone far enough. The Right seemed to ignore that Obama had deported more people than many of the presidents before him. The Left seemed to have turned their sights from the Republican-led Congress that had proposed nothing substantive on immigration and took aim at Obama, who had done something.

Somewhere between race, religion, and politics lay the spaces where we wrestled with whether and to what extent Obama's rhetoric could ever be considered prophetic. Given the entrenched history of the American jeremiad I sketched in chapter 1, questions regarding the relationship between politics and prophetic religion are sometimes obvious, but, at other times, these queries bubble beneath the surface. Contrary to Obama's initial message of hope and change and the expectations many on the Left held that he would be a radically progressive president, I think there was little if any evidence that Obama shared this leftward vision of his potential presidency. From material as sketchy as the PBS biography to his more detailed two-volume autobiography, the attentive reader would have seen Obama as a consensus-seeking pragmatist rather than a changing-making progressive. And the seesawing left to right leaning of some of his policies added credence to this observation. He received the Nobel Peace Prize for enriching America's international relationships; yet he expanded the military drone program, killing untold numbers of civilians.

Still there are moments for nearly every president to potentially speak in a prophetic tone, though not necessarily in an authentic prophetic voice.

I draw a distinction between prophetic tone and actual use of prophetic discourse. I remain decidedly skeptical that most politicians or any president can speak in pure prophetic terms given their binding institutional allegiances. However, politicians of all stripes and stations will confront prophetic moments. For Lincoln, those moments were the Civil War and slavery. For Roosevelt, the times were Pearl Harbor, World War II, and the Japanese interment camps. For Kennedy and Johnson, the prophetic context was the escalating and explosive civil rights movement. And for Obama it was a set of conflicting contexts—postracialism, Christian nationalism, militarism, and wealth protectionism on one hand, and paranoid fears of black criminality, anti-Islamic sentiments, and a growing impoverished and politically disenfranchised population on the other.

Despite his cautious pragmatism, Obama has spoken on the edges of the prophetic—if by *prophetic* one partly means critique of status quo or institutional exclusion. His now infamous "Race Speech" given during the Jeremiah Wright controversy—that traced the historical rationale for black frustration with entrenched racism—was one well-deliberated example. According to rhetorical scholar and cultural critic Vorris Nunley, with the "Race Speech," Obama provided larger American society with a peek into African American hush harbors, spaces like black barbershops, beauty shops, churches, and lodges (to name a few), where African Americans could speak the unvarnished truth about their culture and against racism.[8] Frederick C. Harris rightly notes that while "those unfamiliar with the prophetic tradition in Afro-Christianity" found Wright's condemnation of American military imperialism "shocking," his remarks fell within a long-line of African American prophets like David Walker and Frederick Douglass that challenged American "hypocrisy" about freedom. Writing in the style of the Declaration of Independence, Walker proclaimed in 1829 that American would face the wrath of God for its inhuman treatment of the nation's people of color. During a speech commemorating July 4th, Douglass excoriated America's duplicitous double-speak, which proclaimed liberty on the one hand but promoted slavery on the other.[9]

Obama's relationship to Trinity United Church of Christ and its controversial pastor suggested how the former president's religious commitments were both personal and communal. Given his rational, secular inclination, Obama resisted converting to the Christian faith. Wright's

8. Nunley, *Keepin' It Hushed*, 170–77.
9. Harris, *Price of the Ticket*, 273.

brand of social justice Christianity appealed to Obama and would ideally link him to the historic African American struggle. According to Anna Hartnell, Obama deemed such a link as essential given his Kenyan ancestry and Hawaiian birth. Undoubtedly, Obama saw Wright within the prophetic tradition of Martin Luther King Jr. Unfortunately Obama's opponents did not.[10]

Perhaps the idea of potential prophetic moments and tones cut to the heart of the Obama and King comparison. Did Obama's ethos or actions in any speech remotely rise to the level of King's prophetic voice? And herein lays the proverbial rub. Obama probably never rose to the level of King's prophetic ethos, particularly the mythic King. But more to the point, Obama's rhetoric—and perhaps no politician's, as I suggested earlier—could ever meet the lofty standards of King's prophetic rhetoric. This assessment does not entirely reflect cynicism about the political system or politicians' sophistry. Rather, given the on-the-line, often in-your-face nature of prophetic rhetoric, how could any duly elected, desiring to be reelected, politician consistently speak in this fashion? Elijah would never be a dinner guest at King Ahab's table. The current controversy swirling around the iconic Congressman John Lewis largely stems from the fact that the nation is faced with a former civil rights prophet who presently serves as a politician.

Most Americans now revere King and his rhetoric. However, this was not even close to being the case during his time. In fact, even during the time of King's "I Have Dream" speech, arguably the height of his popularity, scores of people, including some white liberals and blacks of various political leanings, held reservations about the then thirty-four-year-old rising star of the civil rights movement. In our time King's persona has been refashioned as the black man who pleased all but the most bigoted people. Prophets don't fit that bill. King certainly didn't. In short, by word and deed, Obama has been compared to a canonized, mythical MLK, one created and metamorphosed into the image of the conservative or progressive who happens to have been criticizing Obama at that moment. Obama was not the only one who could not measure up. Black society can't, as one could note by surveying conservative pundits' scathing analyses of any measure of African Americans' disgruntlement since the late 1970s.

Similarly, the firestorms surrounding Obama's election and reelection involved a number of complex factors. I mention one in this web of

10. Hartnell, *Rewriting Exodus*, 35–47.

ideologies: the expectation that Obama should have been everything for everybody. Or as most black grandparents and parents have taught their progeny: even if you're twice as good, you'll often only receive one-half the recognition. Most will admit that Obama's biography is exceptional in many ways: he personifies the immigration and migration narratives with a father from Kenya and mother from Kansas. He at once embodies the ethnic diversity and up-by-your-bootstraps drive that we Americans claim to celebrate in a so-called colorblind society. And he is one of the finest orators in history. So why couldn't he catch a break when he was president? I suggest that it is precisely because Obama was exceptional that many took exception with him. In being and bearing, he embodied what racists of all regions and ideological bents have feared: a brilliant brother with swagger. As president, he stood upon and navigated the fault lines of nationality, identity politics, class, and civic religion. Whenever race, gender, or sexual orientation collide with the socioeconomic religiosity of American traditionalism, political earthquakes and aftershocks are inevitable.

That Americans of varying political shades compared the former president with Martin Luther King Jr. was to some extent also understandable. As a lawyer working on Chicago's South Side, Obama labored for civil rights and at community organizing. These actions pleased progressives. The electrifying 2004 Democratic convention speech he gave as a senator echoed King's call that we transcend the differences that divide us. King's notion of a national community that finds common ground beyond ethnic and religious differences registered on higher frequencies as Obama's subsequent speeches crisscrossed differences in politics, economics, race, gender, and sexual orientations. In theory, the spirit of most these speeches pleased both progressives and conservatives. From the 1980s to the present, for instance, black and white neoconservatives have argued that King's primary moral legacy was a society where race does not matter at all. Those conservatives interpret King's call for *content of character over color of skin* as renouncing cultural pride as well as racial prejudice.

At its best the King and Obama connection might have inspired Americans of all ethnicities to celebrate a narrative of racial progress. At worst identifying Obama with King could have muddied the lines between politician and prophet. Depending on how serious or personal the crisis, some citizens would have chosen to ideally transform the president's bully pulpit into a civil religious pulpit where the country becomes the congregation. They would have demanded that the president act like a pastor—instead of a chief executive—when their heartfelt, religious interests were involved. This could have been the case for black religionists who deemed church pastors the ultimate voice in spiritual and sociopolitical matters, as well as for the brand of white neoconservatives who were out-of-the closet evangelicals. Drawing a distinction between politician and prophet, while necessary, is not without its own layers of ideological clutter. No matter how well thinkers such as George Shulman argue for the potential sociopolitical efficacy of the prophetic voice or how strongly I affirmed this notion in the last chapter, those concerned about contingent connections between church and state remain suspicious. Those of us who have reeled at the excesses of the Religious Right remain rightfully leery of any use of religious language within politics.

KING'S FUSION OF THE POLITICAL AND THE PROPHETIC

The "true," radical Martin Luther King, to allude to the subtitle of a Michael Eric Dyson book,[11] could not measure up to King's contemporary saintly iconic status. King is frozen in 1963 on the steps of the Lincoln Memorial delivering his famous and decidedly misunderstood "I Have a Dream" speech. This speech was in fact the apex of King's career at the time, the oratorical culmination of speeches given from the Montgomery bus boycott to the Birmingham campaign. This last campaign could be seen as creating the immediate catalyst for the "I Have a Dream" speech. All that I have explored about the Birmingham mass meeting oratory suggests nuances that may enable a richer reading of that speech, its relationship to religion and politics, as well as to King's contemporary legacy to the civil rights movement. In fact, even a cursory reading of the overlapping themes between King's May 3rd Birmingham mass meeting and "I Have a Dream" speeches underscore the richly complex relationship between the prophetic and political.

Both addresses contain the same core message: racial injustice violates the spirit of democracy and the nature of humanity. The "I Have a Dream" speech was delivered four months after the beginning of the SCLC's formal participation in the Birmingham movement. "I Have a Dream" was set within the context of racial unity, as out of two hundred thousand participants for the March on Washington approximately seventy thousand

11. Dyson, *I May Not Get There.*

were white. This semblance of interracial unity contrasted with the stark perception of disunity in Birmingham—not only between black movement participants and white racists like Bull Connor, but also marked differences between King's cohort and white moderates like the eight Birmingham clergy whom Martin Luther King soundly criticized in the now famous "Letter form a Birmingham Jail."

Like the "I Have a Dream," the May 3rd speech, as I alluded to in chapter 4, exposed how racial prejudices and institutional practices were, more often than not, intertwined. For example, in the May 3rd speech King pressed for a biracial committee to begin addressing some of the racial ills in Birmingham. Southern racism was so deeply institutionalized that King argued for black people selecting the black person to serve on such a committee, subject to the approval of the mayor. King then added a remark that might appear—in a cursory comparison to "I Have a Dream"—uncharacteristically militant: Leaders of the Birmingham campaign did not want blacks on the biracial committee that were chosen exclusively by the white establishment. True democracy entailed not only the rights for black Birmingham to vote, but also their right to sit on special city committees designed to improve or correct the city's racial policies. This might constitute one structural solution to an institutional problem.

Both speeches also highlighted how institutional racism was deeply engrained in American cultural history. King reemphasized the theme of gradualism and, as he did in other speeches, stressed the prophetic urgency of the moment. The founding fathers, so King opined in "I Have a Dream," had drafted a "promissory note" for democracy to which Americans of all races ideally should have benefited. Instead, institutional practices and individual racists' acts had formed a pattern throughout history, so that black checks (promises) for democracy nearly always bounced. Similarly, in the May 3rd speech King critiqued Alabama's resistance to comply with Supreme Court mandates for school integration set out in *Brown* (1954) and *Brown II* (1955). Instead of addressing the matter with "all deliberate speed," as the decision ordered, Alabama was engaged in an "all deliberate crawl."[12]

Nevertheless, for King, time was more than a matter of chronology. Time was a matter of seizing a crucial opportunity. For rhetoricians and theologians, the Greek word is *kairos*. Kairos played out in the May 3rd and "I Have a Dream" speeches, the larger civil rights movement, and theme

12. King, Mass Meeting Speech, 150 (Towns).

of the prophetic. Most of the Old Testament prophets deployed their messages with a sense of urgent, opportune timing, or kairos. The injustices perpetuated by the respective manifestations of power were long overdue in being righted. And King's refrain of "Now is the time," reverberated from Montgomery to Memphis and was radicalized in the rhetoric of the militant members of SNCC who shouted for Black Power. Kairos can be connected to the inevitable rise of the first black president. Even those who did not want Obama to win in 2008 ostensibly applauded the event as historic. Of course kairos moves beyond the historic to include what is fitting for a particular moment. Hence, there was a wide gap between celebrating that America finally had a black president to celebrating Obama. In fact the urgency that characterizes the word *kairos* and most social movements rarely matches the gradual momentum of mainstream politics. Movement and mainstream rarely occupy the same ideological space.

Whether one views King's "I Have a Dream" and May 3rd speeches in terms of institutional racism, cultural history, or kairos, the question of how or whether religion should enter into wider social and political deliberations remains, to put it charitably, a messy problem. At its best, the nation should reject the anti-Islamic theology of the crusades and which surrounded radically conservative reactions to 911, as well as the anti-black theology that animated slavery and segregation. However, these politically oppressive sectarian discourses met their counterparts in the zealous moral suasion that Christian abolitionists espoused and the robust civil rights rhetorical discourses that black Protestants championed. To varying degrees, Catholics, Jews, Muslims, and secularists of all races also embraced the prophetic civil rights rhetoric of the 1960s. Can or should American citizens attempt to excavate the rhetorical, social, and political components of prophetic religion for this time? If yes, how can this be done without marring democracy with the domination, denigration, and dismissal associated with the Religious Right?

I don't intend on addressing the above questions in any conclusive way. Rather I wish to broach how both Obama's presidency and our obsessive desire to compare him with King compels us to face these and other questions afresh. Albeit a formidable undertaking, unraveling often elusive distinctions between politicians and prophets are critical for realistically interpreting the legacy our first black president as well as appreciating the rich rhetorical and cultural history of African Americans. Whereas having expected Obama to be like other presidents trivialized the role of race in politics, having expected him to be like King obscured the role of prophetic religion in the black struggle for liberation.

This is not to say that a politician may not or should not at moments speak in transformative ways—that is speaking against injustices, be they national or global. Or that a prophetic leader does not address political issues. Indeed, we need prophetic leaders in the tradition of Martin Luther King Jr. to shake up the political status quo. But just as Socrates feared sophistic rhetoric, prophetic language in the wrong hands can be oppressive rather than liberating. For every Martin Luther King Jr., there is a Jerry Falwell. And puritanical piety plus patriotism often equals xenophobic politics. Politicians should presumably be tempered by moments of political expediency, while prophetic leaders are driven by a mindset of relentless critique. For example, Martin Luther King Jr. expanded the purview of his critique from civil rights to the Vietnam War and economic inequality. President Lyndon Johnson, arguably the greatest presidential advocate for civil rights, despised King for his anti–Vietnam War stance. Coretta Scott King opined that if her husband had lived, he probably would have eventually supported gay rights or become a vegetarian on ethical grounds. Wrestling prophecy from the exclusive ideological grasps of fundamentalism and American civil religion becomes essential if prophetic language is to advance rather than hinder democracy. This may be partly what James Baldwin meant when he declared that he had to "leave the church to preach the gospel."

OBAMA'S RHETORIC AND THE PROPHETIC LEGACY OF THE CIVIL RIGHTS MOVEMENT

Agree or disagree with Cornel West's criticisms of Obama. West believed those criticisms to be inflected with prophetic authority. So the central questions in light of the emphasis of this book, as well as the readiness with which Obama was compared to King follow: Should we have expected our first black president to have spoken prophetically? Perhaps more significantly, did Obama envision himself within the prophetic or Mosaic leadership role that King was most celebrated for but that other prominent African Americans throughout history have occupied? As I alluded to from the outset of this chapter, there have been ceremonial connections Obama has made to King and the civil rights movement, including direct and indirect references in his speeches and using King's Bible along with Lincoln's during the second inauguration. And while arguably Obama became bolder in his critique of racism, particularly, in his second term, I believe that how he viewed his role as a black politician beholden to the legacy of the civil rights movement did not change substantially from his days as senator.

Senator Obama's March 4th, 2007, speech commemorated the forty-second anniversary of the Selma Voting Rights march. This speech indicated one way that Obama might have perceived his leadership in comparison with King's. Approximately one year after this speech, Obama—like King—would be compared to Moses. Further, on the road to the White House, Obama was explicitly and implicitly cast as Messiah, derisively by people ranging from Hillary Clinton during the 2008 primaries to the McCain camp, and satirically by Jon Stewart and Jaime Foxx. How Obama envisioned himself in relationship to the pervasive cultural image of Moses is vital for teasing out the rhetorical significance of his presidency and the pertinent legacies of the civil rights movement.

Obama delivered his March 4th speech, approximately three weeks after he announced his candidacy for president. The contexts for the speech could hardly be more serendipitous: the anniversary of the voting rights campaign conducted in Selma, Alabama. The Voting Rights campaign, which led to the passage of the Voting Rights Act of 1965, was the last great campaign of the now canonized civil rights movement. Some prominent leaders of and participants in this campaign constituted the audience. If listening to the seventh African American to run for president didn't sufficiently inspire them, perhaps the hope would that a black president might curtail the assaults on civil and voting rights that they had witnessed since the 1980s. Fairly straightforward yet predictably moving, this speech revealed Obama's familiarity with the tropes, narratives, and stylistics of African American sermonic rhetoric.

The address opened with lengthy praise for the politicians, preachers, and laypeople present. He especially focused on Congressman John Lewis, a veteran of the sit-ins, Freedom Rides, and the March on Washington, Jeremiah Wright (Obama's now infamous pastor), and Pastors Joseph Lowry and C. T. Vivian, one of Martin Luther King Jr.'s lieutenants. Obama engaged in mock envy as he mentioned how unfortunate it was for him to be speaking after Lowry and in front of C. T. Vivian, whom Martin Luther King Jr. called "one of the greatest preachers he ever heard."[13] This gesture of mock envy is a staple device visiting pastors deploy in black churches

13. Obama, 2007 Selma speech, para 3.

to commend the local pastor while tacitly establishing their own ethos. Obama further established his ethos by invoking "the spirit to move"[14] or aid him in his delivery. By mentioning the spirit, Obama signaled his understanding of a point I made in chapter 2 regarding oral performances within black church walls: No matter how talented the messengers, no matter how substantively or stylistically sound their messages, ultimately and ceremonially black religious rhetoric must be infused with spiritual energy.

Obama then moved to the central question of his speech. Why should he possess the audacity to run for president? While reminding his listeners about how his decision to make the announcement in the shadow of Lincoln's statue was deliberate, the question did cause Obama pause. However, Obama claimed that his doubts were allayed with a letter he received from Pastor Otis Moss from Cleveland, Ohio, who was the father of one of the pastors serving at Trinity, where Obama attended.

In this letter, Pastor Moss legitimized Obama's run for the presidency, arguing that Obama was a part of the Joshua generation. In biblical lore, Joshua was Moses's protégée and successor. But the two couldn't be any more different from each other. Moses was a major prophet and God's lawgiver. Joshua was a warrior, law enforcer, and leader to the promised land. Notwithstanding Joshua's mention in African American cultural history and rhetoric, he never attained the iconic status that Moses did. That Pastor Moss drew this distinction between the Obama being Joshua rather than Moses was telling. That Obama picked up on and framed his speech around this contrast was even more striking. Obama affirmed that he was in the presence of present-day Moseses who "fought for the American soul across racial lines," challenged "the pharaoh, princes and powers," and "led a people out of bondage . . . then across the seas that folks thought could not be parted."[15]

Next Obama addressed those who might question him as a legitimate heir to the movement or as a member of the Joshua generation. He argued that he should not be written off as a movement outsider because of his mixed racial and national heritage. Indeed, his Kenyan grandfather experienced the demeaning language and humiliating treatment as a cook for the British that black Americans had known under Jim Crow. His grandfather had sensed the global impact of the American civil rights movement early on, and had encouraged Obama's father to take advantage of the Kennedy

14. Ibid., para 4.

15. Ibid., para 11–14

administration's foreign student exchange programs. Obama's dad met his mom, and although they were from different continents and races, and though his mom had descended from an enslaver, they married. Obama definitely considered himself an insider to the movement as well as a member of the Joshua generation.

Obama next laid out five challenges for the Joshua generation. First, the Joshua generation was responsible for maintaining cultural memory. They should never forget, nor should they allow those around them to forget the contributions of the Moses generation—contributions that were so far-reaching that they took black people 90 percent of the way to the border of the promise land. When Obama, therefore, referred to the biblical narrative that Moses did not make it to the promised land, he signaled his tacit knowledge of King's final speech on April 3, 1968. In that speech King fully embraced the mantle of Moses as he declared, "I may not get there with you, but we as a people will get to the Promised Land." According to Keith D. Miller, this last speech compromised a hermeneutical lens, without which one can scarcely appreciate the theological, cultural, political, and rhetorical heft of King's ideas and legacy. With this veiled yet conspicuous reference to King's mountaintop speech, one thrust of Obama's speech became evident: the living members of the Moses generation were not ultimately responsible for contemporary African American advancement. While they should be revered and consulted, and would most likely continue to serve the cause of social justice, the Joshua generation should shoulder the bulk of the load. To do this, the Joshua generation most avoid the "poverty of ambition,"[16] or measuring their progress in terms of material success without community service.

Second, the Joshua generation needed to recognize that incorporating the "principles of equality"[17] was an ongoing battle. Obama criticized President George W. Bush's justice department for its hyperfocus on dismantling affirmative action programs rather than on vigorously enforcing the antidiscrimination laws that the Moses generation help place on the books. Obama took another rhetorical jab at those in the Bush administration given to conservative gradualism when he said about discrimination, "better is not good enough."[18]

16. Ibid., para 27.
17. Ibid., para 28.
18. Ibid., para 30.

Securing economic rights constituted Obama's third call to the Joshua generation. Health care, education, urban renewal, and chronic unemployment represented responsibilities that Joshua generation politicians must take seriously, even though much of the American electorate suffered from a hope or empathy gap. In regard to responsibility, Obama implored the Joshua generation to instill within the current generation the same sense of community accountability and discipline that characterized the Moses generation during the civil right movement. This nod to African Americans taking more personal responsibility, a recurring theme in then-senator Obama's speeches, became a source of controversy. From his time as senator and through his presidency, some have accused Obama of blaming the victim. As one might expect given the pervasive force of religion within the civil rights movement, with his fifth point, Obama encouraged the Joshua generation to above all depend upon God.

However, Obama's adoption of the Joshua ethos did not eliminate the racial, national, and international tensions evoked by the Moses archetype. For Hartnell, this archetype is symbolically rooted in the exodus trope which, in turn, has sprouted in to two narratives: "statist" and "nonstatist." The statist exodus narrative privileges "an America defined by a peculiar mixture of triumphalism and innocence." The nonstatist exodus account depicts "a much more critical portrait of a nation that has yet to make good on its promises."[19] Where the first exodus narrative traces its origins to the founding fathers and the Enlightenment, the later narrative traces its beginnings to African ancestors and slavery. Considered Messiah, Moses, or Joshua, Obama literally embodied two clashing historical accounts of America's beginning in a way that no president had before him.

After the 2007 Selma speech, Obama delivered many addresses that evoked the civil rights movement and flirted with prophetic witness—courting discourse somewhere between prophetic tones and transformative rhetoric. During his second term, Obama expanded, though not thoroughly examined, the legacy of antiracism in remarks about the Trayvon Martin case, Michael Brown, and the demonstrations in Ferguson, Missouri. In the wake of the Trayvon Martin tragedy, Obama personalized a potential prophetic moment. On July 19, 2013, following the verdict in the George Zimmerman case, the president offered remarks that walked the line between the informational and the experiential, between the rule of law and the pull of conscience. While the remarks were brief, they underscored how

19. Hartnell, *Rewriting Exodus*, 37.

difficult it is for any politician, but particularly the first African American president, to speak prophetically. Quite expectedly, Obama began by acknowledging the grief that Martin's parents were experiencing and the dignity they displayed. Further, without directly praising or condemning the verdict in this particular case, he indirectly acknowledged the intricate workings of our judicial system and affirmed the need to respect this legal process. However, given the popular debate that had been swirling around the controversy, Obama felt the need to provide "context" for the way some people felt about the verdict. Interestingly, the former president inserted a personal yet stunning observation as the first layer of this context. He noted that Trayvon Martin could have been his son, or, in fact could have been the president himself thirty-five years ago. As in past speeches, Obama introduced racism without expounding upon or providing a substantive structural critique—let alone solution. Perhaps as significant, this technique was interwoven into a larger rhetorical strategy (again found in his other speeches) whereby Obama juxtaposed facts that might appear objective with the realities constructed from existential narratives. African Americans, he explained, have confronted a set of experiences, including being watched in department stores (the president had experienced this himself) and noticing white women clutching their purses in elevators. Obama rightly noted that these experiences informed how many black Americans interpreted the case.

On the heels on affirming the sentiment that many African Americans held in the Martin case, Obama introduced a critique about young black male criminality that might have assuaged or served as a concession for his white listeners. However, he shrewdly couched those comments regarding black-on-black male crime by noting that African Americans themselves were aware of these dire statistics. Obama obviously walked a rhetorical tightrope of accommodation that a prophet would never be bound to. As difficult as it is for any politician to speak prophetically, I think it is more challenging for a president of a nation to do so. At best, heads of state have had moments—or more precisely—flashes of transformative (rather than strictly prophetic) declaration. This is partly why Americans remember Lincoln and FDR. Overall, Obama's Trayvon Martin speech was not prophetic precisely because it did not challenge the systemic or institutional nature of the problem that led to this young man's death. Essentially the former president called for statistical calculations to determine to the potential prevalence of racial profiling, sensitivity training for the police, and community programs that would instill hope in African American young men. To be fair, Obama did project a backhanded but stinging critique of Florida's stand-your-ground law by querying whether if the tables were turned, society would be okay with Martin standing his ground as Zimmerman had.

Obama faced a similar challenge in his remarks about the Michael Brown case and the aftermath in Ferguson, Missouri. In fact, one could cynically describe Obama's comments on the Brown case in November 2014 as the rhetoric of *more of the same*. He touted themes of law and order, African Americans' despair about the verdict, and the need to improve relations between the police and the black community. Obama did affirm—albeit vaguely—the need for some changes within the American judicial system as well as historical reasons why African Americans might rightfully mistrust this system at worst and be highly suspicious of it at best. However, in the final analysis, Obama's critique of what he perceived to be the occasional injustices operating within the American legal system seem to function as a concession designed to appease black sentiment and curtail violence. As in some of his other race remarks, Obama honed his focus on possible manifestations of black pathology. Intentionally or not, he placed the lion's share of the moral burden for racial unrest upon the African American community. In fact, Obama's remarks were framed with a refrain of Brown's parents' plea for the black community not to express dissent through violence. And as necessary and, to some degree noble, that plea may have been, what moral or ethical burden did Officer Wilson and the police department shoulder? There can be no substantive critique, transformative, prophetic, or otherwise of society where the practices of prevailing institutions are not engaged, held accountable, critiqued, and ultimately transformed.

President Obama's speech commemorating the fiftieth anniversary of the Selma March provided an opportunity to reassess the civil rights legacy vision he casts as a senator some eight years earlier. The speech also afforded a chance to examine whether Obama's presidential rhetoric proved to be connected to the legacy of the civil rights movement beyond a ceremonial level. As was the case at the outset of the first Selma speech, Obama acknowledged and praised civil rights veteran and longtime congressman John Lewis. However, unlike the previous Selma speech, here Obama had little praise for the other dignitaries, including one past American president, members of Congress, and a governor. Perhaps understandably given his subject matter, in contrast to Obama's praise for Lewis, he acknowledged the latter group briefly. In a sense, this gesture set the tone for the rest of the speech. To be sure, the focus of Obama's 2015 Selma speech was heroism. But in practical terms, what did this heroism mean for an American society still plagued by racism? The Selma March and the Edmund Pettus Bridge were the moment and place where Americans of all types and freedom struggles throughout history would crescendo. For Obama, the grassroots heroism enacted in Selma was effective primarily because it usually utilized salt-of-the-earth individuals. While citizens of all races and creeds participated in democratic experiments such as Selma, no particular race or creed was required to do so.

As he had in other speeches, Obama here argued that the change Selma participants marched for was at the heart of American democracy—even if antagonists to the march and movement did not recognize it at the time. Further, once again Obama walked a rhetorical tightrope between claiming that fighting the status quo was necessary and embracing such battles as a reason why America is exceptional. In other words, the fight in Selma opened the doors for other struggles within American history: the struggle for rights by women, Latinos, Asians, gays and lesbians, and Americans with disabilities. But American protest also sparked a fire in South Africa and the rest of the world. In some ways, Obama claimed that the kind and quality of protest represented in Selma was both revolutionary and institutional, cutting-edge and traditional. Consequently, Obama charged twenty-first-century Americans with the peculiar and paradoxical call to change the nation while honoring it as exceptional. Like Americans who have gone before us, contemporary citizens of this republic must work to perfect our union, strive to complete an unfinished narrative.

Obama contended that America's story of freedom was unfinished economically and legally. He returned to the theme of America as a community where we look out for each other. Without being explicit, he challenged his audience to be open to economic policies that ensure the working class an honest and livable wage for an honest day's work. Regarding America's incomplete legal narrative, Obama did not stress the issue of race. However, he does not even allude to the prison industrial complex, which many thinkers link together as the economic and legal reasons for the marginalization of people of color. As writer Michelle Alexander argues, prisons may be the new Jim Crow. The prison industry profits from the labor of black inmates, many of whom will not find jobs upon release, and most of whom will not be able to vote.

As most of Obama's other orations had done, the Fiftieth Anniversary Selma speech generated a range of reactions. Some commentators thought it was one of the most inspiring addresses, not just delivered by Obama, but in the history of American presidential rhetoric. Others bristled at and rejected the speech as eloquent stylistically but empty substantively. Whether they were fans or foes of Obama, the memorial celebration in Selma reminded Americans—of every race and political persuasion—that the march to democracy continued more than fifty years later.

Obama's rhetoric and two-term presidency also force Americans to wrestle with the heterogeneous unity of African American culture, a cosmic quilt with patches of sacred and secular, innovation and tradition, what we know, what we say, how, when and to whom. Or as the sage sisters and brothers of many black churches would opine around good preaching, moving singing, and arguably the best food, "We ain't what we ought to be; we ain't what we gonna be, but thank God, we ain't what we used to be." And as kairos never stops but rather sometimes shapes chronos (sequential time), sacred and secular African American rhetorics ebb and flow from past, present, and future moments of groaning and grandeur. Blacks now, as they always have, "sing America," to borrow from Langston Hughes. But higher ranges of that song cannot be reached if through our political, social, economic, and educational policies if children of color are still wondering "Is America, America to me?"

Obama's claim that American democracy is an ongoing, incomplete narrative was an insightful and potentially efficacious observation. On some levels, the claim sounds prophetic. However, at the core of the prophetic rhetoric practiced during the civil rights movement was a quality of critique that resisted codifying or institutionalization. This is not say that the heirs of the civil rights movement, left leaning and right leaning, have not aligned the civil rights movement with the status quo. However, the civil rights rhetoric of the Birmingham mass meetings was raw, real, and relevant in ways that refused to be contained. This is why, while grounded in religion, Birmingham mass meeting rhetoric—to some extent at least— transcended orthodoxy. While steeped in African American rhetoric, aesthetic, and epistemological traditions, Birmingham mass meeting rhetoric fanned out and embraced multiracial, multicultural, and multifaceted discursive traditions and techniques that promote freedom.

Whereas Birmingham mass meeting rhetoric sought to make American democracy more inclusive and did echo cherished American values, this body of speeches for the most part remained prophetic. Most of the former president's speeches, however, affirmed and touted American exceptionalism. And among the many sociopolitical drawbacks of clinging to American exceptionalism is making exceptions for America's failures. Over and over again, when faced with a prejudicial crime or injustice, Obama would typically opine a variation of this refrain: "But that's not who we are as Americans."

Obama seemed to personify hope about the legacy of King and the civil rights movement that neither he nor the nation could realize in eight years. He accepted the nomination for the presidency on August 28th, 2008, on the forty-fifth anniversary of the March on Washington and King's timeless "I Have a Dream" speech. Many of his speeches before and during his presidency summoned—sometimes explicitly other times implicitly—people, places, memories, and moments from the movement. And he literally embodies the lofty moral goals of that great democratic experiment: a person of biracial, international pedigree who bootstrapped his way through a childhood with an absentee father and a free-spirited mother, through multiple moves into an Ivy League law school, into community service, and ultimately into national politics. Still, notwithstanding his many accomplishments as president, the first black head of state could—at best—merely perform prophecy.

Perhaps comparing Obama, the first black president, to King was destined to be a failed experiment from the start. Beyond the seemingly irreconcilable tensions between a prophet as critic and president as standard bearer of national institutions, Obama bore the burden of fulfilling our expectations about a colorblind and otherwise inclusive society. Americans of all races, creeds, and political persuasions expected more of him largely because King expected more of us, and we saw more in him. For all of Obama's failures, and there have been some, few presidents, if any, could fulfill the high hopes and prophetic demands that Martin Luther King Jr. set in motion during the civil rights movement. Had King become president, I don't think he could have.

7

Birmingham on My Mind

Personal Reflections on Teaching, Scholarship, and Vocation

"I am all too aware that reading about prophets does not automatically lead to action. As the old dictum says, 'Those who can't do, teach.' But teaching and reading may lead to doing."[1]

—Albert J. Raboteau

I was born on May 5, 1962, the year James Meredith entered Old Miss, the sit-in movement spread to Cairo, Illinois, and some white New Yorkers screamed at the U.S. district court about quotas long before affirmative action got a running start. I was born one year and one day after thirteen freedom riders began their bus trip through the South, approximately one year before Kelly Ingram Park, the Dream speech, four murdered girls, and one assassinated president.

The memories of the civil rights movement are a part of my consciousness, whether or not I own up to this reality. At least, that's what my father taught me. Born in 1923 (he passed away in 1988), my father, like countless other African Americans, knew Jim Crow personally. On several occasions, I remember him vividly describing the degradation he faced while growing

1. Raboteau, *American Prophets,* introduction.

up in the 1920s and '30s in a small town outside Shreveport, Louisiana. Like the author Richard Wright, he remembered the emotional strain of being straightjacketed by a set of rules—some known but most tacit—created by the whim and will of the white person whom you might encounter that day. The system was more than physically inhibiting, depriving black Americans of the sociopolitical rights most white Americans took for granted. According to my daddy, it was psychic torture as you realized that even the most innocent gesture, such as complimenting a white woman on her dress or failing to exude the appropriate deference to a white man, could get you badly hurt or killed

Like numerous other African Americans of his generation and before, my father wanted me and my five siblings to know and hear the story of our struggle over and over again, to taste those narratives, bitter as they might be sometimes. An increasing number of Americans across racial lines have retreated from civil rights narratives, insisting that the nation has been ushered into a halcyon period of colorblindness, in which discussions of racism are now the purview of the white supremacist, the black opportunist, or the paranoid. Perhaps this nearsighted faith in the dogma of colorblindness partly accounts for the mania that surrounded Obama. Surely—so this idyllic narrative might continue—Justice John Marshall Harlan, the lone dissenter in *Plessy v. Ferguson*, would rise from his grave to proclaim that Obama was the kind of person that prompted him to declare that "the Constitution is colorblind." *We've come so far* is the rallying cry that circulates within American culture. The only real dangers are spurred by ongoing reflections, not just on racism, but on race. These reflections are perceived as balkanizing to democratic unity at best, and can lead to reverse discrimination against the endangered white male at worst.

This truncated reflection on my dad speaks, and perhaps the figure of Obama also speaks, to the power of time and place, especially in relation to racial identity formation. Obviously who you are and what you become has a lot to do with your surroundings. One need only think of how the rural ruggedness of the South during slavery, the black migration from there during the late nineteenth century and the early twentieth century, and the return to the South post–civil rights movement have nuanced African American identity. Every location has an allure beyond its geographical attributes. The post–civil rights return to the South, for example, is understandable given not only the elimination of de jure segregation but also given what Harlem Renaissance writer Jean Toomer, among others, has observed: For African Americans, the South holds community, the communal, a sense of spirit, an echo of the voices of ancestors.

The crucible for the American civil rights movement was of course the South, and during and since that movement the currents of voices, visions (past, present, future) and place—above all place—flow to, with, and away from each other. Taylor Branch, David Garrow, Clayborne Carson, and David Levering Lewis have crafted historical narratives about how the time and place that was the civil rights movement shaped—indeed permeated—our very concepts of race, nation, and democracy. Keith D. Miller, Michael Eric Dyson, Jonathan Rieder, and Richard Lischer, among a host of others, have focused on the rhetorical prowess of Martin Luther King Jr., his prophetic voice crying from the wilderness of the mid-twentieth-century South.

This chapter conjures up the shifting yet, hopefully, significant connections between researching and teaching the civil rights movement as a popular-culture movement, its relationship to the public sphere and critical citizenry. Said differently, what political and pedagogical difference does viewing civil rights oratory as prophecy make in the here and now? I will make three moves in this chapter. First, I reflect on the first two courses I taught on the civil rights movement—including content, style, some student reactions, and particularly what I discovered to be my personal motivations. I also make a quick yet meaningful detour to discuss my first trip to the South to study the civil rights movement with other professors. Second, I explore what I consider to be a watershed moment for my interest in the civil rights moment: the travel course I taught on the Alabama civil rights movement in 2002. My—and I believe the students'—literal journey to Birmingham, Selma, and Montgomery symbolized the larger intellectual and experiential sojourn we were taking to better understand our personal, cultural, and national identities, and how place shaped the cognitive, affective, and participatory domains of our knowledge. Last, I introduce how my current focus on the oratory of the Birmingham mass meetings can also enrich and expand notions of prophetic discourses of other genres.

A SCHOLAR OF COLOR AND THE COLOR OF TEACHING

I taught my first college-level class on the civil rights movement in the fall of 2000. Since the students at Pepperdine were largely conservative at that time, my unstated purpose was to combat reductive views regarding

151

the legacy of the civil rights movement. Stock views are not confined to right-wing conservatives. Of course a number of liberals, including, Hollywood liberals, have perpetuated myopic perspectives as well, which have emerged literally in a spate of movies—particularly in the 1990s—that collectively could have been easily titled *White Folks Are Good Too*. These films tended to romanticize white roles and black agency during the civil rights movement beyond historical recognition and respectability, thus watering down the force of the real-life interracial coalitions that actually occurred during this time. These films have titles such as *The Long Walk Home* and *Mississippi Burning*. I showed these two films during this first class on the civil rights movement, noted a few historical and conceptual limitations of them, but somehow reserved the panther's share of my critical jabs for the conservative points of view represented in the nonfiction books that I had assigned: Thomas Sowell's *Civil Rights: Rhetoric or Reality?* and Shelby Steele's *Dream Deferred*. I rounded out these ultraconservative perspectives on the contemporary implications of the civil rights movement with Derrick Bell's *Faces at the Bottom of the Well*, as well as a conservative author whose book reads radically progressive in spots, Orlando Patterson's *The Ordeal of Integration*.

I began the course with a series of questions ostensibly designed to open up discussion and my students' minds, the two most pressing of which were (1) Why was the civil rights movement deemed controversial? (2) Why was the government gradual in its response to the black freedom struggle? I divided the class in half, and every student within each half group wrote a five-minute, informal response to one of the questions. After this, they were assembled into two groups, one group discussing their response to question 1, the other their response to question 2. This group discussion continued until the end of the period. I opened the next period by having us discuss the two questions as a class. Of course, these two questions morphed into other questions and comments from the class and me. Unfortunately, or perhaps predictably, these questions ended up vilifying or deifying people from the 1960s, while giving no regard to implications for the present, including political compromises and status quo practices that might disenfranchise people of color on some level.

I am not sure whether I wanted to convert my students to more progressive takes on the contemporary implications of the civil rights movement. Rather, I would have settled for converting them from the assumptions about race, gender, class, and culture that all too often wafted from the waves of talk radio during the 1990s. Hence, I threw in documentaries about Martin Luther King Jr. and Malcolm X to convince them that they didn't know what they thought they did about these well-known icons. I used the documentary series *Eyes on the Prize* to dispense important factual information and to frame the times and places of the movement.

My overt pedagogical intent was to afford these students a student-centered experience in excavating the major people, places, and ideas of the movement. To this end, I allowed them to choose one of the nonfiction texts (Bell, Patterson, Sowell, or Steele) to present on in groups of four. I thought working with their peers and then presenting to the rest of the class would force some critical engagement—however small—with the sacred cow sentiments reflected in their thinking.

There were many other opportunities channeled by what I deemed open-ended pedagogical strategies, in which I thought at least a few students were eventually going to be rabbit-trailed into my leftward way of thinking, However, as Socratic and as student-centered as I planned on being, this, my first experience teaching the civil rights movement—the movement in which I had a personal investment—flopped. Whether conservative students were presenting on the books or shrugging off what they perceived to be a left-leaning class discussion, I was often so bent on my rhetorical intent that some of my questions and comments came across as polemical. I played the teacher card, making them see my point rather than leading them to think through and write about their own positions—including alternative ones—more effectively.

My next foray into experimenting with civil rights pedagogy was in spring 2001. The fact that this second course was upper-division made some difference. In fact, I had a few students taking the course for graduate credit, not as English majors per se, but rather for the English course component for an interdisciplinary master's program in American studies. Nearly all of the graduate students enrolled in the American studies program were secondary school teachers, and the ones in my course were no exception. These students volunteered, diffidently at first but later more directly, their insights into and strategies for teaching the course. I did not mind this, especially since their group presentations modeled some of these effective pedagogical strategies for the undergraduates and me. However, I did mind the talk radio imbued conservative tidbits a couple of my graduate students provided, albeit usually in private. For me the problem with much conservative rhetoric, specifically with regard to social justice and inclusion issues, is how historically reductive it can be in analyzing the civil rights movement—promoting idealism at the risk of minimizing or, in all too many cases, obfuscating realism. Practically any policy, perception, or position that does not get to the bright side in short order (exempting liberal bashing of course), should not occupy one's attention. The two graduate students who embraced the "we have overcome" rhetoric—one more vocal than the other—were not even good at it.

But I intentionally avoided giving corner to any conservative author on this reading list—the sociological and historical texts included James Cone's *Martin & Malcolm & America*, Doug McAdam's *Freedom Summer,* and Cornel West's *Race Matters.* I also included what I considered three in-your-face autobiographies: *The Autobiography of Malcolm X,* which, unknown to me at the time, some scholars think may not actually be an autobiography; *Bus Ride to Justice,* the disjointed, terse, but very informative autobiography of Fred Gray, the principal black attorney for Rosa Parks and Martin Luther King Jr. during the Montgomery protest; and Elaine Brown's controversial *A Taste of Power,* exploring the life of the first female head of the Black Panther Party. Charles Johnson's *Dreamer* and Alice Walker's *Meridian* were the only works of fiction I had the students read.

Upon second blush, the including Brown and Walker may have represented my own inadvertent bias, since I did not include female writers the first time I taught the civil rights movement. This move was particularly odd, especially since the first course included, as this one would, a discussion of how women were marginalized during the civil rights movement. During the first and second times I taught this course, the students were appalled, for example, to learn that Rosa Parks was neither initially photographed on the newly integrated busses after the Montgomery victory nor slated to speak at the March on Washington, an event that could be seen as one culminating moment in a movement she helped get off the ground. As for Brown's and Walker's respective books, the students were struck by the sexist treatment on a number of levels, including the women's personal relationships. The fact that Walker's characters were all fictional didn't diminish the point the novel made about the irony of those experiencing racism choosing to practice sexism.

As I had done in my first course on the civil rights movement, so also in the second course, but perhaps more intentionally, I built an instructional fortress that propped up my views of race, gender, and social justice and left just enough space for the conservative-leaning students to shoehorn in a few of their views, but hardly enough room for them to excavate reflective paths beyond that fortress, even if those paths might lead them to my way of thinking on some of these issues.

Before I would have another attempt to ram "the civil rights movement according to David Holmes" down the throats of another batch of students, I won a fellowship to study the civil rights movement for a month at Samford University in Birmingham, Alabama. A liberal arts college founded by Baptists, Samford had two professors of sociology (both white and native southerners) who had secured funds from the Lilly Foundation to bring in eight scholars—three whites and five blacks—for an intensive study of spirituality and social justice within the civil rights movement. These two ideas may seem incompatible to some and awkwardly or arbitrarily linked to others. But this was a Baptist university after all, and this book has illustrated how spirituality and secular concerns can intersect, occasionally and specifically when truth is being spoken to power.

As a result, I was pleasantly surprised by how liberally the coordinators of this seminar defined *spiritually* and how progressively they defined *social justice*. I was pleased that the broad contours with which the leaders of this workshop sought to define *spiritually* included debates that attempted to uncover the commonplaces of personal reflection, critical engagement with ideas, and sociopolitical responsiveness to be found in multiple religious traditions. "Sociopolitical responsiveness" evolved from the "love your neighbor" notion that preceded and followed the Christian gospel, transcending ritualistic acknowledgement or a token emotional affirmation of diversity and inclusion.

I could recount many experiences from the thirty days that I was a Lilly Fellow; many places, people, and events indeed shaped my teaching philosophy and practice. Among those I would characterize with the overused but here appropriate word *surreal* was my first visit to the Sixteenth Street Baptist Church, where four black girls were killed in a bombing on September 15, 1963. Our tour guide for the building was a close friend to these girls: Carolyn McKinstry, a woman whose conviction was wrapped in calm charisma. As she recalled the moments leading up to the bombing on that Sunday morning, including what might be considered a warning phone call ("Three minutes," Ms. McKinstry remembered the caller saying.), I thought I had reached my emotional and intellectual climax. If I thought I was experientially invested in the civil rights movement before, if I thought I had a hard time detaching my emotions from teaching a class on the movement just long enough to appear objective, how would I hold up after this experience? How would I ever process this experience? I thought there was nothing more that could move me.

I was wrong. Our tour ended with a survey of the church's basement, one wall still marked by small lines and crevices from the explosion. Then we were asked to sit down in folding chairs; a video monitor was turned on, and we watched Spike Lee's *4 Little Girls* in the basement of the Sixteenth Street Baptist Church.

It is difficult to gauge, let alone describe, the emotions I felt. This would probably weigh like hallowed ground for most that are sympathetic to the movement; even the slightest rustle, or the quietest whisper could disturb something in the universe. I remember Ms. McKinstry leading us in a discussion after the film was over. Though she is a woman who comports herself with rare class and dignity, there was an ever-so-slight quiver in her bearing. Sure, she had probably given this lecture many times, but how does one completely detach herself from such a horror? How do you forget what you have been forced to learn, not through schools but through life's fated experiences? Much has been written about collective memory, be it national or cultural. As others have noted many times over, blacks are one of the few groups of marginalized people implored to forget. But we cannot forget the Middle Passage, or Red Summer, or the Tuskegee experiment. We will not forget Emmett, Cynthia, Addie Mae, Denise, or Carol. African Americans should not and must not forget their martyrs—especially the children. Carolyn would not forget her friends.

On the same day we toured the Sixteenth Street Baptist Church, we met Fred Shuttlesworth, the intrepid founder of the Alabama Christian Movement for Human Rights, and the one who invited King and the SCLC to come to Birmingham in 1963. Aside from a slight limp, Shuttlesworth carried his then-seventy-nine years well. He could not have been more than 170 pounds, and his hair was dotted with the slightest flecks of gray. For the briefest moment, it occurred to me that he might have dyed his hair. However, neither did he seem like the type to do so, nor did anything I had read about him lead me to believe he would. His mobility slowed down by the passing of many winters, but ardors of that "fire in him that you couldn't put out," to paraphrase the title of Andrew Manis's biography, remained. He spoke with a conviction beyond cockiness as he recalled the trials of the Birmingham campaign. He maintained the belief that he embraced after his house was bombed on Christmas 1956: that God had called him to lead the movement in Birmingham. This conviction had led many whites, a significant number of blacks in Birmingham, and, as King would discover after he arrived in Birmingham, several other black ministers to the conclusion that Shuttlesworth was a stubborn autocrat at best and stone crazy at worst.

From where I stood, a black California native in his fourth year of a tenure-track job, it was very difficult for me not to romanticize the man and his accomplishments. Critical thinking does not always result in complete detachment from people who share the same ethnic cultural memories. As I alluded to earlier, to claim complete detachment from something so raw and real would be to declare oneself an intellectual robot. Aside from the stack of critical, philosophical, and cultural treatises that suggest we can come to any sort of intellectual enterprise unhampered by personal and community baggage, I wonder, why would we want to if we could?

What impressed me most about my initial meeting with Shuttlesworth was the ways he seemed to combine the most pristine strands of the civil rights tradition. He was clearly a follow-me-as-I-do leader, an activist who would seemingly try almost anything. The history seems to bear this out. In May 1961, when the Freedom Riders took their trip through the South and were brutalized, Shuttlesworth took one of the injured, a white young man, to his home. Of course Shuttlesworth knew the intense hatred Alabama racists held for outside agitators, particularly white ones. Shuttlesworth unflinchingly faced this special danger of housing a "white nigger."

As Shuttlesworth spoke to us, there was very little he mentioned about the Birmingham movement of 1963 that I did not already know, even at this early point in my research, but there was something about his spirit. One of my white colleagues raised the predictable question, "Did you ever come to hate white people during this time?" Shuttlesworth retorted that the struggle in Birmingham was about evil, not black and white races. Of course I was not expecting Shuttlesworth to explore the interworkings of systematic or institutional racism in relationship to the ethics of individual racial bias, but I was a little disappointed that he reduced that discussion to a simple binary. Yet this minor criticism was partly a reason to honor his battle-worn optimism. From his aging and feeble frame, he expressed an enduring commitment to social justice that could not be gainsaid. Indeed, even given his autocratic leanings and fundamentalist worldview, an accusation that Martin Luther King Jr. had leveled against many state and federal officials could not be made against him: Shuttlesworth did not prefer order to justice.

Instead, Shuttlesworth stood within the tradition of the African American jeremiad. Even in 2001, before I had read any books on him or had begun to transcribe his remarks made during the Birmingham mass meetings, I could sense the unrelenting, indomitable spirit of one who wanted to keep the message of integration alive.

The discussion of integration would take on a different hue, literally and figuratively, when we read the book *Blessed Are the Peacemakers*, and heard from the author. While the visiting fellows read several books during our month together, and we heard from the authors, none of these exchanges were as memorable as the one we had with S. Jonathan Bass, author of *Blessed Are the Peacemakers*. Martin Luther King Jr.'s famous "Letter from a Birmingham Jail" is a rhetorically masterful response to eight clergymen who criticized the Birmingham demonstration as ill-timed. Bass's book provided rich biographical portraits of these eight clergymen as well as a detailed account of how King's letter underwent several revisions, and was not composed in one sitting in his cell.

Our discussion with Professor Bass was among the most spirited and emotionally draining academic discussions in which I have ever participated. Two of the five black fellows, one a political scientist and the other a professor of religion, confronted Bass on, to their estimation, his defense of racists. Indeed, in the "Letter from a Birmingham Jail," King held out his sternest criticism, not for the avowed racists, but for the white moderates, the group he felt these clerics represented. For these black professors, Bass's arguments, both in his book and during the presentation, were unconvincing. I expressed sentiments similar those from my fellow participants, but to my subjective recollection, I was a little more charitable in my spirit towards Professor Bass; at least that is what he indicated later.

The opinions on Bass's book were divided along racial lines, although the two white professors who facilitated the Lilly Fellowship remained silent during our discussion. One white fellow, a historian, defended Bass's thesis with mild support, a support that became muted as the black professors' criticisms mounted. Nevertheless, the historian's disturbed detachment perhaps indicated his abiding, though tacit, support for Bass.

Then there was the graduate student in history whose presence was odd because she was the only one accepted as a fellow in this program who did not already hold the doctorate. Be that as it may, she came to a strong defense of Bass while he was in our presence and an even stronger defense in his absence. Shortly after Bass's departure, we continued the spirited, almost fractious discussion about whether those white moderate clergy-men whom King criticized should be given any corner. Without putting too fine a point on it, the graduate student's escalating pleas for Bass and, by extension these clerics, sprang (in my view) from the romantic idealism that stems from colorblind ideology. This ideology, along with the varie-gated permutations that evolve from it, constitutes the major plot line for popularly circulated views of the civil rights movement. According to this popular, conservative view, these religious leaders should have been given a break, though some of their approaches to integration and criticisms of King were off the mark, because ultimately the civil rights movement sought to bring people together across color, to move them into a time when color would not matter at all. Is that not the conclusion King came to a few months later as he delivered his most famous speech on the steps of the Lincoln Memorial? When King states in the "I Have a Dream" speech that his "four little children will one day live in a nation where they will not be judged by the color of their skin but by the content of their character," wasn't King embracing looking past color and its attendant conflicts that the Birmingham eight ultimately wanted?

This follow-up discussion brought our graduate student colleague to tears. Bass's harshest critic, an African American male political scientist, extended an olive leaf and offered to take her to lunch. The entire Bass incident moved my mind down paths that none of us were either aware of or willing to talk about: What did the entire incident say about white privilege? Of course I am not just talking about the privilege the eight white clerics exercised when they presumed, as King suggested, to declare the time of another people's freedom. I am also talking about the privileges of the informal rhetorical stance that my white colleagues exercised during our discussion of Professor Bass's work.

From one white professor's silence to the white graduate student's righ-teously indignant speech, these whites, like the clerics before them, could shape discourse about blacks, regardless of their discursive strategy, aca-demic qualifications, or personal experience. At that moment it occurred to me that such a sense of rhetorical entitlement was not exclusively a part of the conservative backlash some assume to have emerged in the 1980s, gaining a feverish ferocity in the 1990s. This white backlash began evolving shortly after the passage of the Voting Rights Act in 1965 and included a goodly number of racially liberal whites. Urban rioting was the ostensible impetus for the backlash. However, the mainstream assumption that black Americans were ungrateful for all the country had done for them had been circulating a few years earlier. A 1962 Gallup poll found almost 90 percent of whites believing that African American students were treated equally to their white counterparts, while a 1963 poll revealed "roughly two-thirds of whites" affirming that "black were treated equally in white communities."[2] The rhetorical smugness that has historically infused the white psyche with the nerve to speak to what is best for people of color is not just a conservative problem, though this group has mastered and plied the practice with such a voracious innocence.

Another illustration of the elusive, often seductive nature of white privilege surfaced during one field trip during the Lilly seminar. In the mountains of Tennessee we met the first white member of the SCLC, Will Campbell, a longtime liberal clergyperson. Campbell's *Brother to a Dragonfly* charts his Mississippi upbringing in the early part of the twentieth century, his call to the ministry, and his rejection of the mores of Jim Crow. When we met him, I was immediately taken by the contradictions that he embodied: a warm grandfatherly persona and an activist spirit. His down-home demeanor and folksy manners could not disguise the fiercely opinionated fire that burned within him. If I might get ahead of myself a bit, I relished the inscription he placed in my copy of his book, for I got the sense that he would not have penned it merely as a genteel gesture: "For David, our kind of folks. Will Campbell."

As Campbell relayed bits and pieces of his moving story, somehow the term "redneck" came up. He had earlier made the point about the dehumanizing, denigrating power of "nigger." When "redneck" was mentioned, he equated the two. He found that term every bit as dehumanizing as the one applied to blacks. I couldn't disagree more. This assumption constitutes one of the logical flaws of some brands of white liberalism: All prejudice is created equal. Even if I had countered Campbell by arguing the well-documented proposition that majority racism, in America and elsewhere, has been driven, perpetuated, and sustained by power, he would likely have clung to the notion that at its heart racism is primarily a moral problem. This proposition blurs the line between the more inclusive racial ideology of liberals like Campbell and the colorblind naïve narrative of the garden-variety conservative radio talk show host or Fox News television anchor.

2. Wise, *Between Barack*, 34.

It is much easier to speak of the unspeakable actions and words of racism in terms of good and evil. We all long for a cosmic sense of right and wrong to some degree—whether or not we are religious. It is much easier to minimize ethnic differences or racial distinctions in order to hide behind the noble excuse of *e pluribus unum* than to face the reality that race, gender, class, sexual orientation, and other identity markers are resistant to permanent categorization and subjugation.

ALABAMA, HERE WE COME: PLACE AND RADICAL WHITENESS STUDIES

As I have already suggested, Birmingham would leave a lasting impression upon me and my thinking about how I would teach and research the civil rights movement. Of course, the other southern states and their attending struggles called out to my mind and heart, but it would be Alabama—more specifically by May 2002, Birmingham, Montgomery, and Selma—that would captivate my imagination. I must admit that the idea of a travel course, especially after the spring semester of 2002, did not appeal to me. Summer was one of those rare moments in a teaching institution where you could focus some uninterrupted time doing your research, perhaps doing some of that archival work in Birmingham—a notion that had begun to capture my fancy the year before.

A Pepperdine staff member who was working on a doctorate in English pitched the idea of the travel course to me, saying that the trip would be completely funded, but the entire course had to be completed in one month. This prospect made for a pedagogical nightmare logistically. How was I going to teach a class that even remotely introduced the Alabama civil rights movement—not to mention include travel and discussion about cities, two of which I had never been to?

I think the curiosity—intellectual, professional and, above all, personal—finally pushed me over the line of consent. What would it mean to as one of the students later observed "to smell the air" that the civil rights movement participants did? I designed the course so that during the on-campus portion we could cram as many books and films as possible about the Alabama movement into seven days (Monday through Friday, and Monday and Tuesday the following week). The written texts included two biographies, one autobiography, and a collection of critical sketches. The visual texts included three of the *Eyes on the Prize* documentary films and two popular movies: *The Road to Freedom: The Vernon Johns Story*, and *The Long Walk Home*. My major goal was to give the students a taste of selected written and visual texts before they began to experience the *texts* of the Alabama city landscapes. In the other courses I had taught on the civil rights movement and also in this one, I wanted the students to begin their exploration by answering a very basic but essential question: How do the pop-culture films about the civil rights movement contrast with the documentaries about that period and why?

With regard to the *The Road to Freedom* and *The Long Walk Home*, the students had some threads to untangle with the films on their own merits. *The Road to Freedom* portrays the life of Vernon Johns, the pastor who preceded Martin Luther King Jr. at Dexter Avenue Baptist Church. By 1948 when Johns assumed the pastorate at Dexter, he had already garnered a reputation as brilliant, eccentric, and sometimes quick-tempered. His breadth of knowledge in and beyond theology (he was widely read in English poetry, for example) caused congregations, especially elitist ones like Dexter, to overlook Johns's faults—faults like his anger management problems, which led to his itinerant movement from church to church. Upon viewing the film, my students had a difficult time with Johns's militant persona and eclectic sociopolitical postures. Based on the common narratives they had heard about the movement, Johns defied characterization. He synthesized Booker T. Washington's passion for industrial education and agricultural enterprise with W. E. B. Du Bois's insistence on classical education and political activism. Like Washington, Johns believed that black people could make themselves indispensable to their community, not to mention to the larger white world, by "learning to do a common thing well," such as farming and, possibly, selling some of the products. On the other hand, like Du Bois, Johns challenged his black congregation to agitate for their political rights in that present moment. Vernon Johns struck many of my students as militant, some so much so that every scene in which Johns fiercely spoke out they attributed to artistic license. When I assigned a reading on Johns from the first chapter of the exhaustive civil rights history *Parting the Waters*, and my students discovered that, aside from a few embellished details, the tales of Johns's abrasive behavior were not exaggerated, they were stunned. They then more easily connected Johns to the caption emblazoned on the box of the first video version of the film I owned: "Before there was Martin Luther King, before there was Malcolm X, there was Vernon Johns."

And herein lay the proverbial rub for my students. They couldn't imagine how one might reconcile widely accepted readings of Martin Luther King Jr. with Malcolm X. Never mind that many scholars argue that Martin and Malcolm were moving closer to each other in terms of ideology, the former making a more pronounced effort to embrace pan-Africanism, and some level of black consciousness, the latter exploring interracial coalitions and interorganizational efforts at civil rights. By 1965, King was not the unflinching idealist for American integration of the "I Have a Dream" speech, and Malcolm was not inflexible antiwhite black nationalist of "The Ballot or the Bullet" speech. These students found it difficult to reconcile themselves to the ideological tensions embodied in Vernon Johns. I had neither the heart nor the inclination to reveal that, in a way, their attitudes toward Johns's complexity represented mainstream society's simplistic categorizing based on race, class, gender, or sexual orientation. Dominant society has an embedded impulse to find the representative one (or two) of a targeted group, the social equivalent to the token in the professional world. This impulse indirectly speaks to one of the flaws of classical liberalism: Equal opportunity plus radical individualism ensures success, unless you are the other, in which case your individualism is imbrued and subsequently elevated—or denigrated as the case might be—to a different level.

The Long Walk Home is a fictionalized cinematic portrayal of the Montgomery bus boycott. The relationship between Whoopi Goldberg and Sissy Spacek, respectively portraying a black maid and her white employer, drives the plot. Goldberg's and Spacek's characters offered another critical-thinking challenge to my students: How might one assess the contributions of whites to the civil rights movement? After Odessa (Goldberg) begins showing signs of exhaustion walking to work during the boycott, Miriam (Spacek) offers Odessa a ride two days a week, not out of support for the cause, but as a convenient way of getting her maid to work. As a result of a series of unexpected circumstances—including her husband discovering that Miriam is giving Odessa rides to work, and forbidding his wife to "cart around a Nigger maid"—Miriam eventually becomes one of the carpool drivers for the boycott: this leads to a climatic Hollywood showdown with (on one side) the white men who want to shut down the carpool station, and (on the other side) the black women—Miriam and her daughter. (The only black man in this scene is literally pushed offscreen.)

It could be that the premise of the movie is loosely based on the type of observation Jo Ann Robinson, Alabama State University English professor and member of the Women's Political Council, made in her book called *The Montgomery Bus Boycott and the Women Who Started It*. Robinson, who organized the production and distribution of the flyers that precipitated the first day of the boycott, noted that several white women employers were driving their black maids to work. Though I had used Robinson's book in other courses, for some reason I did not for this course; perhaps this was one of my many pedagogical blunders, especially since my class would actually be going to Montgomery.

However, I did have the students read *The Montgomery Bus Boycott: A White Preacher's Memoir* by Robert Graetz. Born and raised in West Virginia, Graetz was characterized by many of Montgomery's white residents as a northern outsider because he had been a pastor for a church in Columbus, Ohio, before being assigned to the all-black Trinity Lutheran Church in Montgomery. According to Graetz, he became involved with the bus boycott shortly after discovering that Rosa Parks had been arrested for refusing to give up her seat to white man. Graetz described his participation as being fraught with humiliations, threats, and dangers, and other historical sources corroborate most of the events he shared.

My original purpose for having my students view *The Long Walk Home* and read Graetz's book was not only to examine the region of Montgomery within the larger Alabama civil rights narrative but also to complicate the role of race within that narrative. In other words, how could I steer them away from a simplistic reading that assumed all white people stood against and all black people for this cause? Given the spirit of service and usefulness that partly describes Pepperdine's ideal student, I wanted them to see how some white Americans served African Americans in unexpected, unpopular, and dangerous ways. Neither of these purposes needed to be stressed, as my students were all too ready—especially given their rearing during the age of white backlash rhetoric—to at least broach the idea that whites, and particularly white men, are sometime given a raw deal, victimized when it comes to their vilification within the history of American race relations.

As a result it was really difficult for the students to grasp how I could still critique the historical Graetz and the fictional Miriam for failing to recognize their white privilege. Helping my students to even hear the question, do well-meaning white people exercise a level of privilege even as they might be engaging in noble acts of inclusion? was one of the greatest struggles of the entire trip.

While we were on campus, I wanted the students to conceptualize how Montgomery, Birmingham, and Selma as places contributed respectively to our grasp of the inception and end of the movement. What were the factors that contributed to the Montgomery bus boycott getting more press than other African American–directed boycotts in the South? How did the Montgomery bus boycott fit within the larger stream of events that inspired the spirit of the movement's beginning, such as *Brown v. Board of Education* and the Emmett Till murder? Why do some scholars view Birmingham as the last stand for the civil rights movement? Why was Birmingham a critical last stand? Would the movement have succeeded if the Birmingham campaign had failed? These and other questions were introduced while we were on campus and then strategically raised again during our travels. Obviously the students' answers changed; very little trumps experientially learning, and "breathing the air they breathed," as one student noted, certainly qualifies as that type of learning. However, I spurred the students to think about why their answers had changed, beyond this obvious reason.

We arrived in Birmingham on May 16, 2002—not the most ideal place from which to start, since the movement climaxed rather than commenced there. Aside from the fact that flying into Birmingham and driving to Montgomery and Selma was the most cost-effective way to travel, I can't remember what precipitated this choice. I just remember my trepidation about what would be lost instructionally by the students' following the paths of the Alabama civil rights movement outside its chronological order. Were it not for the fact that they had done a little reading about the movement, this experience would be comparable to knowing the end of a suspenseful novel or movie before reading or viewing the beginning. But I still worried that my students would find everything after Birmingham's anticlimactic. I particularly felt this way because on the first day the students would experience what I had experienced one year earlier as a Lilly Fellow—a tour of the Sixteenth Street Baptist Church with Carolyn McKinstry.

These otherwise garrulous students were understandably stunned into silence by the recounting of the Sixteenth Street Baptist Church bombing. Through a blend of patience, well-crafted questions, and maternal charm, Ms. McKinstry was able get my students talking.

While planning the course, I anticipated that the students might face a challenge communicating what they observed during the travel portion of the course. This is one reason I required a journal charting their observations. They had written a pre-essay while on campus and before the end of the course would complete a final essay and an oral presentation. Here are a few excerpts from the journal of a white female student I will call Andrea:[3]

> Birmingham, Thursday, May 16—It's crazy to stand and look at a park where over forty years ago kids were hosed down for being black and marching for their freedom . . . Kelly Ingram Park— a place where youth marchers got hosed down and attacked by police dogs. Dr. Holmes just called this a hallowed spot. It's not a happy place to smile in pictures while standing alongside sculp- tures—really memorials for those who gave everything for the freedom of all.

I don't recall calling Kelly Ingram Park a "hallowed spot," though I would not be opposed to such a description. There was something intangi- bly sacred and timeless about the travel portion of this course.

For now, I want to describe the past events of this summer course from 2002 in this present moment. Meet a student I will call Kathy Shields, an erudite and passionate African American junior from inner-city Bal- timore. The product of a single-parent home, she balances confidence in herself with a deep compassion for others, a compassion, however, that is not afraid to confront bigotry when the time and situation demands. In her pre-essay, I hear a resounding reverence for her people:

> It is amazing how a group of oppressed marginalized people found ways to overcome their oppressors . . . so I want to go to the place where all of this happened, where the civil rights movement has its roots.

In her final paper, she reflects cogently:

> There have been many who argued that the civil rights movement was a failure in part because of the widespread crime, poverty, and apathy currently plaguing the black community . . . I believe that if my people could overcome centuries of slavery, segregation, and oppression, we can overcome anything.

One of her concluding sentences evinces her belief that the movement was redemptive:

> The civil rights movement has confirmed my belief that a group of thoughtful, committed individuals can change the world. And I

---

3. For the sake of my former students' privacy, I have assigned them pseudonyms. For this reason, their reflections are not listed in the bibliography.

never want to forget the price that was paid for me to be an American citizen.

A student I'll call John Baird, the only white male to take the course, styles himself a liberal—a designation that his parents, both highly successful, also embrace. Though only a sophomore, he has traveled to twenty countries, is a strong supporter of affirmative action, and loves arguing this point with his counterparts. He envisions the class, in part, as an opportunity not only to broaden his knowledge, but, further, to provide himself with more ammunition to debate his conservative colleagues. His pre-essay reads, in part:

> Through books and videos, our intellectual pursuit can be fed with facts and information that can provide substance for arguments and a basis for one's thoughts.

He seems to identify a convergence between the cognitive and affective when he observes:

> I will leave this course with a strong sense of connection to the subject and with a better sense of the reality of it all. It will be like having a conversation with someone you don't know, and the meeting you have . . . changes your opinion.

The revelation of the course provokes humility in John, as seen in his final paper:

> There is more to be learned from the movement and its players than can ever be learned . . . Prior to the course, I felt that I had an understanding of the movement and its effect on American society . . . I soon found out I was wrong in my premature assumption.

He further moves beyond his former idea of using his knowledge for self-aggrandizement:

> I could use my increasing knowledge of the movement to reevaluate the areas of politics and policy . . . the experience could help me as I continually reform my public policy positions.

Michael Collins, a black junior from San Francisco, was, raised by a two-parent, working-class family. From all indications, he holds to conservative religious but liberal political views, usually projecting a dogmatic persona with either position. This is why the deference suggested in his pre-essay is at once surprising and encouraging:

I realize that you can always learn something new from something that you have already seen, but sometimes you have to work harder to do so. I think that this course will make me think outside the box that my mind has created for the civil rights movement.

That his final paper focused on a less celebrated figure in the broader civil rights movement, Fred Shuttlesworth, demonstrated Michael's effort to "think outside the box." Shuttlesworth's fusion of faith and social responsibility resonated with Michael:

Shuttlesworth's faith gave him social consciousness and brought about political action. My faith has definitely brought about social consciousness . . . As a business major will I choose a job that offers the highest salary or will I choose a job based on my personal calling?

For the white students, the course opened an ongoing dialogue about the role of white Americans in social movements focused primarily on black liberation. Will their role be more about controlling or contributing to social justice for African Americans? They were introduced to courageous whites who participated in the movement, such as Robert Graetz— whom I alluded to earlier—the Lutheran minister from the north who was assigned a pastorate in Montgomery and subsequently became involved in the bus boycott, which resulted in threats and, ultimately, the bombing of his home. They became acquainted with Clifford and Virginia Durr, native-born Alabamans who supported the movement by assisting people such as Rosa Parks and Fred Gray (Martin Luther King Jr.'s first lawyer). The students especially got to know Viola Liuzzo, a woman separated from the black voting rights struggle in Selma, Alabama, not only by race but also by region. The Michigan housewife volunteered to help blacks in the Selma movement. And as she drove from Selma to Montgomery, the Klan shot her for it.[4]

Still, these white students were challenged, both by their colleagues of color and me, to avoid appropriating a patronizing take on their own participation in future civil rights battles. More important, these students were challenged to engage in an open and ongoing critique of the material, yet often tacit and invisible, reality of white privilege.

For Michael and Kathy, the two African American students, I would hope that the course testified to the rich, complex diversity of the African

4. Stanton, *From Selma to Sorrow.*

American experience. African America is an ever-expanding cultural quilt with countless patches of variegated perspectives, rhetorical and discursive strategies—ways of knowing and being. I want them to be comfortable with the material ambiguity of what bell hooks styles "postmodern blackness."[5] I want them to grasp that there's more to fathoming blackness than being born that way.

For all of my students, then, now, later, and of any racial hue, I hope that they not only interpret civil rights differently but also alter their view about access to those rights. I would hope that they are on the road towards understanding Catherine Prendergast's argument in *Literacy and Racial Justice:* that literacy, as one road of access to civil rights, is neither apolitical nor culturally neutral but has historically been deemed white property. Even now projections of affirmative action as reverse discrimination are skewed because they don't take this point into account. I would trust that my students would move on to engaging Bradford Stull's proposition in *Amid the Fall* that their language, in whatever incarnation, should be viewed ultimately as emancipatory.[6] Building on the diverse yet powerfully prophetic rhetorical approaches of Du Bois, King, and Malcolm X, Stull theorizes about how their respective approaches might infuse civically conscious and responsible writing practices.

PROPHECY AS VOCATION: BREAKING THROUGH THE WALLS

As I have taught and researched about the civil rights movement over these past seventeen years, it has been rather difficult, nearly impossible, not to make these gestures personal. Because I am African American and Christian, the civil rights movement and particularly the Birmingham campaign registered to me on "higher frequencies," to paraphrase Ralph Ellison's famous closing of *Invisible Man*. I would like to be able to say that my personal stake has not affected my objectivity as I have dug through the archives, interviewed participants in and spectators of the Birmingham campaign, and even transcribed and analyzed the mass meetings. But I would be fooling no one.

This is not to say that there is something necessarily wrong with autobiographical sentiment inflected into scholarly inquiry. In my primary

5. hooks, "Postmodern Blackness."
6. Stull, *Amid the Fall*, ch. 1.

field, for instance, many fine scholars have shown how autobiography and rhetorical scholarship can be blended to great ends. Keith Gllyard's *Voices of the Self* remains one of the few insightful linguistic coming-of-age narratives, artfully harmonizing how he experienced multiple levels of literacy and how scholars explain this phenomenon. Since and arguably because of Gilyard's work, the lines between marginalized personal experiences and traditional academic knowledge within the field of rhetoric and composition have been thankfully blurred.

Still, the lines between objective analysis and autobiographical connection are not the only walls that have collapsed for me as a result of this project. While this project has focused on the prophetic range and power of Birmingham mass meeting oratory, the implications of my analysis extend beyond the spatial walls of the mass meetings and the discursive boundaries of oratory. If the history of rhetoric as composition largely rests on the premise that discussions about classical oratory can be extended to written, digital, and other technological modes of communication, then without little question the same could be said about Birmingham mass meeting oratory. Imagine if Twitter had existed during the time of the civil rights movement, particularly given King's ongoing strategy to publicize the virtues of the movement and the vices of its opponents. One need not imagine too far afield, as movements of varying degrees of sociopolitical significance—like Occupy Wall Street, the Tea Party, and Black Lives Matter—have maximized their respective messages through social media. My reading both of the Birmingham oratory and Black Lives Matter rhetoric leans toward viewing Black Lives Matter as prophetic, not in terms of its every demonstration or declaration, but in terms of the group's overall intent to address the extent to which racial injustices are institutionalized within the public sphere. As much as some try to demonize Black Lives Matter for hyperactivism, this organization's strategy of publicly spotlighting institutional injustices was King's principal strategy. Without the media—newspapers but mostly television—the institutional injustices perpetuated in 1963 Birmingham would have never been exposed. No exposure, no Civil Rights Act of 1964. No Civil Rights Act, no Voting Rights Act of 1965. In the aggregate all lives matter, but in critical times, some lives matter particularly: black lives, refugee lives, chronically unemployed white Midwestern lives, homeless lives—any lives that society allows to linger in the shadows of injustice.

Birmingham mass meeting oratory models how democratic discussion can take place, to be certain. But it also models tropes, commonplaces, and other sundry rhetorical figures that can be translated into writing and other communicative modes. I have focused on the prophetic force of the selected speeches that I have analyzed. Prophecy, as I have explored throughout this book, stretches broadly across a number of styles and ideological orientations. And while prophetic rhetoric by the nature of its own default public function operates within the realm of politics, this rhetoric need not necessarily be compromised by politics. As this chapter has included my personal reveries on teaching and my professional study of the civil rights movement, one question that remains to be broached is, how do I justify intellectually the need for the current use of prophetic rhetoric within classrooms and the public sphere?

Fortunately, my field of rhetoric and composition is rife with research that I would describe as prophetic. For one thing, the vast body of scholarship in this field, which is strongly inclusive of and rooted in African American linguistic and rhetorical traditions, grows directly out of the civil rights movement. Geneva Smitherman, Shirley Wilson Logan, Jacqueline Jones Royster, Keith Gilyard, and Victor Villanueva are senior scholars whose incomparable body of work has advanced a prophetically inflected, civically engaged, and democratically inclusive pedagogy. Younger prophetic voices (explicitly designated as such or not) that speak of composition instruction and practices as the direct legacy of the civil rights struggle include Elaine Richardson, Gwen Pough, Adam Banks, Carmen Kynard, Vorris Nunley, Tamika Carey, Stephen Schneider, and Rhea Estelle Lathan. I consider these scholars *prophets* or prophets in the making because they envision their research as representing more than an obligation to the academy. Rather their respective bodies of research reflect their radically democratic commitment to incessantly work through and work out what Martin Luther King Jr. called the "beloved community." As a result, these thinkers believe and teach that writing must be more than grammatically correct and aesthetically polished. Writing should be a means of social engagement. At its loftiest, writing must mean something to the writer and the people to whom she writes—especially if those people reside in the margins of our great republic.

BRIDGING TWO BIRTHS

I was born again in February 1977. Initially my spiritual freedom obfuscated the physical freedom I took for granted as son of the American civil rights movement. Nine months after accepting the Lord, I began preaching at the tender age of fifteen. For African American clergy, preaching emphasizes two of the five classical cannons of rhetoric: memory and delivery. The more Scripture one could recite, the better. And a soulful and stylistic sermon delivery was a must. Not because substance did not matter, but rather because style and substance, pathos and logos, are joined at the hip in the black homiletic tradition.

My experience as a boy preacher expanded my passions beyond the pulpit. But I shall never forget that were it not for that experience my ardor for language, literature, cultural studies, and rhetoric would not burn as brightly as it yet does. Before I luxuriated in the syncopated rhythms of Langston Hughes's poetry, my soul would rest in the images, idioms, and parallelisms within the Psalms. Before Zora Neale Hurston's narratives transported me across Florida and into the Caribbean, the Gospels shuttled me across the dusty roads of Judea and Galilee. My conception of myself as a Christian scholar was born in the cradle of a South Central Los Angeles African American church.

Curiously the idea of becoming a Christian scholar would not capture my imagination until the early 1990s. From 1987 to 1993, I taught middle and high school in the inner city. During this time my conception of myself both as a teacher and Christian blossomed and remained intact, but secretly. I knew there were Christian colleges. (I had attended one as an undergraduate.) But I never overtly connected the vocational dots between my secular teaching profession and my Christian walk. I knew that my upbringing in the church had fueled my passion for and commitment to teaching. But I remained in the closet about affirming teaching as my Christian profession even to my closest acquaintances.

Perhaps even more curiously, the notion of becoming a Christian scholar was planted in my mind while I was still teaching high school. The preacher at the church I was attending at the time taught at Pepperdine. With powers of persuasion still in some ways inexplicable to me, he convinced to leave secondary school teaching and pursue my doctorate. While attending USC, I was older than many of my colleagues. I believed that working on a PhD with two children in tow and a supportive wife was a blessing from God. I also knew that I must honor God in my studies. However, just as I had in my teaching, I kept any connection between my growing faith and burgeoning scholarship to myself.

But it's hard to remain in the closet as a Christian scholar when you teach at a place like Pepperdine. From the time I arrived here, first as a visiting instructor in 1993 then on tenure track in 1997, the university has encouraged me to critically think through my profession as Christian vocation. And that beat goes on. The older I get, the more integrated my sense of myself as a Christian scholar-teacher is becoming. Put another way, my sensibilities as a son of the civil rights movement and a child of God spur an ongoing, sometimes uncomfortable dialogue between my head and heart, soul and body.

An eclectic, almost contradictory range of sources has contributed to my understanding of Christian scholarship. From Longfellow's poetry to Lincoln's speeches; from Mark's servant gospel to Micah's straightforward demand "to act justly and love mercy"; from the sacred reality to be found in the spirituals to the secular spirituality to be unearthed in the R&B, hip hop, the blues, and country music. Diverse texts, some explicitly Christians, others not, have increased my comfort level with tensions that might frighten some religious fundamentalists or radical secularists. These tensions include the expressive and epistemic, literacy and orality, the legal and the subversive, the sacred and the secular. The writers who seem to haunt me in timeless fashion include the following: James Joyce (his playful use of language is serious business), James Baldwin (whose nonfiction I actually enjoy decidedly more than his fiction). In *The Fire Next Time,* Baldwin, a teenage preacher turned humanist, posits that our conception of God should not shroud our view of humanity. If so, we may need to rethink our vision of God. Thomas Merton, a Catholic mystic and theologian, who views the study of the Bible as part of an ongoing conversation with texts of Eastern and Western traditions, also haunts me, as does David Hume, the renowned Scottish philosopher that I read as a rhetorician. Why does he haunt me? After all, he was a religious skeptic who believed that Africans were genetically inferior. However, his prose brims with such constrained passion that I am compelled to read and reread him. If a man that deep could reason his way into racism, then anybody could.

For the past several years, I have been much more comfortable about being out of the closet with my Christian scholarship. Several years ago I was invited to give a lecture at Florida State University, which houses an impressive graduate program in rhetoric. During the Q&A, I was asked, what was the greatest personal influence in my work with civil rights rhetoric? I replied, "My relationship with Christ." After the lecture, one doctoral student approached me to directly commend but indirectly chide me. "Dr. Holmes, I wonder whether you're able to make this profession because you are a tenured professor and an established scholar."

I still wrestle with this question. I pray that my vocation as a Christian scholar, that my being out of the closet, is not a matter of convenience but a matter of core values—values like robust dialogue, social justice, and personal redemption: I realize that in the final analysis being a Christian scholar is about a lot of things, yet perhaps high on that list should be deliberating incessantly about thinking and living nobly and purposefully.

My teaching, scholarship, and service have always been a personal more than a professional matter for me. As I approach my midfifties, these activities have become matters of being. The sweep of African American history but particularly the Birmingham movement haunt me, inspiring me to do better by my students, my profession, my country, and my world, and interrogating me when I don't. My consciousness of spirituality and social justice are deeply rooted in my experiences as a child of God and son of the civil rights movement. However, as I have tried to demonstrate in this book, Birmingham mass meeting speeches illustrate a quality of discourse that cannot be contained in categories of race, region, gender, class, sexual orientation, or religion. Since the year 2000, the courses that I have taught on the civil rights movement have illustrated some of this complexity. These courses respectively have focused on women, lesser known people and places, white participants, fiction, cinema, and, recently, Sidney Poitier's films that overlap with key moments in civil rights history.

Civil rights memory cannot be confined to one political point of view. While American history may strongly suggest a progressive tilt when it comes to the civil rights movement, King and most of his company were determined not to be controlled by Democrats or Republicans. Prophetically, that was a good idea then and remains a good idea now. Contemporary prophets hailing from the Birmingham mass meeting tradition must perch themselves above the political fray. Not in a holier-than-thou posture, but from a place of ongoing challenge to status quo and institutional injustices—wherever and from whomever they might be found. George Shulman makes a similar assessment concerning how one might apply King's prophetic views to contemporary political and religious discussions.

> Then a political response to the Christian New Right should be, not a rigid defense of liberal distinctions between sacred as private and secular as public, but an effort to rework pervasive religious

language to foreground its democratic features and challenge its theocratic interpreters. The problem therefore is not religiosity as such but fundamentalism as a practice and the failure to generate countervailing power by contrasting visions.[7]

The contemporary prophet's perch is not a place to stand permanently, but it is a landing to return to frequently. Perches, like mountains, have to be descended from so that prophetic citizens can be of service in the valley—standing up, moving forward, and speaking out when necessary. Every form of writing and speaking—from the classical forms to forms using the range of technologies currently constituting social media—may be used prophetically. Authentic and liberating prophecy is more about the message than the medium; in fact, prophetic discourse is more about the message than it is about the messenger—no matter how principled that messenger might be. This is the way I read George Shulman's notion of prophetic "office." The ethos of the prophet is derived from the profound weight of the message.

In 1965 at Cambridge University, James Baldwin debated the celebrated conservative William F. Buckley Jr. The question for the debate was "Has the American dream been achieved at the expense of the American Negro?" While Buckley made his case in the negative by marshalling a stockpile of facts and figures into a coherent, sequential argument, Baldwin communicated his counterclaim with a fiery pathos ignited by personal experience. From the standpoint of Western rationality, Buckley made his point. But Western rationality was not the point upon which Baldwin was standing. Surely his claims were reasonable and rung with a fidelity born of having experienced the American dream as unreachable. And yet, Buckley's facts and figures did not compose the foundation upon which Baldwin grounded his ethos. Baldwin did not base his credibility on his use of Eurocentric logic. Rather he began his speech by seizing the role of the prophet Jeremiah for that critical moment. Baldwin had long since left the church as well as any traditional notions of theistic faith. However—for religious believers and righteous unbelievers—prophecy constitutes the noblest vocabulary for true justice, the precise diction for naming society's indescribable horrors, and the emphatic voice of those who have been, or feel like they have been, silenced.

7. Shulman, *American Prophecy*, 130.

Bibliography

Abernathy, Juanita. Interview with author, June 16, 2009.

Abernathy, Ralph David. *And the Walls Came Tumbling Down: An Autobiography.* New York: Harper & Row, 1990.

———. Speech at Mass Meeting. Sixteenth Street Baptist Church, Birmingham, Alabama, May 3, 1963. CD provided by Birmingham Civil Rights Institute. Original recording made by C. Herbert Oliver. Transcribed by David G. Holmes.

———. Speech at Mass Meeting. Sixth Avenue Baptist Church, Birmingham, Alabama, May 2, 1963. CD provided by Birmingham Civil Rights Institute. Original recording made by C. Herbert Oliver. Transcribed by David G. Holmes.

Aristotle. *The Art of Rhetoric.* Translated by John Henry Freese. Loeb Classical Library 193. Cambridge: Harvard University Press, 1991.

Banks, Adam J. *Race, Rhetoric, and Technology: Searching for Higher Ground.* NCTE-LEA Research Series in Literacy and Composition. Urbana, IL: National Council of Teachers of English, 2006.

———. *Digital Griots: African American Rhetorics in a Multimedia Age.* CCCC Studies in Writing & Rhetoric. Carbondale: Southern Illinois University Press, 2011.

Bass, S. Jonathan. *Blessed Are the Peacemakers: Martin Luther King, Jr., Eight White Religious Leaders, and the "Letter from Birmingham Jail."* Baton Rouge: Louisiana State University Press, 2001.

Belafonte, Harry, with Michael Shnayerson. *My Song: A Memoir.* New York: Knopf, 2011.

Bell, Derrick. *Faces at the Bottom of the Well: The Permanence of Racism.* New York: Basic Books, 1993.

Bercovitch, Sacvan. *The American Jeremiad.* Studies in American Thought and Culture. Madison: University of Wisconsin Press, 2012.

Bevel, James. Speech at Mass Meeting. Sixteenth Street Baptist Church, Birmingham, Alabama, April 12, 1963. CD provided by Birmingham Civil Rights Institute. Original recording made by C. Herbert Oliver. Transcribed by David G. Holmes.

Birmingham Police Department. Inter-Office Communication regarding Meeting of the Alabama Christian Movement for Human Rights, Sixteenth Street Baptist Church, April 25th, 1963. (April 29th, 1963). Housed in Birmingham Public Library Archives.

———. Inter-Office Communication regarding Meeting of the Alabama Christian Movement for Human Rights, Sixth Avenue Baptist Church, April 22nd, 1963. (April 23rd, 1963). Housed in Birmingham Public Library Archives.

Bibliography

———. Inter-Office Communication regarding Meeting of the Alabama Christian Movement for Human Rights, Sixteenth Street Baptist Church, April 12th, 1963. (April 18th, 1963). Housed in Birmingham Public Library Archives.

———. Inter-Office Communication regarding Meeting of the Alabama Christian Movement for Human Rights, Sixteenth Street Baptist Church May 3rd, 1963. (May 7th, 1963). Housed in Birmingham Public Library Archives.

———. Inter-Office Communication regarding Meeting of the Alabama Christian Movement for Human Rights, Sixth Avenue Baptist Church, May 2nd, 1963. (May 3rd, 1963). Housed in Birmingham Public Library Archives.

Blackmon, Douglas A. *Slavery by Another Name: The Re-Enslavement of Black Americans from the Civil War to World War II*. New York: Anchor, 2008.

Bonilla-Silva, Eduardo. *Racism without Racists: Color-blind Racism and the Persistence of Racial Inequality in America*. Lanham, MD: Rowman & Littlefield, 2014.

Boulware, Marcus H. *The Oratory of Negro Leaders 1900–1968*. Westport, CT: Negro Universities Press, 1969.

Branch, Taylor. *Parting the Waters: America in the King Years, 1954–1963*. New York: Simon & Schuster, 1988.

———. *Pillar of Fire: America in the King Years, 1963–65*. New York: Simon & Schuster, 1998.

Brown, Elaine. *A Taste of Power: A Black Woman's Story*. New York: Anchor, 1994.

Bryant, Nick. *The Bystander: John F. Kennedy and the Struggle for Black Equality*. New York: Basic Books, 2006.

Burke, Kenneth. *A Rhetoric of Motives*. Berkeley: University of California Press, 1969.

Campbell, Will. *Brother to a Dragonfly*. New York: Seabury, 1977.

Carey, Tamika L. *Rhetorical Healing: The Reeducation of Contemporary Black Womanhood*. SUNY Series in Feminist Criticism and Theory. Albany: State University of New York Press, 2016.

Chappell, David L. *A Stone of Hope: Prophetic Religion and the Death of Jim Crow*. Chapel Hill: University of North Carolina Press, 2004.

Cone, James H. *A Black Theology of Liberation*. 40th anniversary ed. Maryknoll, NY: Orbis, 2010.

———. *Martin & Malcolm & America: A Dream or Nightmare?* Maryknoll, NY: Orbis, 1990.

———. *The Spirituals and the Blues: An Interpretation*. Maryknoll, NY: Orbis, 1991.

Crowley, Sharon. *Toward a Civil Discourse: Rhetoric and Fundamentalism*. Pittsburgh Series in Composition, Literacy, and Culture. Pittsburgh: University of Pittsburgh Press, 2006.

Douglass, Frederick. *Narrative of the Life of Frederick Douglass & Other Writings*. Meijer Family Classics. Ann Arbor: Ann Arbor Media Group, 2004.

Dudziak, Mary L. *Cold War Civil Rights: Race and the Image of American Democracy*. Politics and Society in Twentieth-Century America. Princeton: Princeton University Press, 2000.

Dyson, Michael Eric. *I May Not Get There with You: The True Martin Luther King, Jr.* New York: Simon & Schuster, 2000.

Else, Jon, and Judith Vecchione, prods. *Eyes on the Prize*. Vols. 1, 2, and 3. VHS. PBS. 1995. Original broadcast, 1987–1990.

Eskew, Glenn T. *But for Birmingham: The Local and National Movements in the Civil Rights Struggle*. Chapel Hill: University of North Carolina Press, 1997.

Bibliography

Fallin, Wilson, Jr. *The African American Church in Birmingham, Alabama, 1815–1963: A Shelter in the Storm.* Studies in African American History and Culture. New York: Garland, 1997.

———. Interview with author, May 24, 2006.

———. *Uplifting the People: Three Centuries of Black Baptists in Alabama.* Religion and American Culture. Tuscaloosa: University of Alabama Press, 2007.

Farmer, James. *Freedom When?* New York: Random House, 1965.

———. *Lay Bare the Heart: An Autobiography of the Civil Rights Movement.* New York: Plume, 1986.

———. Speech at Mass Meeting. Sixth Avenue Baptist Church, Birmingham, Alabama, May 2, 1963. CD provided by Birmingham Civil Rights Institute. Original recording made by C. Herbert Oliver. Transcribed by David G. Holmes.

Fink, Kenneth, dir. *The Vernon Johns Story: The Road to Freedom.* Written by Leslie Lee et al. Produced by Big Apple Films, Laurel Entertainment Inc., and Tribune Entertainment. 1994. DVD. Las Vegas: Hollywood International, 2006.

Fisher, Walter R. *Human Communication as Narration: Toward a Philosophy of Reason, Value, and Action.* Studies in Rhetoric/Communication. Columbia: University of South Carolina Press, 1987.

Garrow, David. *Bearing the Cross: Martin Luther King, Jr., and the Southern Leadership Conference.* New York: Morrow, 1986.

Gilyard, Keith. "African American Contributions to Composition Studies." Reprinted in *True to the Language Game: African American Discourse, Cultural Politics, and Pedagogy*, 61–76. New York: Routledge, 2011.

———. "Aspects of African American Rhetoric as a Field." In *African American Rhetoric(s): Interdisciplinary Perspectives*, edited by Elaine Richardson and Ronald Jackson II, 1–18. Carbondale: Southern Illinois University Press, 2004.

———. *Voices of the Self: A Study of Language Competence.* African American Life. Detroit: Wayne State University Press, 1991.

Glaude, Eddie S., Jr. *In a Shade of Blue: Pragmatism and the Politics of Black America.* Chicago: University of Chicago Press, 2007.

Graetz, Robert. *A White Preacher's Memoir: The Montgomery Bus Boycott.* Montgomery: Black Belt, 1999.

Gray, Fred. *Bus Ride to Justice: Changing the System by the System; The Life and Works of Fred Gray.* Montgomery: NewSouth Books: 1995.

Harris, Fredrick C. *The Price of the Ticket: Barack Obama and the Rise and Decline of Black Politics.* Transgressing Boundaries. New York: Oxford University Press, 2012.

Harris, James H. *The Word Made Plain: The Power and Promise of Preaching.* Minneapolis: Fortress, 2004.

Hartnell, Anna. *Rewriting Exodus: American Futures from Du Bois to Obama.* London: Pluto, 2011.

hooks, bell. "Postmodern Blackness." In *Yearning: Race, Gender, and Cultural Politics*, 23–31. Women's Studies, Black Studies. Boston: South End, 1990.

Howard-Pitney, David. *The African American Jeremiad: Appeals for Justice in America.* Philadelphia: Temple University Press, 1990.

Hoyt, Thomas. "Interpreting Biblical Scholarship for the Black Church Tradition." In *Stony the Road We Trod: African American Biblical Interpretation*, edited by Cain Hope Felder, 17–39. Minneapolis: Fortress, 1991.

Hubbard, Dolan. *The Sermon and the African American Literary Imagination.* Columbia: University of Missouri Press, 1994.

Hughes, Langston. "Let America Be America Again." In *The Collected Poems of Langston Hughes,* edited by Arnold Rampersad and David Roessel, 189–91. New York: Knopf, 1994.

Huntley, Horace. Interview with Fred Shuttlesworth. Oral History Project. Birmingham Civil Rights Institute, December 10, 1996.

Jarratt, Susan C. *Rereading the Sophists: Classical Rhetoric Refigured.* Carbondale: Southern Illinois University Press, 1991.

Johnson, Charles. *Dreamer: A Novel.* New York: Scribner, 1999.

Karenga, Maulana. "Nommo, Kawaida, and Communicative Practice: Bringing Good into the World." In *Understanding African American Rhetoric: Classical Origins to Contemporary Innovations,* edited by Ronald L. Jackson II and Elaine B. Richardson, 3–22. New York: Routledge, 2003.

King, Martin Luther, Jr. "I Have a Dream." In *A Call to Conscience,* edited by Clayborne Carson and Kris Shepard, 75–88. New York: Warner, 2001.

———. Speech at Mass Meeting. Sixteenth Street Baptist Church, Birmingham, Alabama, April, 22, 1963. CD provided by Birmingham Civil Rights Institute. Original recording made by C. Herbert Oliver. Transcribed by David G. Holmes.

———. Speech at Mass Meeting. Sixteenth Street Baptist Church, Birmingham, Alabama, May 3, 1963. In *"We Want Our Freedom": Rhetoric of the Civil Rights Movement,* compiled by W. Stuart Towns, 147–51. Westport CT: Praeger, 2002.

———. *Stride toward Freedom: The Montgomery Story.* New York: Harper & Row, 1958.

Kynard, Carmen. *Vernacular Insurrections: Race, Protest, and the New Century in Composition-Literacies Studies.* Albany: State University of New York Press, 2013.

LaRue, Cleophus J. *The Heart of Black Preaching.* Louisville: Westminster John Knox, 2000.

Lathan, Rhea Estelle. *Freedom Writing: African American Civil Rights Literacy Activism, 1955–1967.* Studies in Writing & Rhetoric. Urbana: Conference on College Composition and Communication/National Council of Teachers of English, 2015.

Lee, Spike, dir. *4 Little Girls: The Story of Four Young Girls Who Paid the Price for a Nation's Ignorance.* Produced by 40 Acres & A Mule Filmworks and Home Box Office (HBO). 1997. DVD. Burbank, CA: Warner Home Video, 2010.

Lischer, Richard. *The Preacher King: Martin Luther King Jr. and the Word That Moved America.* New York: Oxford University Press, 1995.

Mailloux, Steven. *Disciplinary Identities: Rhetorical Paths of English, Speech, and Composition.* New York: Modern Language Association of America, 2006.

Manis, Andrew M. *A Fire You Can't Put Out: The Civil Rights Life of Birmingham's Reverend Shuttlesworth.* Religion and American Culture. Tuscaloosa: University of Alabama Press, 2009.

———. *Southern Civil Religions in Conflict: Civil Rights and the Culture Wars.* Macon, GA: Mercer University Press: 2002.

Marable, Manning. *Black Leadership: Four Great American Leaders and the Struggle for Civil Rights.* New York: Columbia University Press, 1998.

McAdam, Doug. *Freedom Summer.* New York: Oxford University Press, 1988.

McWhorter, Diane. *Carry Me Home: Birmingham, Alabama; the Climatic Battle of the Civil Rights Revolution.* New York: Simon & Schuster, 2002.

Bibliography

Miller, Keith D. *Martin Luther King's Biblical Epic: His Final, Great Speech*. Race, Rhetoric, and Media Series. Jackson: University Press of Mississippi, 2012.

Mitchell, Henry H. *Black Preaching: The Recovery of a Powerful Art*. Nashville: Abingdon, 1990.

Morris, Aldon D. *The Origins of the Civil Rights Movement: Black Communities Organizing for Change*. New York: Free Press, 1984.

Moses, Wilson Jeremiah. *Black Messiahs and Uncle Toms: Social and Literary Manipulations of a Religious Myth*. University Park: Penn State University Press, 1993.

Murphy, Joseph M. *Working the Spirit: Ceremonies of the African Diaspora*. Boston: Beacon, 2003.

Niven, David. *The Politics of Injustice: The Kennedys, the Freedom Rides, and the Electoral Consequences of Moral Compromise*. Knoxville: University of Tennessee Press, 2003.

Nunley, Vorris. *Keepin' It Hushed: The Barbershop and African American Hush Harbor Rhetoric*. African American Life Series. Detroit: Wayne State University Press, 2011.

Obama, Barack. *The Audacity of Hope: Thoughts on Reclaiming the American Dream*. New York: Three Rivers, 2006.

———. *Dreams from My Father: A Story of Race and Reconciliation*. New York: Three Rivers, 1995.

———. Fiftieth Anniversary Selma Speech. https://www.whitehouse.gov/the-press-office/2015/03/07/remarks-president-50th-anniversary-selma-montgomery-marches/.

———. Forty-Second Anniversary Selma Speech. http://civilrightsleader.com/barack-obama-speech-selma-alabama-2007/.

———. "Knox College Commencement Address." In *Great Speeches by African Americans*, edited by James Daley, 143–50. Mineola, NY: Dover, 2006.

———. Remarks by the President after Announcement of the Decision by the Grand Jury in Ferguson, Missouri. https://www.whitehouse.gov/the-press-office/2014/11/24/remarks-president-after-announcement-decision-grand-jury-ferguson-missou/.

———. Remarks by the President on Trayvon Martin. https://www.whitehouse.gov/the-press-office/2013/07/19/remarks-president-trayvon-martin/.

Parker, Alan, dir. *Mississippi Burning*. Written by Chris Gerolmo. Produced by Orion Pictures. DVD. Santa Monica, CA: MGM Home Entertainment, 2001.

Parker-Brooks, Maegan. *A Voice that Could Stir an Army: Fannie Lou Hamer and the Rhetoric of the Black Freedom Movement*. Race, Rhetoric, and Media Series. Jackson: University Press of Mississippi, 2014.

Patterson, Orlando. *The Ordeal of Integration: Progress and Resentment in America's "Racial" Crisis*. Washington, DC: Civitas, 1997.

Pauley, Garth D. "Truman and the NAACP: A Case Study in Presidential Persuasion on Civil Rights." *Rhetoric and Public Affairs* 2/2 (1999) 211–41.

Pearce, Richard, dir. *The Long Walk Home*. Written by John Cork. Produced by Dave Bell Associates and New Visions Pictures. 1990. DVD. Santa Monica, CA: Lionsgate/Miramax, 2013.

Pipes, William H. *Say Amen, Brother! Old-Time Negro Preaching*. African American Life Series. Detroit: Wayne State University Press, 1992.

Pitts, Walter F. *Old Ship of Zion: The Afro-Baptist Ritual in the African Diaspora*. Religion in America Series New York: Oxford University Press, 1993.

Pough, Gwen. "Empowering Rhetoric: Black Students Writing Black Panthers." *College Composition and Communication* 53/3 (2002) 466–86.

Bibliography

Prendergast, Catherine. *Literacy and Racial Justice: The Politics of Learning after Brown versus Board of Education*, with a foreword by Gloria Ladson-Billings. Carbondale: Southern Illinois University Press, 2003.

Raboteau, Albert J. *American Prophets: Seven Religious Radicals and Their Struggle for Justice*. Princeton: Princeton University Press, 2016.

Ransby, Barbara. *Ella Baker and the Black Freedom Movement: A Radical Democratic Vision*. Gender & American Culture. Chapel Hill: University of North Carolina Press, 2003.

Rieder, Jonathan. *The Gospel of Freedom: Martin Luther King, Jr.'s Letter from Birmingham Jail and the Struggle that Changed the Nation*. New York: Bloomsbury, 2013.

———. *The Word of the Lord Is Upon Me: The Righteous Performance of Martin Luther King, Jr.* Cambridge: Belknap, 2008.

Roberts, Gene, and Hank Klibanoff. *The Race Beat: The Press, the Civil Rights Struggle, and the Awakening of a Nation*. New York: Knopf, 2006.

Robinson, Jo Ann. *The Montgomery Bus Boycott and the Women Who Stared It*. Knoxville: University of Tennessee Press, 1987.

Roosevelt, Franklin D. Speech at Madison Square Garden, October 31st, 1936. *The American Presidency Project*. http://www.presidency.ucsb.edu/ws/?pid=15219/.

Rowe, Karen. "Painted Sermons: Expanding the Scope of Explanatory Rhetoric." In *Sizing Up Rhetoric*, edited by David Zarefsky and Elizabeth Benacka, 296–310. Long Grove, IL: Waveland, 2008.

Royster, Jacqueline Jones, and Jean C. Williams. "History in Spaces Left: African American Presence and Narratives of Composition Studies." *College Composition and Communication* 50/4 (1999) 563–84.

Schneider, Stephen A. *You Can't Padlock an Idea: Rhetorical Education at the Highlander Folk School, 1932–1961*. Studies in Rhetoric/Communication. Columbia: University of South Carolina Press, 2014.

Selby, Gary S. *Martin Luther King and the Rhetoric of Freedom: The Exodus Narrative in America's Struggle for Civil Rights*. Studies in Rhetoric and Religion 5. Waco: Baylor University Press, 2008.

———. "Scoffing at the Enemy: The Burlesque Frame in the Rhetoric of Ralph David Abernathy." *Southern Communication Journal* 70/2 (2005) 134–45.

Shulman, George M. *American Prophecy: Race and Redemption in American Political Culture*. Minneapolis: University of Minnesota Press, 2008.

Shuttlesworth, Fred. Fifth Annual Presidential Address. Alabama Christian Movement for Human Rights, June 5, 1961. Obtained from Birmingham Public Library Archives.

———. Presiding Remarks at the Mass Meeting. Sixteenth Street Baptist Church, Birmingham, Alabama, April 25, 1963. CD provided by Birmingham Civil Rights Institute. Original recording made by C. Herbert Oliver. Transcribed by David G. Holmes.

———. Presiding Remarks at the Mass Meeting. Sixth Avenue Baptist Church, Birmingham, Alabama, April 22, 1963. CD provided by Birmingham Civil Rights Institute. Original recording made by C. Herbert Oliver. Transcribed by David G. Holmes.

———. Sixth Annual Presidential Address. Alabama Christian Movement for Human Rights, June 5, 1962. Reprinted in *Rhetoric, Religion, and the Civil Rights Movement*, edited by Davis Houck and David E. Nixon, 465–66. Waco: Baylor University Press, 2006.

Bibliography

Simon, Paul. "The Sounds of Silence." On *Monday Morning, 3 A.M.: Exciting New Sounds in the Folk Tradition*, performed by Simon & Garfunkel. Columbia CL 2249. 1964. 33 1/3 rpm.

Smitherman, Geneva. *Talkin and Testifyin: The Language of Black America.* 1977. Reprint, Detroit: Wayne State University Press, 1986.

Sowell, Thomas. *Civil Rights: Rhetoric or Reality?* New York: Morrow, 1985.

Stanton, Mary. *From Selma to Sorrow: The Life and Death of Viola Liuzzo.* Athens: University of Georgia Press, 1998.

Steele, Shelby. *A Dream Deferred: The Second Betrayal of Black Freedom in America.* New York: Harper Perennial, 1999.

Stull, Bradford. *Amid the Fall, Dreaming of Eden: Du Bois, King, Malcolm X, and Emancipatory Composition.* Carbondale: Southern Illinois University Press, 1999.

Thornton, J. Mills, III. *Dividing Lines: Municipal Politics and the Struggle for Civil Rights in Montgomery, Birmingham, and Selma.* Tuscaloosa: University of Alabama Press, 2002.

Walker, Alice. *Meridian.* New York: Harcourt Brace Jovanovich, 1976.

Walker, Wyatt Tee. *"Somebody's Calling My Name": Black Sacred Music and Social Change.* Valley Forge: Judson, 1979.

West, Cornel. *Democracy Matters: Winning the Fight against Imperialism.* Black Thought and Culture. New York: Penguin, 2004.

———. *Race Matters.* New York: Vintage, 1994.

Wiegman, Robyn. "Whiteness Studies and the Paradox of Particularity." *Boundary* 2/26 (1999) 115–50.

Wilkins, Roy, with Tom Mathews. *Standing Fast: The Autobiography of Roy Wilkins.* New York : Da Capo, 1994.

———. Speech a the Mass Meeting. Sixteenth Street Baptist Church, Birmingham, Alabama, April 25, 1963. CD provided by Birmingham Civil Rights Institute. Original recording made by C. Herbert Oliver. Transcribed by David G. Holmes.

Wilson, Kirt H. "Interpreting the Discursive Field in the Montgomery Bus Boycott: Martin Luther King, Jr.'s Holt Street Address." *Rhetoric and Public Affairs* 8/2 (2005) 299–326.

———"Rhetoric and Race in the American Experience: The Promises and Perils of Sentimental Memory." *Sizing Up Rhetoric*, edited by David Zarefsky and Elizabeth Benacka, 20–39. Long Grove, IL: Waveland, 2008.

Wimbush. Vincent L. "The Bible and African Americans: An Outline of Interpretive History." In *Stony the Road We Trod: African American Biblical Interpretation*, edited by Cain Hope Felder, 81–97. Minneapolis: Fortress, 1991.

Wise, Tim. *Between Barack and a Hard Place: Racism and White Denial in the Age of Obama.* Open Media Series. San Francisco: City Lights, 2009.

Woods, Abraham. Interview with the author, June 2005.

Woods, Calvin. Interview with the author, June 2005.

———. Speech at Mass Meeting. Sixth Avenue Baptist Church, Birmingham, Alabama, April 22nd, 1963. CD provided by Birmingham Civil Rights Institute. Original recording made by C. Herbert Oliver. Transcribed by David G. Holmes.

Woods, Jeff. *Black Struggle, Red Scare: Segregation and Anti-Communism in the South, 1948–1968.* Baton Rouge: Louisiana State University Press, 2004.

Index

Index

Birmingham Children's Campaign, 51,
74–75
Birmingham Civil Rights Institute, 30
Birmingham Herald (newspaper), 84
Birmingham Police Department, 63, 70
Birmingham World (newspaper), 84
Birth of a Nation (film), 85
Black heroism examples, in Bevel's
April 12 speech, 63–65
Black Lives Matter, 170
Black Panther Party, 154
Black pathology, 117–20
Blanton, Thomas Edwin, Jr., 90
Blessed Are the Peacemakers (Bass), 158
Bond, Julian, 44
Bonilla-Silva, Eduardo, 17
Boulware, Marcus, 32–3, 35, 98–99
Boutwell, Albert, 75
Branch, Taylor, 2, 151
Brooks, Maegan Parker, 2
Brother to a Dragonfly (Campbell), 160
Brown, Elaine, 154
Brown, Michael, 145
Brown v. Board of Education, 46, 89,
137, 165
Bryant, Nick, 45, 48
Buckley, William F., Jr., 175
Burke, Kenneth, 43, 79, 100
Bush, George W., 142
Bus Ride to Justice (Gray), 154

Call-and-response rituals, 86–87
Calverton, V. F., 94
Cambridge University, 175
Campbell, Will, 160
Camp meetings of Second Great Awak-
ening, 6
Carey, Tamika, 171
Carmichael, Stokely, 10
Carson, Clayborne, 2, 151
Cedar Grove Academy (Pritchard, AL),
30–31
Chambliss, Robert "Dynamite Bob," 90
Chappell, David, 4, 14–20, 24–25
Cherry, Bobby Frank, 90
Christian realism, prophetic, 13, 20
Civil Rights Act of 1964, 2, 127
Civil rights movement

book overview, 25–26
evoked by Obama, 143–47
mass meeting sources on, 4–9
overview, 1–4
prophecy as mass meeting theory
and practice, 9–26
Cornel West on, 11–14, 24–25
David Chappell on, 14–20, 24–25
George Shulman on, 20–25
jeremiad, 9–11
teaching about, 151–61
unity issues in, 102–4
Civil Rights: Rhetoric or Reality?
(Sowell), 152
Clergy, Bevel's criticism of, 62–64
Clinton, Hillary, 140
Collins, Addie Mae, 90
Color blindness, ideology of, 122
Combined memory, 32
Committee of Racial Equality (CORE),
96–97
Communist Party, 42, 45–46
Complacency, force of, 50
Cone, James, 12, 23, 57, 154
Congress of Racial Equality (CORE),
97–98, 100
Connor, Eugene "Bull," 46, 61–62, 75
Constantinian Christianity, 12
Cooperation, rhetoric of, 43
Crisis (NAACP publication), 113
Critique, rhetoric of. *See* Abernathy,
Ralph
Crowley, Sharon, 4, 15–16, 38
Cultural knowledge, of white America,
113–15

Daughters of the American Revolution,
107
Davis, Angela, 10
Democracy, gospel of, 121–22
Democracy Matters (West), 12, 38
Democratic Party, black support shifts
to, 45
Desegregation, Ku Klux Klan view of,
40
Dewey, John, 13, 15
Dexter Avenue Baptist Church, 162

Index

Direct action, law-and-order approach *versus*, 62–63
Dixon, David, 2
Dogma, prophecy divorced from, 4
Douglass, Frederick, 58, 107, 133
Dream Deferred (Steele), 152
Dreamer (Johnson), 154
Du Bois, W. E. B., 162
Dudziak, Mary, 101
Durr, Clifford, 168
Durr, Virginia, 168
Dyson, Michael Eric, 7, 136, 151

Economic status impact, 57–59
Elasticity, cultural, 32
Ellison, Ralph, 169
Enlightenment, 15
Eskew, Glenn T., 2
Exceptionalism, American, 11
Exodus narrative, 57–58
Eyes on the Prize documentary series, 29–30, 61, 153, 161

Faces at the Bottom of the Well (Bell), 152
Fallin, Wilson F., Jr., 1, 7, 16, 74, 112
Falwell, Jerry, 38, 139
Farmer, James
    antiblack racism discussed in speech of, 104–6
    authentic freedom in speech of, 106–8
    background of, 92–94
    as Birmingham campaign speaker, 98–101
    civil rights organization unity called for, by, 102–4
    as Congress of Racial Equality director, 97–98
    in Fellowship of Reconciliation, 96
    human rights struggle in speech of, 101–2
    John F. Kennedy criticized by, 44
    Lay Bare the Heart, written by, 94–95
    mentors of, 95–96
    in NAACP, 96–97
    overview, 3

Fellowship of Reconciliation (FOR), 96–97
Fire Next Time, The (Baldwin), 20, 173
First Great Awakening, 10
Fisher, Walter, 68
Florida State University, 173
Force of complacency, 50
Foxx, Jaime, 140
Freedom Democratic Party of Mississippi, 64
Freedom Rides of 1961, 44–45, 98
Freedom Summer (McAdam), 154

Gallup polls, 160
Gandhi, Mahatma, 95
Garfunkel, Art, 91
Garrow, David, 2, 151
Gaston, A. G., 52, 57, 69, 104
Gilyard, Keith, 9, 34, 170–71
"Glacial change" approach to civil rights, 43
Glaude, Eddie, 27–28
Goldberg, Whoopi, 163
Gospel of democracy, 121–22
Graetz, Robert, 164, 168
Graham, Billy, 4
Grassroots agency. *See* Bevel, James
Gray, Fred, 154, 168

Hamer, Fannie Lou, 19, 64
Harlan, John Marshall, 48, 150
Harlem Renaissance, 85, 108
Harris, Frederick C., 133
Harris, James Henry, 33–34, 36
Hartman, Thom, 130
Hartnell, Anna, 134
Hatch, John, 2
Height, Dorothy, 92
Holmes, Oliver Wendell, 104
Holt Street Baptist Church, 4–5
Houck, Davis W., 2
Howard-Pitney, David, 10
Howard University, 94
Hoyt, Thomas, Jr., 36–37
Hubbard, Dolan, 32, 36
Hughes, Langston, 107–8, 122–23, 147, 172

187

Index

Human rights struggle, civil rights struggle as, 101–2
Hume, David, 173
Humor, Abernathy's use of, 79
Hurston, Zora Neale, 172
Hush harbor rhetoric, 89, 133

I Have a Dream speech (King), 136–38, 159
Illegitimacy, economics of, 118
Improvisation, narrative, 32
Improvisational poetics and hermeneutics, 33–37
Institutional racism, in organized religion, 94
Instruction, rhetoric of. *See* Abernathy, Ralph
Integration as true justice (Bevel's April 12, 1963, speech), 70–72
Invisible Man (Ellison), 169

"Jack-leg preacher," 93
Jarratt, Susan, 35
Jefferson, Thomas, 127
Jeremiad tradition, 9–11, 120
Johns, Vernon, 162
Johnson, Charles, 154
Johnson, Lyndon B., 45, 139
Joshua generation, 142–43
Journey of Reconciliation, 98
Justice, integration as (Bevel's April 12, 1963, speech), 70–72
Juvenile delinquency, myth of, 117–18

Kairos (crucial opportunity), 137–38
Keepin' It Hushed (Nunley), 77
Kennedy, John F., 43–45, 48
Kennedy, Robert F., 44, 109, 114, 123–24
King, A. D., 81, 90
King, Coretta Scott, 139
King, Martin Luther, Jr.
  assassination of, 2
  in "Big Six" of civil rights movement, 92
  Billy Graham consulted by, 4–5
  Birmingham arrest of, 53–55, 63
  on Birmingham mayor Boutwell, 75

in Birminham campaign, 3
divergent opinions welcomed by, 52
on force of complacency, 50
Fred Gray as attorney of, 154
global concerns of, 10, 42, 101
John F. Kennedy criticized by, 44
Letter from a Birmingham Jail of, 158
in Louis Harris poll of 1963, 44–45
Malcolm X and, 163
Obama, Barack, association with, 128–30, 135–36
political and prophetic fused by, 136–39
political theology of, 23
on politicians, 126
prophetic discourse of, 20–22
on racism, militarism, and poverty threats, 40
Shuttlesworth invitation to (1963), 28–29
Stride toward Freedom of, 79
stylistic contrasts with Abernathy, 77–79
"Kingdom of God" discussion (Bevel's April 12, 1963, speech), 56–57
Klibanoff, Gene, 84
Ku Klux Klan, 29, 40, 90
Kynard, Carmen, 171

La Haye, Tim, 38
Lathan, Rhea Estelle, 171
Law-and-order approach, direct action *versus*, 62–63
Lay Bare the Heart (Farmer), 94
Leadership, Wilkins on, 50
Lee, Spike, 156
Let American Be America Again (Hughes), 107
Letter from a Birmingham Jail (King), 158
Lewis, David Levering, 151
Lewis, John, 75, 92, 134, 140, 145
Liberalism, lack of neutrality in, 17
Lilly Foundation, 155, 158
Lincoln, Abraham, 130–31
Lincoln, C. Eric, 7
Lischer, Richard, 2, 5–7, 78, 93, 151

Index

Index

Index

Index

Till, Emmett, murder of, 71, 165
Tolson, Melvin, 94–95
Toomer, Jean, 150
Toward a Civil Discourse (Crowley),
  15, 38
"Tragic-comic hope," 12, 16
Trinity United Church of Christ, 133
Truman, Harry S., 42, 101, 123

University of Alabama, 109, 114
University of Mississippi, 41, 64–65,
  123
Unwanted pregnancies, economics of,
  118
*Uplifting the People: Three Centuries of
  Black Baptists in Alabama* (Fallin),
  16

Verbal performance, hermeneutical
  function of, 35
Vernacular prophecy, 23–24
Villanueva, Victor, 171
Vivian, C. T., 140
Voices of the Self (Gilyard), 170
Voting Rights Act of 1965, 2, 127, 140,
  159

Walker, Alice, 154
Walker, David, 57, 133
Walker, Wyatt, 54
Wallace, George, 65, 109, 114–17, 123
Ware, J. L., 52, 62
Washington, Booker T., 89, 162
Watts, Eric King, 2
Wesley, Cynthia, 90
West, Cornel
  Christian fundamentalists critiqued
    by, 38
  liberal pragmatism connected to
    black revivalist prophecy, 27–28
  on prophecy as mass meeting theory
    and practice, 4, 8, 11–14, 24–25
  Race Matters by, 154
West African Griot, 77

West African spirituality, 6
White Citizens Council, 117
White cultural knowledge, 113–15
White narrative privilege, 41
Wiegman, Robyn, 30
Wiley College, 94
Wilkins, Roy
  African American sense of worth in
    speech of, 120–21
  black pathology attacked by, 117–20
  Christian church associated with,
    110–11
  gospel of democracy in speech of,
    121–22
  influences on, 122–23
  John F. Kennedy criticized by, 44
  on leadership, 50
  mainstream values represented by,
    108–10
  overview, 3
  political power and, 123–25
  on politicians, 126
  renunciation of white cultural
    knowledge in speech of, 113–15
  situating himself as "visitor," 111–13
  Wallace, as viewed by, 115–17
Williams, Robert, 89
Wilson, Kirt, 2, 5, 34, 128
Wimbush, Vincent L., 28, 57, 60, 68
Witness, prophetic, 12–13
Wood, Abraham, 1
Woods, Calvin, 27, 121
Woods, Jeff, 43
Worth, sense of, in African Americans,
  120–21
Wright, Jeremiah, 133–34, 140
Wright, Richard, 150

Young, Andrew, 53, 55
Young, Whitney, 92

Zarefsky, David, 2
Zimmerman, George, 143, 145